"The loss of a biblical vision of the local church—indeed the collapse of biblical ecclesiology in many congregations—is the greatest threat to Baptists. *Restoring Integrity in Baptist Churches* is a book urgently needed and well timed. The writers of this book are some of the brightest theologians and scholars in Baptist life today, and they are deeply committed to the recovery of integrity in Baptist life and in Baptist churches. We have needed this book for a long time."

—R. Albert Mohler Jr.
President, The Southern Baptist Theological Seminary

"Restoring integrity in Baptist churches. Formidable assignment! Formidable scholars! Formidable proposals! I believe the Lord will use this book by committed conservative scholars to return our churches to New Testament integrity."

—Jerry Vines
Pastor Emeritus, First Baptist Church, Jacksonville, FL
Past President, Southern Baptist Convention

"In a day when many believe the most important ingredients to effective ministry are intellect, intensity, and insight, this volume restores our faith in the fact that it is really integrity in the local church. Integrity is rooted in our private lives, reflected in our personal lives, reinforced in our professional lives, and ultimately revealed in our public lives as churchmen. *Restoring Integrity in Baptist Churches* . . . read it and reap!"

—O. S. Hawkins
President and Chief Executive Officer, Guidestone Financial Resources

"My favorite verse in the Bible is Proverbs 20:7, which magnifies integrity. The church will be blessed by our heavenly Father in direct proportion to its integrity. This book will chart the path that leads to the place of knowing His hand on the church's work. What we are in the inward parts is what matters most."

—Johnny Hunt
Pastor, First Baptist Church, Woodstock, GA

"Southwestern professors White, Duesing, and Yarnell offer in this edited volume a critical restatement of Baptist concerns for free church ecclesiology. Professors from several Southern Baptist seminaries and one pastor-theologian have combined to give an essential resource for Baptist churches and schools."

—Paige Patterson
President, Southwestern Baptist Theological Seminary

Restoring Integrity

IN BAPTIST CHURCHES

THOMAS
WHITE,

JASON G.
DUESING,

AND

MALCOLM B.
YARNELL III

EDITORS

JOHN HAMMETT AND MARK DEVER
ON CHURCH MEMBERSHIP

DANIEL AKIN, DAVID ALLEN,
THOMAS WHITE, AND JASON LEE
ON BAPTISM

THOMAS WHITE AND EMIR CANER
ON THE LORD'S SUPPER

GREGORY WILLS AND R. STANTON NORMAN
ON CHURCH DISCIPLINE

MALCOLM B. YARNELL III
ON THE PRIESTHOOD OF BELIEVERS

KREGEL
MINISTRY

Library of Congress Cataloging-in-Publication Data
Restoring integrity in Baptist churches / by Thomas White, Jason G. Duesing, and Malcolm B. Yarnell, editors.
    p. cm.
  Includes indexes.
  1. Southern Baptist Convention—Doctrines. 2. Baptists—Doctrines. 3. Baptism—Baptists. 4. Baptists—Discipline.
I. White, Thomas. II. Duesing, Jason G. III. Yarnell, Malcolm B.
BX6462.7.R47   2008   286'.173—dc22   2007044986

ISBN 978-0-8254-4113-4

Printed in the United States of America

*To the faithful believers who through God's grace
have preserved the New Testament witness of integrity
in the local church for more than two thousand years.*

Contents

Acknowledgments

This volume would not be possible were it not for the efforts of the Center for Theological Research and the Smith Center for Leadership Development at Southwestern Baptist Theological Seminary. Both of these centers put time and resources into the second Baptist Distinctives Conference held at Southwestern's Fort Worth campus during September of 2006.

The Smith Center for Leadership Development is a 55,000-square-foot conference center with fifty-five guestrooms. It attempts to bring positive change to the local churches through hosting theologically organized events addressing culturally significant topics. More information on the Smith Center, including information for scheduling conferences, may be found at http://www.swbts.edu/center.

The Center for Theological Research is currently engaged in a monumental task that will benefit all Baptists. The Web site http://www.BaptistTheology.org makes available to the broader public "White Papers" addressing current theological issues, as well as rare or out-of-print Baptist works online. By providing ready access to these important Baptist resources, the center seeks to preserve Baptist heritage and help educate a new generation concerning the biblical ways of our Baptist forefathers.

The editors wish to express their deep appreciation to the administration of Southwestern Baptist Theological Seminary, especially President Paige Patterson, for their support of the Baptist Distinctives Conference and this publication, and to Jon Wood, who helped with the indexes. The Baptist Distinctives Conference is a yearly endeavor scheduled to occur each fall at the Fort Worth campus of Southwestern Seminary.

Contributors

Daniel L. Akin (Ph.D., University of Texas at Arlington) is president of Southeastern Baptist Theological Seminary, as well as professor of theology and preaching. He has published many works, including *God on Sex: The Creator's Ideas About Love, Intimacy, and Marriage* (Nashville: Broadman & Holman, 2003) and *Discovering the Biblical Jesus: Evidence from an Empty Tomb* (Nashville: Lifeway Press, 2003), and recently edited *A Theology for the Church* (Nashville: B & H Publishing Group, 2007).

David Allen (Ph.D., University of Texas at Arlington) is the dean of the School of Theology and professor of expository preaching at Southwestern Baptist Theological Seminary. He has published numerous works, including two forthcoming projects: *Hebrews* in the New American Commentary series, and *The Authorship of Hebrews: The Case for Luke* (both Nashville: Broadman & Holman).

Emir F. Caner (Ph.D., University of Texas at Arlington) is dean and professor of history at The College at Southwestern. He is coauthor of *The Costly Call: Modern-Day Stories of Muslims Who Found Jesus* (Grand Rapids: Kregel, 2005), *The Sacred Desk: Presidential Addresses of the Southern Baptist Convention Presidents* (Nashville: Broadman & Holman, 2004), *Unveiling Islam: An Insider's Look at Muslim Life and Beliefs* (Grand Rapids: Kregel, 2002), and *More Than a Prophet: An Insider's Response to Muslim Beliefs About Jesus and Christianity* (Grand Rapids: Kregel, 2003).

Mark Dever (D.Phil., University of Cambridge) is pastor of Capitol Hill Baptist Church. He is the author of numerous works, including *The Message of the Old Testament* (Wheaton, IL: Crossway Books, 2006), *The Message of the New Testament*

(Wheaton, IL: Crossway Books, 2005), *Nine Marks of a Healthy Church* (Wheaton, IL: Crossway Books, 2004), *Polity: Biblical Arguments on How to Conduct Church Life* (Washington, DC: Center for Church Reform, 2005), and *The Deliberate Church: Building Your Ministry on the Gospel* (Wheaton, IL: Crossway Books, 2005). He is also the founder of 9Marks Ministries.

Jason G. Duesing (Ph.D. candidate, Southwestern Baptist Theological Seminary) is chief of staff in the Office of the President, Southwestern Baptist Theological Seminary. He recently coedited *First Freedom: The Baptist Perspective on Religious Liberty* (Nashville: B & H Publishing Group, 2007).

John S. Hammett (Ph.D., Southern Baptist Theological Seminary) is professor of systematic theology at Southeastern Baptist Theological Seminary, and has authored many publications, including *Biblical Foundations for Baptist Churches: A Contemporary Ecclesiology* (Grand Rapids: Kregel, 2005).

Jason K. Lee (Ph.D., University of Aberdeen) is currently associate professor of historical theology at Southwestern Baptist Theological Seminary. He has authored *The Theology of John Smyth* (Macon, GA: Mercer University Press, 2003) and *The Selected Works of John Smyth* (Scottdale, PA: Herald Press; Ontario, Canada: Pandora Press, forthcoming).

R. Stanton Norman (Ph.D., Southwestern Baptist Theological Seminary) is currently vice president for development at Southwest Baptist University. He has coedited *Perspectives on Church Government: Five Views of Church Polity* (Nashville: Broadman & Holman, 2004) and has authored *More Than Just a Name: Preserving Our Baptist Identity* (Nashville: Broadman & Holman, 2001).

Thomas White (Ph.D., Southeastern Baptist Theological Seminary) is vice president for student services and a faculty member at Southwestern Baptist Theological Seminary. He is the editor of *Selected Writings of James Madison Pendleton* (Paris, AR: Baptist Standard Bearer, 2006).

Gregory A. Wills (Ph.D., Emory University) is currently professor of church history and director of the Center for the Study of the Southern Baptist Convention at the Southern Baptist Theological Seminary. He has authored many works, including *Democratic Religion: Freedom, Authority, and Church Discipline in the Baptist South, 1785–1900* (New York: Oxford University Press, 2003).

Malcolm B. Yarnell III (D.Phil., Oxford University) is assistant dean for theological studies, director of the Center for Theological Research, director of the
Oxford Study Program, and associate professor of systematic theology at Southwestern Baptist Theological Seminary. He is the author of *The Formation of Christian Doctrine* (Nashville: B & H Publishing Group, 2007).

Introduction

THOMAS WHITE

In the locker room of a popular gym, I sat talking with friends. We had just finished lifting weights. After months of lifting one hour a day, four days a week, we had experienced only minimal gains in the amount of weight that we could lift. I had hit a plateau and could not seem to break through it. Another guy in the gym came up to me and told me that he had something that could help me break through my barrier. I sat up in anticipation, thinking this guy was about to give me the secret to eternal youthfulness, when he pulled a bottle out of his pocket—a small glass bottle with a space in the top for a needle to withdraw the fluids. The label on the bottle read "testosterone." I realized that I had a choice to make. I could compromise my integrity by taking steroids and reap the rewards of gaining pounds on my bench press and my squat, or I could maintain my integrity and struggle for gains the old-fashioned way. Was lifting weights all about the numbers, or was it more about the process? Was my goal to be bigger and better or simply to keep my body in shape? I struggled with the answers to these questions for many months. I watched as others grew much faster while I worked much harder. It did not seem fair.

The local church faces a similar dilemma. It can grow by using any number of tactics. A church can grow by appealing to consumerism, by creating a "trendy" atmosphere, by reaching out to felt needs, by not offending members, and by attempting to please all those people who enter the door. These "guaranteed" methods to achieve church growth can do harm to the corporate body, just as drugs that guarantee the growth of human muscle can harm the individual's body. A church must ask some tough questions: Does this mentality compromise the integrity of the local church? Are numbers the most important thing? Does the church only want to be "bigger and better," or would it be satisfied to maintain its integrity even if that meant sacrificing some growth or growing at a slower rate?

At this point, you may be thinking, How is the church in danger of losing its integrity for the sake of growth? Think about what has happened to Baptists over the past 150 years. Since the 1850s, the skewed emphasis of soul competency and the priesthood of the "believer" (rather than "believers"), the loss of church discipline in most Baptist churches, the changing view from closed or close Communion to a more open position, and the failure to continue defending our distinctive of believer's baptism by immersion have occurred. How have these affected Baptists?

Two main areas of discussion are needed, and these two, highlighted in this introduction, will guide the reader throughout the remainder of this work. First, this work will examine how events or trends have challenged the Baptist church's integrity and purpose. Second, this work will demonstrate how one can maintain or regain the integrity of the local church and theological purity while addressing the challenges of modern culture. With these two areas of discussion in mind, experts in Baptist life were sought to make presentations on these important topics.

CHALLENGES TO BAPTIST ECCLESIOLOGY

The following challenges that have shaped Baptist ecclesiology are not listed in order of importance, and they are not documented in this introduction. The documentation of these challenges will occur in subsequent chapters. This section simply will introduce the reader to several factors that have influenced Baptist churches to arrive at their current condition.

First, extreme individualism and the belief in the priesthood of the "believer" rather than "believers" has created congregations who feel each person possesses a right to his or her opinion. Extreme individualism allows members to believe that they can live life on their own terms without the encouragement or admonition of the body of believers. In addition, the priesthood of the "believer" provides theological nomenclature for defending whatever one wants to believe and admonishing those who deny the legitimacy of such belief. Baptists are neither free now nor have they ever been free to believe whatever they want. Baptists are bound by Scripture and should follow the plain meaning of Scripture without twisting hermeneutical spirals to support personal agendas. Self-determined positions undermine church discipline (where one member is confronted by others), closed Communion, and the defense of one position as the right position on baptism.

Second, theological denigration has affected many Baptist churches. The demise of sound theology, and more specifically ecclesiology, whether intentional or not, has occurred. Church discipline rarely occurs in the majority of Baptist churches. This loss of church discipline has affected the Baptist belief in regenerate church membership. With Baptist churches no longer guarding regenerate church membership, congregational polity becomes problematic, as unspiritual members continue contributing to spiritual decisions. This problem has led some to abandon congregational government rather than correcting the problem at the source by reimplementing church discipline and meaningful membership. Baptist church rolls contain the names of many people who rarely if ever enter the doors of the church. The loss of church discipline and the minimization of regenerate church membership functionally demonstrate the ecclesiological slide of Baptist churches.

Third, the emergence of the megachurch introduces unique and new challenges to Baptist ecclesiology. For example, how does a church carry out discipline when more than five thousand people attend every Sunday? That is fifteen hundred more people than live in my hometown of Honea Path, South Carolina. In addition, how can one properly guard the Lord's Supper when most members do not know each other and the pastoral staff certainly cannot have a personal relationship with everyone? The megachurch to some extent allows members to become anonymous, receiving the benefits of attending church without the duties of dedicating themselves to the ministry of the church. This is not to claim that the megachurch is wrong. After all, the first church at Jerusalem had three thousand people added in one day. But it brings unique challenges to Baptist ecclesiology that deserve discussion.

Fourth, a consumer-driven culture has created challenges for Baptist churches. Part of this has been prompted by churches seeking to entertain people in order to gain attendance. And part of the problem arose over members desiring to implement what the world offers in the local church. This consumer attitude perhaps is best exhibited by the "church hopper," who moves his or her membership from one church to another at the first whim. Such a person focuses more on personal happiness and felt needs than contributing to the ministry of the local church. The churches, by accepting these members so easily, reinforce this behavior. Another action that reveals the consumer culture is Christians driving past theologically sound churches near their homes to attend "popular" churches much farther away without valid theological justification. If someone attends a church farther away from his or her home because of preference or "commercial attraction," and not belief, that person is likely exhibiting a consumer mentality rather than a servant mentality. I drive farther to eat at certain restaurants because of preference. I drive farther to shop at certain stores because of preference, but I should not choose a church in the same way I choose a restaurant or a department store. Consumers will never understand meaningful membership or experience the local church as the body of Christ while focusing on their individual felt needs. Leaving one's local church body should be a painful and unpleasant experience. But with "church hoppers," meaningful connections never tend to form, and accountability rarely occurs. Rather, personal preference rules the day.

Fifth, perhaps the biggest challenge confronting Baptist churches is the "seeker-sensitive" movement. This movement positively seeks to remove unneeded barriers to reaching people with the gospel of Jesus Christ. At the same time, most seeker-focused churches do not practice church discipline. Few things could be less seeker-oriented than the act of publicly disciplining a member for improper behavior. Most, if not all, seeker churches do not practice the strictest form of Communion, limited to members only, and many do not practice Communion with like faith and practice, commonly called close Communion. Seeker churches tend to practice open Communion, with a few not making any statement at all about the Lord's Supper being for believers only. Restrictions placed on the Lord's Table could come across as not being seeker-friendly to many visitors. Controversial doctrines like believer's baptism by immersion do not receive extensive discussion in seeker-sensitive churches. This clearly biblical doctrine historically has been very important to the Baptist tradition but does not fit nicely within the seeker-sensitive tradition.

With these five challenges in mind, how can one seek to maintain a distinctive Baptist ecclesiology in today's culture? The presentations in this book seek to confront these challenges and show how a church can maintain proper ecclesiology while remaining relevant to culture. These discussions address the issue of maintaining the integrity of the local church by upholding necessary theological beliefs while operating in a seeker-sensitive world. Many of the challenges I have listed possess positive characteristics that do not conflict with theological integrity. The difficult task of the presentations in this book is to identify the balance between proper theology and practical relevance.

THEOLOGICAL IMPORTANCE OF ADDRESSING MODERN CULTURE

This volume addresses and emphasizes several areas of theological belief and practical application that will benefit the local church and bring some sense of discovery to the quest for theological purity amidst modern culture. These chapters have not been organized in any order of importance, partially because the elements are all intertwined to some degree. The essays are organized thematically according to five broad categories: church membership, baptism, the Lord's Supper, church discipline, and universal priesthood.

First, meaningful church membership must be regained. Meaningful membership will counter the culture of consumerism that the church faces. In addition, a congregation full of members who understand their role will result in a well-balanced church with more than the usual 20 percent of the members doing 80 percent of the work. In order for the members to take membership seriously, biblical expectations must be placed on them. This works in conjunction with church discipline and enforcing the expectations on those who malevolently or ignorantly fall short. Membership also can be emphasized by proper teaching on the Lord's Supper and baptism. For any church to function properly, its membership must see its role as meaningful.

An emphasis on the importance of regenerate church membership must be recovered. A proper theological understanding of the believers' church will affect the way the members see their individual roles in the local church. Correspondingly, the baptism of believers protects regenerate church membership by making baptism the door to the local church and the public profession of faith. Only those participating in this ceremonial act may be accepted into the membership of the local church. Thus, baptism properly understood protects the entrance to the church, while church discipline protects the continued integrity of the church. Without proper church discipline, no church can maintain meaningful and regenerate membership. The successful maintenance of regenerate church membership allows congregational church government to function properly. Regenerate membership is perhaps the most crucial and central element of polity in the life of Baptist churches.

Second, Baptist churches must regain, and act on, the proper understanding of baptism. The doctrine from which the denominational name arose has fallen into anonymity. With challenges from less-than-conservative churches questioning the importance of baptism and with seeker churches minimizing its importance, many younger pastors and church workers have not been properly equipped to defend the doctrine of baptism. Thus, this book dedicates discussion to the following aspects of baptism: baptism must be of believers, baptism must be by immersion, baptism is the outward symbol of the inward change, baptism is the public profession of faith, baptism is the door to the local church, and baptism begins the covenant relationship among the believers in a local congregation. The presentations will positively present proper theology and at the same time address current issues challenging the importance of the biblical doctrine of baptism.

Third, Baptist churches must understand and maintain the proper view of the Lord's Supper. A proper view of the Lord's Supper celebrates the ordinance meaningfully and not just as a necessary quarterly addition to the end of the church service. The Lord's Supper celebrates the memory of Christ on the cross, the fellowship and unity of the body, and the anticipated triumphant return of Christ, while denying the errors of transubstantiation and consubstantiation. In addition, the Lord's Supper, understood correctly, cannot be separated from church discipline and the regenerate nature of the congregation. This emphasis immediately creates tension with seeker-sensitive organizations that minimize such connections or celebrate the Lord's Supper only during services when few seekers are present, such as a Wednesday night service.

Fourth, Baptist churches must regain the proper practice of church discipline, which always seeks restoration. Church discipline easily can be twisted and used as a political tool to root out those with differing views or as a legalistic hammer with which one may beat others over the head. These misuses do not exemplify biblical church discipline, which intentionally confronts members in sin seeking both individual restoration and the maintenance of a pure body of believers. The loss of biblical church discipline is why many onlookers conclude that the church is no different than the world. This should never be the case; by requiring meaningful membership reinforced by biblical church discipline, the church will look very different from the world. A church will never successfully gain meaningful membership or maintain regenerate church membership without the consistent practice of church discipline. In addition, biblical church discipline necessarily correlates with the Lord's Supper, as we are not to celebrate the ordinance with those who practice immorality.

Finally, Baptist churches must address emerging and seeker groups pointing out specific challenges to Baptist theological practice. Without dismissing the very important emphasis on community and the desire for evangelism, Baptists must examine proper theological practice in light of the success these movements have achieved. While the local church needs a measuring stick for success other than numbers, the conversion of lives does represent the mission of the church. Traditional Baptist church order that follows and flows from Scripture can reflect in a real way the emphasis on community expressed by emerging groups and the emphasis on evangelism of seeker groups. Perhaps both of these movements in some way have recognized missing aspects of the local church—aspects missing because of an incomplete theology of the church. Community and a focus on evangelism can receive proper emphasis while maintaining traditional Baptist and biblical theology. This book demonstrates how a proper and complete understanding of Baptist church doctrine can guard the integrity of the local church while operating successfully in a seeker-sensitive world.

1

Regenerate Church Membership

JOHN S. HAMMETT

There are two generally recognized lists of marks of the church. The first list, which may be called the classical marks of the church, is found in the Nicene Creed, which describes the church as "one, holy, catholic, and apostolic."[1] The second list comes from the Reformers, who commonly agreed that a true church was found where there was the pure preaching of the Word and the right administration of the sacraments. In both cases, it seems these lists were derived, not from inductive study of Scripture on the nature of the church, but from polemical needs to distinguish the true church from contemporary rivals. Glenn Hinson says of the classical marks, "This formula took shape chiefly in efforts of the church to define themselves in relation to the Montanist, Novatianist, and Donatist schisms."[2] Similarly, the Reformation marks highlighted the understanding of the gospel that distinguished the Reformation churches from the Catholics, for the pure preaching of the Word was the preaching of the gospel, and the right administration of the sacraments was directed against the Catholic view of the sacraments, which the Reformers saw as obscuring or denying the gospel.

The topic of this chapter is what may be justly called the Baptist mark of the church, the principle of regenerate church membership. Like the classical and Reformation marks, this mark served to distinguish Baptist churches from the state churches that surrounded them. However, perhaps more so than the other two lists, the Baptist mark emerges obviously from biblical teaching on the church and has been central in the development of Baptist ecclesiology. This chapter will look

---

1. Though found in the Nicene Creed today, this description of the church was not found in the form of the creed developed at Nicaea in 325, but was added following the Council of Constantinople in 381.
2. E. Glenn Hinson, introduction to *Understandings of the Church*, trans. and ed. E. Glenn Hinson (Philadelphia: Fortress, 1986), 4.

first at the biblical rationale for regenerate church membership, then trace its rise and fall in Baptist life, argue for its centrality in Baptist ecclesiology, and suggest ways that it may be recovered in Baptist churches today.[3]

THE BIBLICAL RATIONALE FOR REGENERATE CHURCH MEMBERSHIP

The case for regenerate church membership from Scripture is overwhelmingly, even embarrassingly, clear. The following are only some of the major lines of evidence.

THE WORD EKKLESIA

There are two Hebrew words for God's people in the Old Testament: *edah* and *qahal*. The Greek term *ekklesia* is only used to translate *qahal*, never *edah*. Lothar Coenen distinguishes the two terms in this way: "There is always something indefinable about the *qahal*; for it embraces only those who have heard the call and are following it. *Edah*, on the other hand, is the permanent community into which one was born."[4] Thus, early Christians chose a term for their gatherings that suggests one did not join by birth but by response to a call. The way the New Testament uses the word *ekklesia* confirms this. While the importance of the etymology of *ekklesia* may be debated, the fact is that the church is referred to numerous times as those "called" (*kletos*) by God (e.g., Rom. 1:7; 1 Cor. 1:2; Jude 1).

BIBLICAL DESCRIPTIONS OF THE CHURCH

It is difficult, if not impossible, to find any text in Acts that suggests that anyone ever became associated with one of the churches described in it apart from a response to the gospel. Rather, churches are composed of those who "accepted his [Peter's] message" (Acts 2:41), those "who were being saved" (Acts 2:47), those who "believed" (Acts 4:4), and those who were "won" to discipleship (Acts 14:21).[5] The opening words of most of Paul's letters indicate that he thought he was writing to groups of believers. He calls them "those sanctified in Christ Jesus" (1 Cor. 1:2), "the faithful in Christ Jesus" (Eph. 1:1), and "the holy and faithful" (Col. 1:2), and more than sixty times he calls those in these churches "saints" or those set apart as devoted to God.

The New Testament uses a number of images to describe something of the church's nature, and all of them presuppose that the church is composed of genuine believers. How could the church be "the people of God" if the people did

---

3. A fuller development of many of these points may be found in John S. Hammett, *Biblical Foundations for Baptist Churches: A Contemporary Ecclesiology* (Grand Rapids: Kregel, 2005), 81–131.
4. Lothar Coenen, "Church," in *New International Dictionary of New Testament Theology*, ed. Colin Brown (Grand Rapids: Zondervan, 1975), 1:295.
5. All Scripture quotations in this chapter are from the New International Version (NIV).

not, in fact, belong to God? How could the church be "the body of Christ" if the members of that body were not, in fact, joined to Christ? How could the Holy Spirit make the church "a holy temple" in which God dwells and is worshipped if, in fact, God did not dwell in the individuals composing the church?

BIBLICAL EXPECTATIONS OF CHURCH MEMBERS
The church is given assignments that require it to be a body of believers. For example, the premise behind church discipline is that the church is to be a holy body. Furthermore, the members of the churches to whom the New Testament letters were addressed were commanded to pray for one another, to teach and admonish one another, to counsel one another, to edify and encourage one another, to love and forgive one another, and to serve and bear one another's burdens. In fact, there are at least thirty-seven specific "one another" commands in the New Testament.[6] It is hard to believe such commands would be issued to bodies that the authors did not believe were composed of regenerate individuals.

THE RISE AND FALL OF REGENERATE CHURCH MEMBERSHIP
The strong biblical rationale for regenerate church membership raises the question of how any alternative understanding of the church ever could have developed. Why was it left to Baptists to highlight this aspect of the church's nature? Why was it neglected for so long? The historical context preceding Baptists shows that while regenerate church membership had been practiced to a degree in the early church, a variety of factors contributed to the loss of regenerate church membership in the millennium prior to Baptists. Sadly, history also records that though regenerate church membership was at the heart of the origin of Baptists and was for most of Baptist history central to Baptist ecclesiology, it dramatically declined in Baptist life in the twentieth century and is in desperate need of recovery today.

THE DEVELOPMENT OF THE CORPUS PERMIXTUM
There is evidence that the early church maintained the biblical pattern of regenerate church membership for much of the patristic period. Perhaps the strongest evidence is the catechumenate, or the training process for new Christians, especially that used in many churches of the second and third centuries.[7] This material was designed for those "who have exercised faith in [the gospel message] and are

6. For a listing of thirty-one "one another" commands in the New Testament, see Jeremy Oddy, "Christian Fellowship: A Theological Study of *Koinonia* in the Local Church" (Th.M. Guided Research Report, Southeastern Baptist Theological Seminary, 2004), 23.
7. The standard source for the catechumenate of the early church is the *Apostolic Tradition*, usually attributed to Hippolytus of Rome (A.D. 170–235). For a recent translation , see Paul F. Bradshaw, Maxwell E. Johnson, and L. Edward Phillips, *The Apostolic Tradition* (Minneapolis: Fortress, 2002).

now taking the step to commit themselves to a rigorous course of study, prepare for baptism, and join the community of believers."[8] This preparation, which could last up to three years, was for those who were regenerate and was designed to lead to church membership. It seems to reflect a strong commitment to regenerate church membership and was "a universal feature" in the early church.[9]

Beyond this practice, the persecution of churches in the Roman Empire discouraged casual membership in churches. With the conversion of Constantine and the legalization and then imposition of Christianity, a new approach to church membership developed. Historians note that prior to Constantine's conversion, Christians numbered about 10 percent of the population of the Roman Empire, but within a century, that number jumped to 90 percent.[10] It seems safe to say that many were admitted to church membership without passing through the catechetical process. Sociologist Rodney Stark, commenting on the relaxing of standards, says, "The Church made it easy to become a Christian—so easy that actual conversion seldom occurred."[11]

Of course, this decline in commitment called forth a number of protests,[12] one of them being the Donatist movement in North Africa. The Donatists were especially concerned about the ease with which the church received back into her midst priests and bishops who had denied Christ or handed over the Scriptures during earlier times of persecution. They wanted the church to manifest visible holiness in its members, and they separated themselves from the Catholic Church to maintain holiness. Augustine regarded the Donatist sin of schism as far worse than anything done by those who succumbed under persecution and argued that the holiness of the church is that of her Head, Jesus Christ, which becomes visible in the members of the body only in the *eschaton*.

To illustrate the church in the world, Augustine used a parable of Christ, one that was to be used for centuries, that of the wheat and tares. He argued that in the church as we see it today, unbelievers and believers are mingled. It is a mixed body (*corpus permixtum*). Only at the final judgment will they be separated. Of course, the obvious objection to this argument is the fact that Jesus identifies the field

---

8. Clinton Arnold, "Early Church Catechesis and New Christians' Classes in Contemporary Evangelicalism," *Journal of the Evangelical Theological Society* 47, no. 1 (March 2004): 42. Arnold draws some fascinating parallels and differences between the practice of the early church and what numerous evangelical churches do today in new member or new Christian classes.

9. Ibid., 53.

10. Robert G. Clouse, Richard V. Pierard, and Edwin Yamauchi, *Two Kingdoms: The Church and Culture Through the Ages* (Chicago: Moody, 1993), 109.

11. Rodney Stark, *For the Glory of God: How Monotheism Led to Reformations, Science, Witch-Hunts, and the End of Slavery* (Princeton and Oxford, UK: Princeton University Press, 2003), 40.

12. Ibid., 40–41. Stark believes, and this author agrees, that the monastic movement was the largest form of protest against the decline in piety and commitment in the church.

in which the wheat and tares grow together as the world, not the church (Matt. 13:38). But Augustine's influence prevailed, and the accepted view of the church came to be that of the mixed body, a view that was maintained for more than a thousand years.[13]

REGENERATE CHURCH MEMBERSHIP IN BAPTIST LIFE

Once the Bible became readily available and the sole normative source for theology among Protestants, regenerate church membership almost immediately reappeared with the Anabaptists in Zwingli's Zurich. Regenerate church membership also was championed by the early English Baptists of the seventeenth century. While believer's baptism was the most visible mark of the Baptists, the more fundamental issue for the early Baptists and Anabaptists was the nature of those who were to compose the church. Leon McBeth says, "Perhaps the origin of Baptists is best explained as a search for a pure church. They sought a church composed of 'visible saints,' that is, true believers."[14]

Early Baptist statements of faith give repeated emphasis to this concern.[15] The Somerset Confession of 1656 is emphatic in charging churches to maintain regenerate church membership as a duty and matter of faithfulness: "In admitting of members into the church of Christ, it is the duty of the church, and ministers whom it concerns, in faithfulness to God, that they be careful they receive none but such as do make forth evident demonstration of the new birth, and the work of faith with power." Well into the nineteenth century Baptists maintained their zeal for the purity of the church, and as late as 1905, at the first meeting of the Baptist World Alliance, J. D. Freeman could say of Baptists, "This principle of a regenerated Church membership, more than anything else, marks our distinctiveness in the Christian world today."[16]

But danger signs had long been apparent. For example, Baptist churches in the South in the early nineteenth century typically had attendance well in excess of the number of their members. The children of members were present but rarely were seen as fit subjects for baptism and church membership prior to their teenage years. Moreover, many adults would regularly attend but not seek church membership

---

13. For more of the historical background, see G. G. Willis, *Saint Augustine and the Donatist Controversy* (London: SPCK, 1950).

14. Leon McBeth, *The Baptist Heritage* (Nashville: Broadman Press, 1987), 75.

15. Examples of such concern can be found in virtually all English Baptist confessions of the seventeenth century. See the examples in William Lumpkin, ed., *Baptist Confessions of Faith* (Philadelphia: Judson Press, 1959). Further examples from the eighteenth and nineteenth centuries can be seen in the texts gathered in Mark Dever, ed., *Polity: Biblical Arguments on How to Conduct Church Life* (Washington, DC: Center for Church Reform, 2001).

16. J. D. Freeman, "The Place of Baptists in the Christian Church," in *The Baptist World Congress: London, July 11–19, 1905, Authorised Record of Proceedings* (London: Baptist Union Publication Department, 1905), 27.

because the standards associated with membership and a regenerate life were daunting to them. A church with 100 members might well have 200 to 300 attendees. But in the early nineteenth century, evangelical church membership across the South, in Baptist, Methodist, and Presbyterian churches, began to increase, not due to a rise in piety, but to a relaxing of standards in the churches.[17]

American Christianity had long been a democratic, egalitarian, populist movement and as such had generally accommodated popular culture. In other words, American evangelical Christianity was becoming market driven before there was marketing.[18] For example, one study of the Second Awakening in America concludes that evangelical churches grew "largely because the price was right and the streets were filled with vendors."[19] The individualism so strongly characteristic of America began to be reflected in churches less willing to examine very closely the genuineness of the professions of faith of prospective members and less willing to discipline those whose professions were denied by their lives.[20]

The same problems endure to this day. Some suggest that the reason Christianity has remained so popular in America is that it makes so few demands.[21] This is a problem that cuts across the divisions of traditional, contemporary, seeker, and emerging churches. Whenever a church wants passionately to grow, the temptation comes to tailor the message to what will appeal to the audience.[22]

---

17. Christine Heyrman, *Southern Cross: The Beginnings of the Bible Belt* (New York: Alfred A. Knopf, 1997), 27.

18. The populist, market-driven nature of American Christianity is recognized by many American church historians. See John Woodbridge, Mark Noll, and Nathan Hatch, *The Gospel in America: Themes in the Story of America's Evangelicals* (Grand Rapids: Zondervan, 1979); Nathan Hatch, *The Democratization of American Christianity* (New Haven and London: Yale University Press, 1989); Gregory A. Wills, *Democratic Religion: Freedom, Authority, and Church Discipline in the Baptist South 1785–1900* (New York: Oxford University Press, 1997); and, Mark Noll, *America's God: From Jonathan Edwards to Abraham Lincoln* (Oxford and New York: Oxford University Pres, 2002).

19. Hatch, *Democratization of American Christianity*, 15, citing the study of Terry D. Bilhartz, *Urban Religion and the Second Great Awakening: Church and Society in Early National Baltimore* (Rutherford, NJ: Fairleigh Dickinson University Press, 1986), 98–99.

20. The decline in discipline is documented by Wills, *Democratic Religion*. Other factors are explored in John S. Hammett, "From Church Competence to Soul Competence: The Devolution of Baptist Ecclesiology," *Journal for Baptist Theology and Ministry* 3, no. 1 (Spring 2005): 145–63.

21. Woodbridge, Noll, and Hatch, *Gospel in America*, 179.

22. This critique has been leveled against Willow Creek Community Church by G. A. Pritchard, *Willow Creek Seeker Services: Evaluating a New Way of Doing Church* (Grand Rapids: Baker, 1996), 242–59; against Saddleback Community Church by Jonathan R. Wilson, "Practicing Church: Evangelical Ecclesiologies at the End of Modernity," in *The Community of the Word: Toward an Evangelical Ecclesiology*, ed. Mark Husbands and Daniel J. Treier (Downers Grove, IL: InterVarsity Press, 2005), 63–72; and against all "growth-oriented churches" by Alan Wolfe, *The Transformation of American Religion: How We Actually Live Our Faith* (New York: Free Press, 2003), 36, 166–67.

Today, a denomination like the Southern Baptist Convention maintains the theology of regenerate church membership in its official statements, but in reality its churches show little evidence of regeneration in the behavior of their members. It is widely known that divorce and moral problems are as common among church members as nonchurch members. Even the very modest index of attendance at Sunday morning worship shows close to two-thirds of Southern Baptist church members missing on any given Sunday morning.[23] Regenerate church membership cannot be seriously maintained as characterizing most Baptist churches in North America today.

REGENERATE CHURCH MEMBERSHIP AS THE CENTER OF BAPTIST ECCLESIOLOGY

Despite the loss of regenerate church membership in practice, it remains central to Baptist ecclesiology. In fact, the loss of regenerate church membership is directly related to problems in other areas of Baptist ecclesiology, for, as Justice Anderson has said, regenerate church membership is the "cardinal point of Baptist ecclesiology, and logically, the point of departure for church polity."[24] Charles Deweese likewise argues for the centrality of regenerate church membership to Baptist ecclesiology: "A direct relationship exists between a regenerate church membership and five other areas of Baptist life—church covenants, the ordinances, church discipline, evangelism, and small groups."[25] In the following we attempt to trace the connection between regenerate church membership and four aspects of Baptist ecclesiology.

REGENERATE CHURCH MEMBERSHIP AND BELIEVER'S BAPTISM

As noted above, while believer's baptism may be the most visible Baptist distinctive, it is supported by the logically prior principle of regenerate church membership. Baptists accepted the view of virtually all the churches around them that baptism is the ritual associated with entering into church membership. Where they differed was in their insistence that the church was to be composed of regenerate persons, or believers, only. Therefore, the only persons they would baptize and accept as members were believers. This logical argument was supported by their understanding of biblical teaching on baptism, which they saw as pointing unequivocally to believers as the only proper subjects of baptism.

---

23. For 2005, out of a total of 16,270,315 members in 43,699 Southern Baptist churches, only an average of 6,052,321, or 37.2 percent, attended Sunday morning worship.
24. Justice Anderson, "Old Baptist Principles Reset," *Southwestern Journal of Theology* 31 (Spring 1989): 5–12.
25. Charles Deweese, *A Community of Believers: Making Church Membership More Meaningful* (Valley Forge, PA: Judson Press, 1978), 13.

Not only have Baptists seen the logic of regenerate church membership and Scripture as requiring believer's baptism prior to church membership, but they have also seen the requirement of believer's baptism as a way to safeguard regenerate church membership. Almost a hundred years ago, Baptist theologian A. H. Strong argued that infant baptism undermines and eventually destroys regenerate church membership, for while some infants may experience regeneration as they mature, others will not and yet will remain members of the church. Over time, nonregenerate membership will become common.[26]

Today, some Baptist churches have contemplated accepting into membership those who give clear evidence of regeneration but have not experienced believer's baptism. If clear evidence of regeneration is required, such a practice would not necessarily destroy regenerate church membership, but it would involve a surrender of the traditional Baptist view that sees baptism, not as an optional step, but as a clear command of Christ to be obeyed by every believer. Mark Dever says that if a church receives into its membership someone who refused to obey such a clear command of Christ, it would have no choice but to discipline such a person.[27] Keeping believer's baptism and regenerate church membership together safeguards the latter and recognizes the importance of the former.

REGENERATE CHURCH MEMBERSHIP AND CONGREGATIONAL CHURCH GOVERNMENT

A second area where regenerate church membership is foundational to Baptist ecclesiology is congregational church government. Here the former is clearly prerequisite to the latter. J. L. Reynolds gave the rationale for congregationalism with these words in 1849: "If churches are composed only of such as give credible evidence of having been taught by the Spirit of God, they may be safely entrusted with the management of their own interests."[28] Moreover, a number of early Baptist confessions reflect the belief that churches composed of regenerate persons were capable of self-government, not just because the individuals composing them were regenerate and thus indwelt by the Spirit, but also because Christ gives a special gift of what they called "church power" to the corporate body gathered according to his instructions; that is, to churches composed of regenerate members.[29]

In recent years there has been a movement among some Baptists toward abandoning congregational government and adopting elder rule. This has been fueled

---

26. A. H. Strong, *Systematic Theology* (Philadelphia: Judson Press, 1907), 958.
27. Mark Dever, *A Display of God's Glory: Basics of Church Structure*, 2nd ed. (Washington, DC: Center for Church Reform, 2001), 52–53.
28. J. L. Reynolds, "Church Polity or the Kingdom of Christ, in its Internal and External Development," reprinted in Dever, *Polity*, 345.
29. For more on this, see Hammett, "From Church Competence to Soul Competence," 148–51.

by the difficulties pastors encounter in trying to get congregations composed of a mixture of regenerate and nonregenerate persons to govern themselves responsibly. But the problem is not with *congregationalism* as a system of church government but with *congregations* no longer composed of regenerate members. Congregational church government demands regenerate church membership.

REGENERATE CHURCH MEMBERSHIP AND CLOSED COMMUNION

Historically, most Christian groups have seen baptism as properly preceding participation in the Lord's Supper. Since most churches from the fifth century to the fifteenth century baptized infants, this order seemed obvious and was never challenged. Baptists agreed with this order but saw infant baptism as no baptism at all. They required believer's baptism prior to participation in the Lord's Supper. Moreover, Baptists have seen the Lord's Supper as not just for any group of baptized believers, but specifically for churches. Thus, churches composed of baptized believers (i.e., churches composed of regenerate members) are those for whom the Lord's Supper is intended. The link between baptism, church membership, and the Lord's Supper is made clear in the most recent Baptist confession, the Baptist Faith and Message (2000). Of believer's baptism, it says, "Being a church ordinance, it is prerequisite to the privileges of church membership and to the Lord's Supper." This position is called closed or close Communion, since participation in the Supper is closed or limited to church members. Some churches limit participation to members of that particular local church, but more often members of other Baptist churches who are visiting are also allowed to partake (a position sometimes called transient Communion or closed intercommunion).

Recently, some Baptists have adopted the position of open Communion, the view that any believer who is present may partake of the Supper. While such a position may seem more hospitable, historically Baptists have rejected it for at least two reasons. First, they have seen it as denigrating the importance of believer's baptism. Nineteenth-century Baptist theologian J. L. Dagg concludes his defense of closed Communion with that very point: "Why should baptism be trodden under foot, to open the way of access to the eucharist?"[30] Second, Baptists have seen a connection, not just between baptism and the Supper, but also between the church and the Supper. In the influential Second London Confession, Baptists called the Lord's Supper "a bond and pledge of their communion with him [Christ], *and with each other*."[31] Contemporary Baptist theologian Stanley Grenz makes the same

---

30. J. L. Dagg, *Manual of Theology, Second Part: A Treatise on Church Order* (Charleston, SC: Southern Baptist Publication Society, 1858; reprint, Harrisonburg, VA: Gano Books, 1982), 225. Dagg has one of the most thorough defenses of closed communion, considering and rejecting ten objections to it.
31. Emphasis added.

point, saying, "The Lord's Supper is not only a symbol of present community with Christ but also with one another within Christ's fellowship."[32]

How does this view of the Lord's Supper relate to regenerate church membership? If the Lord's Supper is given to the church and is designed to deepen and express the unity and communion believers experience with Christ and one another, two conclusions seem clear. First, the Lord's Supper is only for regenerate persons, for only they can experience communion with Christ. Second, the horizontal aspect of the Lord's Supper, the deepening and expression of communion with other believers, can be fully experienced only by persons who do in fact have such a relationship with one another; that is, members of a local church. Thus, it seems that the fullest experience of the Lord's Supper would be among the regenerate members of a local church. The historic Baptist understanding of the Lord's Supper and the Baptist view of regenerate church membership fit together, with the former reinforcing the latter. Charles Deweese states, "The heart and vitality of a regenerate church membership hinge heavily on the intensity with which Christians remain true to their baptismal and Lord's Supper vows."[33]

REGENERATE CHURCH MEMBERSHIP AND CHURCH DISCIPLINE

Church discipline and regenerate church membership are related in that the former can be effectively practiced only by a congregation composed of the latter, and that the latter can be maintained only if the former is consistently practiced. One of the objections sometimes made against regenerate church membership is the difficulty of identifying those who are regenerate. While Baptists have acknowledged that regeneration is an internal and invisible work, they have interpreted the Bible as assuming that regeneration will have visible results. Their confessions speak repeatedly of "visible saints" as those suitable for church membership.

Moreover, earlier Baptists saw congregations composed of regenerate persons as competent to evaluate the evidence (or nonevidence) of regeneration in a person's life and extend church membership or practice church discipline accordingly. Perhaps the fullest statement of this idea of church competence comes from the very important and influential Second London Confession. It states, "To each of these Churches thus gathered, according to his mind, declared in his word [i.e., churches composed of regenerate members], he [Christ] hath given all that power and authority, which is in any way needful, for their carrying on that order in worship, and discipline, which he hath instituted for them to observe; with commands, and rules for the due and right exerting of that power."

---

32. Stanley Grenz, *Theology for the Community of God* (Nashville: Broadman & Holman, 1994), 701.

33. Deweese, *Community of Believers*, 41.

This power to carry on discipline was specifically associated with Christ's words in Matthew 16:19, concerning "the keys of the kingdom." The power of the keys was seen as the power "to receive in or shut out of the Congregation"[34] and was specifically committed to "every visible congregational church."[35] The two early Baptists cited here, Benjamin Keach and Benjamin Griffith, were reflecting the common Baptist view that Baptist churches could properly practice church discipline precisely because they were a properly gathered church, composed of regenerate believers, to whom Christ had granted a measure of authority. Regenerate church membership is a prerequisite for the proper exercise of church discipline.

Church discipline is also a protection to regenerate church membership, for human judgment is fallible and churches will eventually admit as members some whose lives later contradict their profession. The initial and primary hope in the exercise of church discipline is that the member under consideration for discipline will repent and experience restoration in his relationship with both God and the church. However, in cases where repentance is not forthcoming, discipline serves a protective function. It allows the claim of churches to be genuine gatherings of Christ's regenerate people to be credible, rather than subject to the critique— accurate of many contemporary churches—that they are full of hypocrites and members whose lives are no different from those of nonbelievers.

Baptist commitment to church discipline and regenerate church membership continued well into the nineteenth century among Baptists in America. In fact, Greg Wills states of nineteenth-century Georgia Baptists, "They placed discipline at the center of church life. . . . Not even preaching the gospel was more important to them than the exercise of discipline."[36] However, in the latter part of the nineteenth century, the practice of church discipline began to decline among Baptists, and in the twentieth century it virtually disappeared. The results with regard to regenerate church membership, a corresponding decline and virtual disappearance, were entirely predictable.

TOWARD THE RECOVERY OF REGENERATE CHURCH MEMBERSHIP

No doubt any attempt to move toward a recovery of membership that is meaningful, and that involves genuine commitment and evidence of regeneration, is fraught with dangers. Is such a recovery even possible for Baptist churches in North America today? Could one not argue that earlier Baptists were too exclusive

---

34. Benjamin Keach, "The Glory of a True Church and Its Discipline Display'd," in Dever, *Polity*, 71.
35. Benjamin Griffith, "A Short Treatise Concerning a True and Orderly Gospel Church," in Dever, *Polity*, 99.
36. Wills, *Democratic Religion*, 8.

and unnecessarily turned people away? Would people not be offended and driven away from our churches today if we were to return to serious questioning of those coming for baptism and to a regular practice of church discipline? Is this even a battle worth fighting? These are all serious questions that deserve careful consideration.

I certainly would encourage any pastor attempting changes in these areas to move slowly, building trust with his people and adding to their understanding of biblical truth as he proceeds. Particularly, church discipline as redemptive rather than punitive should be clearly explained. Nevertheless, it seems to me that the time is ripe for change in this area. I am encouraged by anecdotal evidence of a small but growing number of churches adopting new member classes, requiring commitment to a church covenant, and some even beginning to practice church discipline.[37] I want to offer four reasons why I think recovering meaningful membership is a battle worth fighting and then three practical suggestions for beginning such a recovery in a local church.

WHY RECOVER MEANINGFUL MEMBERSHIP?

First, I think the recovery of meaningful church membership should be the highest priority of Baptist churches today because of the effect it will have on our corporate witness. Imagine being able to respond to the common excuse, "Your church is full of hypocrites," by saying, "Well, we're not perfect, but we are committed to following Christ," and knowing that the lives of church members backed that up. Rather than driving people away, meaningful membership could be the most attractive witness a church could offer. Greg Wills notes that from 1790 to 1860, when Baptist churches maintained high rates of discipline, they also maintained high rates of growth, growing at a rate twice that of the population. But in later years, as their discipline fell, so did their growth.[38] Could the recovery of meaningful membership allow the light of the gospel to shine through us with greater clarity and beauty? Rick Warren and Mark Dever, though in quite different contexts, both speak of the evangelistic impact of a congregation comprised of people whose lives are being changed.[39] Our corporate witness would be greatly enhanced by the recovery of meaningful membership.

---

37. One instructive example is Capitol Hill Baptist Church in Washington, DC. They invite pastors and church leaders to come for a weekend conference in which they describe the process of recovery of regenerate church membership in their congregation and allow the visitors to observe their membership classes and members' meetings and to talk with staff about the issues related to regenerate church membership. See http://www.9marks.org.
38. Wills, *Democratic Religion*, 36.
39. Mark Dever, "Pastoral Success in Evangelistic Ministry: The Receding Horizon" in *Reforming Pastoral Ministry: Challenges for Ministry in Postmodern Times*, ed. John H. Armstrong (Wheaton, IL: Crossway), 255. Dever states, "If you can get a reputation in the community as a church in which people's lives are actually changed, you will begin to see some amazing things." Rick

Second, our corporate health will be strengthened. How can the church live the life it is commanded to live—loving one another, praying for one another, encouraging one another—if many of its members are unregenerate? How can churches govern themselves responsibly if members are not walking in fellowship with Christ and one another? Ephesians 4:16 and Colossians 2:19 indicate that the body grows only when each part does its work, but if parts of the body are not regenerate, they will tear down the body rather than build it up.

A third reason for doing the hard work involved in recovering meaningful membership is the potential for awakening literally millions of lost church members. Many chronically absent church members whose lives give no evidence of regeneration may be trusting in their church membership to get them to heaven. A recovery of meaningful church membership would involve a challenge to such members. Sooner or later, they would have to be confronted with the fact that they are not living as followers of Christ and members of his body should. The administration of loving but firm church discipline, after repeated attempts to bring these individuals to repentance, would be the most serious way a church could attempt to awaken them to their perilous condition. Such an action would be far more loving than the current policy of allowing such members to continue in an apparently lost state without a word of warning.

Finally, recovering meaningful church membership will honor Christ. Ephesians 5:25–27 describes how Christ died for the church in order to present her to himself as a holy, radiant church. If such was the goal of Christ's crossbearing, such must also be the goal of our ministries. Christ is honored when his bride is holy, but he cannot be so honored as long as many of the members making up that bride live like lost people. The Charleston *Summary of Church Discipline* says that when churches allow unconverted people to crowd into them, they "make the church of Christ a harlot."[40] Christ is honored when churches are composed of people whose church membership means, first of all, a genuine, vital commitment to Christ and, second, a commitment to the people of that local body. Christ is honored when church membership is meaningful.

How Can Regenerate Church Membership Be Reclaimed?

How can regenerate church membership become a reality in a church with a membership of 600 but an average attendance of 200, and where half of the 400 absentees have been absent so long that only a few senior citizens even

---

Warren, *The Purpose Driven Church: Growth Without Compromising Your Message and Mission* (Grand Rapids: Zondervan, 1995), 247, concurs: "What *really* attracts large numbers of unchurched to a church is changed lives—a lot of changed lives" (emphasis in original).

40. James Leo Garrett Jr., *Baptist Church Discipline* (Nashville: Broadman Press, 1962), 36.

know who they are? How can a pastor or church leader begin to inculcate the idea of meaningful church membership? Where can he start? Let me make three suggestions.[41]

RETURNING TO CHURCH COVENANTS

Charles Deweese notes that Baptists throughout their history "have written and used hundreds, and perhaps thousands, of church covenants."[42] These documents are different from confessions of faith in that conduct is emphasized more than doctrine, though doctrine is often mentioned secondarily. For all their variety, covenants tend to have a remarkable similarity in terms of contents and purposes. Deweese says that a commitment to church fellowship, an acceptance of the authority of the church's discipline, a pledge to support the worship of the church and personal devotion, and a commitment to mutual care one for another appear in virtually all Baptist church covenants.[43]

Furthermore, one of the major purposes for the use of church covenants is precisely to safeguard regenerate church membership. In the past, churches constituted around the commitments involved in adopting a church covenant. Becoming a member involved "owning" the church covenant. Deweese comments, "Baptists have stated forcefully and repeatedly that the covenant idea is essential to the nature, definition, and constitution of a church."[44] Church covenants did not require perfection; indeed, they required nothing that is not explicitly or implicitly commanded in Scripture, but they did make clear that church membership involved a commitment that any regenerate person should accept.

In the late nineteenth and early twentieth century, the practice of covenanting declined. A number of factors contributed to this decline, among them the sacrifice of the ideal of regenerate church membership to the ideal of numerical growth, the general secularization of American society, and the unwillingness of church members to hold one another accountable. Deweese also suggests that Baptists may have been the victim of the extreme popularity of the 1853 church covenant written by J. Newton Brown, which was widely adopted by Baptist churches in America. Deweese states:

> Covenantal decline also likely resulted from a growing tendency
> of churches simply to adopt standardized, uniform covenants

---

41. For more specific suggestions on recovering regenerate church membership, see Mark Dever and Paul Alexander, *The Deliberate Church: Building Biblically in a Haphazard Age* (Wheaton: Crossway, 2005), especially 33–74, dealing with church covenants, new member classes, church discipline, and numerous related topics in a practical, nuts-and-bolts fashion.
42. Charles W. Deweese, *Baptist Church Covenants* (Nashville: Broadman Press, 1990), v. In this volume Deweese prints seventy-nine of these covenants as a representative sample.
43. Ibid., 55.
44. Ibid., 97.

printed in external sources, rather than to write their own indi-
vidualized statements. Throughout Baptist history covenantal
value and dynamic have correlated closely with the degree of
input that churches have exercised in arriving at the covenants
they have used.[45]

He adds, "Baptist presses and publications which have sponsored model covenants have apparently contributed to the weakening of congregational discipline by making it unnecessary for churches to think through, struggle with,
and write down covenantal responsibilities to which they are willing to commit
themselves."[46]

I would suggest, then, that a church seeking to recover a meaningful membership of regenerate individuals begin by discussing among themselves who and
what they are as a church and what type of commitment Scripture calls them
to make to one another as a body of believers.[47] These discussions would move
the church toward adoption of a church covenant. Examples of the covenants of
other churches may be consulted,[48] but churches would do well to personalize and
individualize their covenant so that the congregation as a whole owns it as *their*
covenant, not one imposed upon them.

Then, when the church has developed a covenant that expresses their commitment to one another and to Christ as his church, the church would vote to dissolve
the present membership and reconstitute around those who sign their names to
the church covenant.[49] This would be preceded by several announcements of the
proposed signing day. I would even encourage the pastor to send a letter to every
member of the congregation with the proposed covenant and the decision of the
church to reconstitute around it.

There is a biblical precedent for such action in Nehemiah 9–10. After a time of
renewal and confession in Nehemiah 8–9, Nehemiah records the decision of God's
people: "We are making a binding agreement, putting it in writing, and our leaders, our Levites and our priests are affixing their seals to it" (9:38). After listing

---

45. Ibid., 36.
46. Ibid., 89.
47. Deweese, *Community of Believers*, 28–40. Deweese gives a helpful outline of some of the practi-
    cal steps to take in the preparation and implementation of a church covenant.
48. For example, the covenants of Saddleback Community Church and Capitol Hill Baptist Church
    are available in a number of places, including Hammett, *Biblical Foundations*, 128–29.
49. Alan Neely, "Church Membership: What Does It Mean? What Can It Mean?" in *Proclaiming
    the Baptist Vision: The Church*, ed. Walter B. Shurden (Macon, GA: Smyth & Helwys, 1996), 47.
    Neely commends the example of a Mennonite church that erased their membership list every
    three years and asked those who wanted to continue in the fellowship of the church to sign their
    names, indicating the renewal of their commitment. I would only change their practice by mak-
    ing it annual rather than triennial.

all the leaders by name, the text states that the rest of the people joined with them (10:28–29). Their "binding agreement," or covenant, specified the areas of their lives that needed specific commitments. In that context, the key issues were avoiding intermarriage with the surrounding pagans, conducting no business on the Sabbath, and supporting the temple worship (10:30–39). Contemporary covenants would list the areas of commitment contemporary churches see as central to their life together. The people in Nehemiah's day concluded with a summary statement of their commitment, "We will not neglect the house of our God." Adopting a church covenant is one way God's people today can say, "We will not neglect our church."

This biblical example gives a beautiful model for contemporary church covenants. The covenant would be their "binding agreement," specifying areas of their commitment to Christ and one another. At the conclusion of a service celebrating the adoption of the covenant, the church leadership could be invited to come and sign their names to a roster attached to the church covenant. Then all who are willing to accept the covenant responsibilities would be invited to come and sign. The same document and roster would be taken to shut-in members who are not able to come but are still committed to the church. Those who sign would become the church's membership. Part of the process for adding subsequent members would involve the signing of the covenant, and existing members would be asked to sign their commitment afresh every year. It could become an annual church renewal event.

I like this approach for three reasons. First, it is biblical. It follows a biblical pattern and calls for a biblical commitment. Second, it deals with the huge backlog of absentee members in a practical way. Rather than having the church sort through and make decisions about who to retain and who to purge from their membership, this procedure places the burden on the individual. The church does not "kick out" or "excommunicate" anyone. It does, however, respect the decision of individuals who choose not to come and sign the church covenant. They have chosen not to be members of the church. Third, it will go a long way toward accomplishing the goal of restoring a regenerate membership. It is not sufficient alone, but it is a good starting point.

What about those who do not come and sign the covenant? In most churches, their number will be considerable.[50] Those who choose not to come and sign should become the object of the congregation's love and concern. They should be visited to ascertain why they did not come. Efforts should be made to reclaim them, but

---

50. For example, when the First Baptist Church of Union, Missouri, reorganized around the signing of a church covenant in 1997, their membership immediately dropped from more than 1,200 to 333, but then it began to grow.

not on just any terms. They should be welcomed into Christ's church on Christ's terms, which include commitment to Christ and to his people, which is what the church covenant expresses. Many of these people may not be saved, but it is not the job of the church to pronounce upon that. God alone knows the heart.

What the church can and should say is that a Christian, who loves Christ and wants to be part of his people, should have no trouble committing to the church covenant and that the church is deeply concerned over the spiritual state of all those who do not manifest a commitment to Christ. Indeed, it is the duty of the church to warn such people of the danger they are in. But it would be less than honest not to acknowledge that chronic church absentees are some of the hardest people to reach. Many, perhaps most, will not respond to efforts to win them. They will simply choose to no longer be part of the church. In truth, they have not been part of it since they dropped out. Their decision not to sign simply recognizes what the reality has been. The adoption of a church covenant, with annual renewal, is a good start, but it is not the only step needed to recover and preserve regenerate church membership.

REFORMING BAPTISM AND CHURCH MEMBERSHIP

Early Baptists had a robust confidence that the church was competent to examine a prospective baptismal candidate and find evidence of regeneration prior to administering baptism and welcoming the baptized believer into the church's membership. Today, many churches and, no doubt, many Christians do not share that confidence. They fear the development of a judgmental attitude that repels those who may be seeking Christ and drives people away, and they know all too well that all human judgment is fallible. Yet I think there are some measures churches may take to be responsible as well as hospitable in baptizing and welcoming new members.

The first such measure is to make a clear separation between welcoming someone who applies for membership and the official granting of membership itself. In most Baptist churches in North America today, what happens when someone comes forward at the end of a service and asks for membership? There may be a few moments of whispered conversation, but after a few perfunctory questions the person is presented for a church vote. The problem is that the church members have no basis for voting on such a person. No one would think of opposing their request for membership, so the vote becomes a meaningless gesture, a relic of an earlier time when churches took membership more seriously. A better approach is to welcome such a person, rejoicing over the decision made, whether it is to transfer membership or to seek baptism and then church membership, but to delay a vote on the request for membership until a later time, when other requirements for membership have been met.

One such requirement could be the completion of a class. Such classes, called variously new Christian's classes or new member's classes, are becoming more common in Baptist churches today and bear some resemblance to the catechumenate of the early church, a time when new converts were taught the basic elements of the Christian faith before and as preparation for baptism.[51] Among many Baptist groups outside of North America such classes are standard.[52] They serve several important purposes. They provide a natural context for new prospective members to meet others and develop relationships. They provide an opportunity to introduce these individuals to the various ministries of the church. And, most importantly, they provide a context for discussion of each individual's spiritual condition, for a key component of such classes should be a review of each person's understanding of the gospel. Even those coming from other churches need to be given the opportunity of sharing how they came to know Christ and how they understand the gospel, for in some churches the gospel is not clearly explained. For those coming as new converts and requesting baptism, such a review of the gospel is essential.

Once prospective new members have completed this class, those who conducted the class can recommend admitting them for baptism and/or church membership, and members can vote with some confidence, based on such a recommendation. I know of cases where prospective new members were converted in the new member's class, and other cases where prospective new members came to understand the gospel for the first time in the new member's class and rejected it. They had responded emotionally to a gospel message in a worship service, but when they understood the commitment involved in trusting Christ, they were unwilling to put their faith in him. But I think it is far better to know and reject the gospel than to be baptized and think one is somehow safe without ever coming to an understanding of the gospel or what it means to place saving faith in Christ.

An objection often raised to such classes, especially in the case of those who are new converts and seeking baptism, is the claim that the New Testament pattern was baptism immediately following conversion, with no intervening class. That is in fact the case on most of the occasions recorded in the book of Acts (Acts 2:41; 8:12, 36–38; 10:48; 16:32–33), but in some cases the time element is not clear (e.g., 18:8), or baptism is not mentioned in connection with conversion at all (4:4; 5:14; 13:48; 14:1, 21). In any case, there is no command regarding the immediacy of baptism anywhere in the New Testament. By the second century, the early church

---

51. Deweese, *Community of Believers*, 43–48. Deweese sees such "pre-baptismal classes" as vitally important for regenerate church membership.
52. For example, during three years as a missionary in Brazil, I encountered no Baptist church that did not have a new convert's class.

began to institute the catechumenate to insure that those they baptized were indeed converted.[53] That is still the motivation behind new member's classes.

One place where caution is especially appropriate is in the case of very young children. Anyone who works with children knows that five-year-olds will readily ask Jesus into their hearts, but until very recently Baptists would never have considered baptizing them. Believer's baptism was seen as virtually synonymous with adult baptism. To request baptism was regarded as a decision requiring a fair degree of maturity. For a church to baptize someone was to welcome that person into the responsibilities of church membership, which would include participation in the governance of the church, which seems inappropriate in the case of preschoolers. Overseas, most Baptists delay baptism until the teen years, but it is difficult to avoid arbitrariness in setting any specific minimum age for baptism.

I think some churches have taken a step in the right direction in requiring a class before baptism and limiting that class to those seven years of age and older. This should be accompanied by clear teaching that God can save any child whenever he chooses and that baptism is in no way necessary for salvation. So, if some children are saved before the age of seven, delaying their baptism will not somehow endanger their salvation. Instead, it will give their decision time to take root and grow, so that when they are baptized it will be more meaningful for them. It also should reduce the growing number of rebaptisms, those performed when church members realize later in life that their baptism as a child was not, in fact, believer's baptism.[54] It also should be another helpful step toward recovering regenerate church membership.

Others think even seven is too young an age for baptism. While he states that setting an arbitrary age for conversion is a mistake, William Hendricks also says, "It is highly doubtful that many children below the age of nine can express or have experienced despair for sin as radical separation from God. One cannot be 'saved' until he is aware he is 'lost.'"[55] This raises the issue of the age of accountability or age of moral responsibility. In Judaism, that age was twelve. At the ceremony of the bar mitzvah, a child assumed adult spiritual responsibilities.[56] That may be the

---

53. Arnold, "Early Church Catechesis and New Christians' Classes," 42.
54. Art Murphy, children's pastor at First Baptist Church, Orlando, Florida, says, "We have found that most children who make that decision [of baptism] under the age of 7 tend to need to make another decision later," referring to rebaptisms. See Art Murphy, "Leading a Child to Christ," *SBC Life* (June–July 1998), 9.
55. William L. Hendricks, *A Theology for Children* (Nashville: Broadman Press, 1980), 249.
56. See David Alan Black, *The Myth of Adolescence* (Yorba Linda, CA: Davidson Press, 1999), 59–67, for a discussion of the important transitions that occur at the age of twelve. Black draws upon the Jewish traditions surrounding the bar mitzvah, the account of Jesus in the temple at the age of twelve, the findings of developmental psychologists such as Piaget and Erikson, and the study of stages of faith by James Fowler.

context for Paul's statement in Romans 7:9, "Once I was alive apart from law; but when the commandment came, sin sprang to life and I died." The commandment came to a Jewish boy at his bar mitzvah. This is the closest I have found to a biblical indication of the age of accountability, and that age is twelve. That was also when Jesus first began to manifest his special calling (Luke 2:41–50). Furthermore, in groups that practice infant baptism, the ceremony of confirmation is usually around the age of twelve. Finally, most developmental psychologists agree that children reach full moral decision-making ability around the age of twelve.

For these reasons, some see twelve as the appropriate minimum age for baptism. This is the course taken by Grace Community Church of Sun Valley, California, and their pastor John MacArthur. They believe baptizing a child who is not genuinely regenerate does that child a disservice and poses a danger, especially if that child takes his or her baptism as proof of salvation. Therefore, they think it is wiser to "wait for more significant evidence of lasting commitment" and for "evidence of regeneration that is independent of parental control."[57] Their practice is to wait until a child is at least twelve to look for such evidence.[58] Whatever choice a church makes about the appropriate age for baptism, our concern here is to encourage a thoughtful approach to receiving children as candidates for baptism and church membership, one that takes seriously the Baptist commitment to believer's baptism and regenerate church membership.

So what does a pastor do when a very young child comes forward with his parents during the invitation? Certainly he should pray with the child and his parents but say to them and the congregation something like this: "We want to celebrate with Johnny and his parents. Today he is taking an important step in his relationship with Jesus. We're going to talk with Johnny and his parents more about this, and at the appropriate time we will be presenting him as a candidate for baptism and church membership. Today we invite you to come by and congratulate him and his parents on the step he has taken today." This affirms the child and allows the church to congratulate him and celebrate his decision, but it does not prematurely conclude that the decision made has moved the child from lost to saved, nor does it commit the church to baptizing the child. But even with these precautions,

---

57. Grace Community Church, *Evangelizing Children* (Sun Valley, CA: Grace Books International, 2003), 6. Also available at http://www.gracechurch.org/ministries.

58. It is also interesting to note that in a 2001 survey of 2000 worshippers in Southern Baptist churches, of those who affirmed that they had experienced conversion, more indicated that they had experienced conversion at the age of twelve than at any other age. Indeed, the number who experienced conversion at that age were more than twice the number for the ages of eleven and thirteen combined. See "Research Report: Conversion and Witnessing Among Southern Baptists" (Alpharetta, GA: North American Mission Board, SBC, 2002), 2, available at http://www.nambnet/research.

which seek to make as sure as humanly possible that the church brings in regenerate members only, there is still a need to deal with members who either are brought in mistakenly in an unregenerate state or begin sometime after joining to live like an unregenerate person. Therefore, there needs to be a third step to restoring meaningful, regenerate church membership.

RESTORING REDEMPTIVE CHURCH DISCIPLINE

A strong emphasis on church discipline was a notable characteristic of early Anabaptists and Baptists. It appeared pervasively in their confessions of faith as a key exercise of congregational government. It was widely practiced in their churches to maintain purity, and it was a popular subject of discussion among their theologians. It persisted well into the nineteenth century and is still present among Baptists outside North America. However, as we noted above, church discipline among Baptist churches in North America declined in the late nineteenth century and nearly disappeared in the twentieth century. It has faced some of the same obstacles as regenerate church membership as a whole: the overall secularization of American society, American individualism, the fear of appearing judgmental, and the desire for increasing numbers. Redemptive church discipline and regenerate church membership have fallen together. Yet there is a strong biblical basis for church discipline[59] and an evident need for it in our churches. Polls on virtually every social index show little difference between the church and the world. As John L. Dagg said perceptively over a hundred years ago, "It has been remarked, that when discipline leaves a church, Christ goes with it."[60] How might pastors go about reinstituting discipline in churches today? In a word, they should do so *carefully*.[61]

I do not think restoring church discipline should be the first step a pastor takes upon entering a church. The people need to see and know that their pastor loves people, lest they think his ideas about church discipline are the product of a hateful heart. He needs to lay a biblical foundation for church discipline by preaching and teaching on the texts dealing with church discipline and to illustrate the teaching with examples of traditional Baptist support for this practice. Hopefully, these actions will spark some discussion of the issue. That discussion should lead to

---

59. Matthew 18:15–20 and 1 Corinthians 5:1–13 are the classic texts, but it also appears in Galatians 6:1; 2 Thessalonians 3:14–15; 1 Timothy 1:20; and 5:19–20.

60. John L. Dagg, *Manual of Church Order* (Charleston, SC: Southern Baptist Publication Society, 1858; reprint, Harrisonburg: Gano Books, 1990), 274.

61. Deweese, *Community of Believers*, 74–80, offers nine practical, helpful suggestions as to how contemporary churches might restore the practice of church discipline. The Winter 2000 issue of *The Southern Baptist Journal of Theology* is devoted to a discussion of church discipline, with six very helpful articles. Both these resources recognize both the importance and the dangers involved in implementing church discipline.

incorporating some official statements about church discipline in key documents such as the bylaws and church covenant.

In these documents, it should be clearly stated that becoming a member of the church and signing the church covenant involves an acknowledgment of the church's authority in matters of discipline. Such statements can protect the church from lawsuits by members who are disciplined. They also should describe the goal of discipline as restoration for the one who is disciplined and protection for the church and its corporate witness in the community. Furthermore, it should be clearly explained that discipline is not for the weak one who falls but repents and wants to grow in Christ, but for the strong one who rebels defiantly. It also should be stated that discipline is not an excuse to get revenge for personal offenses. Some things should be covered over with brotherly love (1 Peter 4:8).

Sins that threaten the unity of the church, the purity of the church, or the church's doctrine are issues that call for church discipline. With such persons, the church should follow the pattern of Matthew 18. The individual who sees the problem should confront the offending brother individually and in all humility. Individual visits can continue as long as the confronter thinks progress is being made. But eventually, if the brother is not won over, two or three others (pastors, staff, friends) are to go together to appeal to the offender again. Only if repeated small-group efforts prove to be in vain is the issue to go before the church.

It bears repeating that the reintroduction of discipline will not be an easy task. James Leo Garrett Jr. said a generation ago, "Those who would lead in the renewal of discipline must be thoroughly convinced of its terrible urgency."[62] I would add they also must see clearly the wonderful benefits that could come in terms of a powerful corporate witness, spiritual growth, the reclamation of wandering brothers, the awakening of lost church members to their peril, and the recovery of meaningful church membership.

CONCLUSION

This chapter has examined what may historically be called the Baptist mark of the church, regenerate church membership. However, today, most Baptist churches are far from exemplifying that mark. In fact, the epidemic of obesity in the American population is matched by the obesity of many American churches. Many can boast large numbers of members, but the majority of those members are like fat cells, not contributing to the church's life and health but constituting a threat to it. I pray that those who read this book will be among those who will faithfully labor to see changes that would make Paul's doxology ring true, that God would

---

62. Garrett, *Baptist Church Discipline*, 25.

be glorified in the church: "Now to him who is able to do immeasurably more than all we ask or imagine, according to his power that is at work within us, *to him be glory in the church* and in Christ Jesus throughout all generations, for ever and ever! Amen" (Eph. 3:20–21, emphasis added).

2

Regaining Meaningful Church Membership

MARK DEVER

D id you hear the one about the Baptist church and their problem with squirrels? The squirrels had infiltrated the church building, up in the attic, even down into the kitchen. Finally, someone came up with a solution. They baptized the squirrels, and now they only see them on Christmas and Easter!

That is the sad reflection of the culture in many of our churches. Few today remember "Transfer Church Membership Week." This was inaugurated by the Southern Baptist Convention in 1953 as an attempt to deal with the large percentage (almost 30 percent) of Southern Baptists who were identified as nonresident members. A few years later, in 1962, James Leo Garrett Jr. wrote that "inactive and nonparticipating church members and the problem of nonresident membership have become major Southern Baptist difficulties."[1] If this is accurate, it was not a recent development. In the 1938 Southern Baptist Convention meeting at Richmond, Virginia, concern was expressed about this problem, and a committee appointed to investigate it. And, decades later, the problem remains.

In fact, the problem of nonresidential membership seems to have worsened and perhaps to have given way to the even greater problem today of two-thirds of Southern Baptists being nonattending members. One certainly appreciates the fact that any church may have members not in attendance on any given Sunday. Perhaps they are on the mission field or in a retirement home. Some are ill and permanently at home. Others may have moved and simply not yet moved their membership. Some are in the military or another overseas government service, and others are in college for part of the year.

---

1. James Leo Garrett Jr., *Baptist Church Discipline* (Nashville: Broadman Press, 1962), 1.

I fear, however, that most of our members are perfectly able on most Sundays to attend church, either here or elsewhere. But they do not. They should join where they attend. And if they are able and do not attend, then they should not be allowed to be a member of a Christian church. They are, in fact, in sin. Hebrews 10:25 instructs us not to be like those who forsake the regular assembling of themselves together. Disobeying this clear instruction does not inspire confidence in the ongoing repentance and faith of nonattenders.

A member's regular, tolerated nonattendance begins to raise further questions. What kind of leadership must a church have to allow such a misrepresentation to arise and flourish? What expectations are being communicated to those who are joining? What discipline is practiced, if any? In fact, tolerated noninvolvement among members may even call into question the kind of evangelism being done and the church's understanding of conversion, even of the gospel itself. Allowing such nonattending members to retain their membership would seem to be such blatant disobedience to Scripture, and such a brazen disregard of the spiritual health of those concerned, that it would even call into question the teaching that has brought about such an unhealthy tolerance in the body.

This, then, is a difficult topic—regaining meaningful church membership. How do you regain what is not understood? How do you make meaningful something that you don't believe? After all, many Bible-believing Christians today deny that church membership is biblical, as quickly and easily as Jehovah's Witnesses deny the Trinity or Muslims Christ's divinity! "Show us the verse," they say. But the truth God has revealed in his Word is not limited to simple, explicit statements. Much of the most important teaching of Christ, his relationship to his Father, and the Spirit's relationship to the Father and the Son is best and most clearly understood when passages are compared and the teaching systematically constructed. And so it is with church membership. But then, today, we must ask, what does membership mean in such an amorphous group as today's local church? Among many today, from popular writers to mission strategists, even the definition of the local church has faded. This is a difficult topic, but even more significant than its difficulty is its importance.

The plan for this chapter is first to define the church. Much of the work that needs to be done is in this initial and foundational work. Then, the membership of the church must be defined. Reasons for the practice of membership and requirements for specific members must be considered. One cannot regain what one does not even understand has been lost. Finally, when we have considered what particularly constitutes membership as meaningful, we will consider what steps can be taken by a local congregation to regain such meaningful membership. In summary, we will consider the church, membership in it, and how it is by definition meaningful and then conclude with steps one can take to regain for a congregation an appreciation of the meaning of membership. All of this is undertaken with a desire to see local congregations built up to the glory of God.

DEFINITION OF A CHURCH

What is a church? It is commonplace that a church is not a building. And it is true that churches do not need to have buildings. For their first few centuries, Christian congregations owned no buildings. They met in private homes. A misunderstanding of salvation and the church that grew up in the patristic period led to the church being conceived of as regularly requiring specific, consecrated space. But during the Reformation, it again became apparent that a building was not required for a Christian church. But what was required for a Christian church was members!

A church is composed of regenerate members. Those members may meet in a building owned by them corporately (a "church") or individually (a home), or in a rented space, but it is the people that are essential. Without a specific community of people, a Christian church does not exist. Samuel Jones defined a church well in his *Treatise of Church Discipline*: "A particular gospel church consists of a company of saints incorporated by a special covenant into one distinct body, and meeting together in one place, for the enjoyment of fellowship with each other and with Christ their head, in all his institutions, to their mutual edification and the glory of God through the Spirit."[2]

What are these "institutions" of Christ? They are, fundamentally, the preaching of the gospel, the practice of baptizing believers, and the regular celebration of the Lord's Supper. Why did Christ institute them? He did so for the benefit of Christians, to supply advice and edification, to have the gospel preached among them by word and sign, by lip and life.

A church conducts the public worship of God and works to extend the kingdom of Christ through witness and evangelism. With Christ as its head, such a body is able to choose its elders and deacons, admit and dismiss its members, administer discipline to members as it sees fit, and follow Christ together in whatever ways they discern God's Word teaches. A Christian church is independent of outside

---

2. Samuel Jones, *Treatise of Church Discipline*, in *Polity: Biblical Arguments on How to Conduct Church Life*, ed. Mark Dever (Washington, DC: Center for Church Reform, 2001), 118. Note that "church discipline" was not historically associated only with corrective actions taken by a church with a member (e.g., rebuke, excommunication). *Discipline* carried a wider meaning, approximating "polity" and "practice," a usage still continued in some circles. For example, *The Book of Discipline of the United Methodist Church* (Nashville: Abingdon Press, 2005) is hardly about their practices of excommunication! A *disciple* is "a follower"; a *discipline* is "a way of following, of living, and, for a local congregation, of living together." It is, therefore, roughly equivalent historically to the words *polity* and *practice*.

control but is naturally in a relationship of peace, love, prayerful mutual concern, and action with other Christian congregations. Denominations are not churches but rather are merely parachurch organizations of local churches, made to facilitate the obedience and growth of the local congregations in their number.

A local congregation is instructed by Scripture in all the ways it must organize its life together (e.g., electing elders and deacons, preaching, baptizing, observing the Lord's Supper). Other matters of organization that might seem useful (e.g., the creation of an office such as church clerk) are allowable but not necessary. The local church is able to handle its own affairs in organizing its internal business, receiving and disbursing funds and other assets, and reporting on such to the church congregation.

So, a church is required to worship and serve God, bear witness to his Word, evangelize, administer baptism and the Lord's Supper, serve Christians, live life together with love, holiness, and unity, govern its own affairs, and show goodness and mercy, especially to its needy members. The church is to show itself to be united around the truth, loving God and each other, and marked by a holiness of life that reflects to the world God's own holiness. The church has a mission to be a display of God's glory to his creation (John 13:34–35; Eph. 3:10–11; Phil. 2:14–16). It is an exclusive community in that it is only those who have been adopted into God's family by faith in Christ who have a rightful place in it. That place is called membership.

DEFINITION OF MEMBERSHIP

Positively, how does the Bible present the Christian life? It is a life not lived in isolation but lived out with other Christians. Christianity is personal but not private. Truly following Christ is committed and regular, not casual and occasional. This is what we mean when we think of being a church member. It is a formal commitment to love and to be loved by those Christians we live around, whom we regularly interact with, whom we desire to hold accountable, and to whom we are held accountable. A certain assembly has accepted the responsibility to teach us, to lead us, to love us, to care for us, and to correct us when we need it. The local church is not a natural group of homogeneous friends. In fact, carnal homogeneity obscures the supernatural unity that draws and holds Christians together and that displays the gospel to the surrounding world.

When church membership is properly understood, it is an expression of the common life Christians share (e.g., 1 John 1:3). It is an expression of relationship, as we together comprise one spiritual house, one home (1 Peter 2:5). It is a relationship that implies a partnership in the gospel (as in Phil. 1:5; Gal. 2:9). It involves the kind of fellowship that we see in the early church in Acts 2. Our sharing with each other reflects the way that God has so graciously given to us.

Church members are to be those who have been called into fellowship with Jesus Christ. That is what Paul assumed as he wrote his letters in the New Testament (e.g., 1 Cor. 1:9; cf. Ps. 27:4). Christians are called to be in Christ, and to abide in Christ (John 15:4–5; cf. Col. 2:6–7). Daily communion with God is to be expressed in our regular fellowship with the same community of Christians. This is how the image of the local church as the body of Christ becomes a reality (see Rom. 12:5). Christians share the same Spirit indwelling; we are called to live that out in our concern for each other (1 Cor. 12:25).

The love we share as a result of sharing in the Spirit is to shape our life together as Christians. While we could say that all Christians are to be characterized by obeying certain duties toward each other, individual Christians cannot live out these duties to all other Christians. In reality, we live them out most fully to those we are regularly around, and especially to those we have committed to work with in our local congregations. In this context especially, we are to honor each other (Rom. 12:10), correct one another (Rev. 3:19), pray for one another (James 5:16), and encourage one another (Heb. 3:13). We should build one another up by teaching God's Word to each other (e.g., 1 John 1:1–3; Ps. 119:13; Prov. 27:17) and by being open to and accountable with one another (James 5:16; Col. 3:16; Eph. 5:21).

Individual friendships and small-group Bible studies may satisfy some aspects of these commands, but the biblical pattern from Acts 2 on is for Christians to be made members of local congregations, with whom they are responsible to live out the Christian life corporately. Even as he did in the Old Testament, so more fully and obviously in the New Testament, God dwells in the middle of his people. Built together, we are God's temple, the "place" where his Spirit especially dwells.

If we are members of a congregation, we will be working together for the spread of the gospel (Phil. 1:3–5). We will give money to this end and pray to this end. We will, as Peter says, "use whatever gift" we have been given "to serve others, faithfully administering God's grace in its various forms" (1 Peter 4:10).[3] God is glorified by the local body being built up through the gifts that God has entrusted to it. Love for each other also will lead church members to sacrifice for each other's good (e.g., Heb. 13:16; cf. Rom. 12:13; 15:26–27; 2 Cor. 8:4; 9:13; 1 Tim. 6:18). By so doing, we obey God's commands, we experience something of his joy, and we bring God glory. Church members are those who are committed to sharing their material provisions with their teacher and so providing for his ministry (Gal. 6:6; cf. 1 Cor. 9:14).

---

3. All Scripture quotations in this chapter are from the New International Version (NIV).

Church members are also those who are committed to sharing in Christ's sufferings, not in any way helping Christ to atone for the world's sins, but rather in following him in faithfulness, and so experiencing the world's rejection (e.g., Phil. 3:10). We are called to suffer for and with Christ and with other believers, whether because of our own sin, or the sin of others. And we are called to serve one another in love (Gal. 5:13), and even to enjoy one another's company (Acts 2:42; cf. Luke 15:23; 1 Cor. 10:31).

To consider church membership another way, consider who defined the membership of a Christian congregation in the New Testament. Did the individual himself? It appears not. The man in 1 Corinthians 5 had no right simply to decide that he himself would remain a member of the Corinthian church. That was the congregation's responsibility; thus Paul addressed the congregation as a whole in his letter, not the man in sin.

Most fundamentally, of course, God defines the membership of a local congregation. In Acts 2 it was the Lord who added to their number daily those who were being saved. In a secondary sense, however, the local church is entrusted with the responsibility of defining its own membership. In 2 Corinthians 2:6 we find Paul appealing to the church members to readmit a disciplined member who had repented. In 1 Corinthians 5 and Matthew 18 it was the congregation who had to act publicly to properly define who composed their membership, because they decided who was to be excluded from it. So, for example, in the case of the adulterous man in Corinth, the congregation evidently had decided to allow him to remain a member, and it is precisely for this decision that the apostle takes them to task and rebukes them.

In none of these cases did the individual himself have the simple power to make himself a member of a congregation, in the way regular attenders in our own day often simply consider themselves members by virtue of their choice to attend. Joining was a congregational act. An individual's desire was necessary but not sufficient. Once the individual was willing, the willingness of the congregation still had to be secured. In the New Testament, it was the church members who admitted and excluded members, because it was the congregation and their leaders who would have to give account for them (e.g., Heb. 13:17).

Who chose the leaders of a congregation? It was the church members (see Acts 6:2–6). Who adjudicated differences? The church members (Matt. 18:15–17; 1 Cor. 5–6). Who finally discerned the orthodoxy of the preaching? The church members (Gal. 1:6–9; 2 Tim. 4). Who commissioned missionaries? Church members (Acts 13:1–3). Who acted together with their leaders to do important business for the kingdom? Church members (Acts 15:22). Publicly defined church membership is an idea implicit in the New Testament.

Essentially, the membership of a church is composed of those who are regularly admitted to the Lord's Table. In chapters 5 and 6 of 1 Corinthians, Paul excoriated the congregation for allowing unrepentant sinners to remain in their number. In chapter 11, he specifically criticized their undisciplined practice of the Lord's Supper. And in 2 Corinthians, Paul refers to one who had been punished "by the majority" (2:6), evidently referring to an action of a majority of a defined group—the members of the church at Corinth.

Occasionally, the truly regenerate may be discouraged from coming to the table and hypocrites admitted, but the intent of a local church should be to admit to the Lord's Supper those whom they take to be regenerate and are not known to be living in any way contrary to the gospel, or the Word of God. This is the bare outline of membership. It presumes that the people are not in any unrepentant sin. It presumes that they have been baptized. It presumes, too, that they are in regular attendance (with a few, particular exceptions). And, it presumes furthermore a level of relationship being developed in which one is known honestly and transparently and known to be repenting. Christian churches are only for sinners and, among sinners, only for repentant sinners.

From the earliest of times, Baptist churches have tended to summarize such duties in church covenants.[4] These Christians accepted that they had duties to pray for their pastors, to pay them as they could, to respect them, to obey them (Heb. 13:17), and to defend them. They usually took these covenants publicly as a way of making themselves accountable to fulfill their duties. They also acknowledged in them that they had a duty to the other members of the congregation, to care for them and watch over them. That care included confronting and even working to excommunicate if the attempt to bring the sinning member to repentance failed. By covenant, they would pledge personal holiness, carefulness for each other, prayer, burden bearing, working together to advance the gospel, and regularly meeting together on the Lord's Day. Such covenants gave a summary shape to what they understood church membership—and indeed, the Christian life—to involve.

According to article XXV of the Somerset (southwest England) Baptist Confession of 1656, a host of Scriptures encouraged these framers to exhort their readers that "in admitting of members into the church of Christ, it is the duty of the church, and ministers whom it concerns, in faithfulness to God, that they be careful they receive none but such as do make forth evident demonstration of the new birth, and the work of faith with power." In John 3:3 Jesus taught that no one would

---

4. E.g., "The Solemn Covenant of the Church of Christ, meeting in White-street, at its Constitution; June 5, 1696" (1697), in Dever, *Polity*, 90–91.

see the kingdom of God unless he or she was born again. In Matthew 3 John's baptism was administered only upon confession and repentance. The confession also cited God's condemnation of Israel for bringing those "uncircumcised in heart and flesh" into his sanctuary (Ezek. 44:6–7) as presaging the regenerate nature of the church. Of course, Peter's reply in Acts 2:38 also was used to show the initial commands of repentance and baptism that Christians (by implication, church members) were to obey. The confession cited Paul's assurance in 2 Corinthians 9:14 of God's grace having been given to the Corinthians as evidence that they practiced a regenerate church membership. David's refusal of fellowship with the wicked in Psalms 26 and 101 also was taken as foreshadowing a believing church.

In summary of this point, the Bible's teaching about church membership is occasional, implicit, and yet clear. Churches are obligated to define those for whom they will take responsibility. Christians normally are obligated to attend and to join a gospel-preaching church near them. It should be noted, too, that Baptists in particular have been leaders in the sixteenth and seventeenth centuries in recovering such New Testament practices. Their rejection of infant baptism made the inclusive geographical units of the Roman church (parishes, dioceses) practically impossible. They recovered the radically voluntary nature of association with a local congregation as being composed of believers only. Such commitment implied duties to fellow members and their pastors. Every member ministry appeared vigorously in this acting out of the doctrine of the priesthood of all believers.

Clarity regarding believing church membership is the chief contribution of Baptists to the wider Christian community. And yet it is this very clarity that has been sacrificed in the pragmatism and reductionism of Baptist church life in the last century, especially in seeking numerical growth. The local church itself is undermined by an evangelistic fervor that ends up tolerating and even pandering to an individualistic consumerism. And a large body of nominal Christians will subvert the church's ministry in the world, in itself, and even in their own lives.[5]

---

5. In the nineteenth century, J. L. Reynolds wrote elegantly and movingly of the importance of a regenerate church membership:

> It becomes the disciples of the Saviour to guard well the door of admission into their fraternity. Upon their fidelity, in this respect, depend its efficiency, prosperity, and safety. An accession of nominal Christians may enlarge its numbers, but cannot augment its real strength. A Church that welcomes to the privileges of Christ's house, the unconverted, under the specious pretext of increasing the number of his followers, in reality betrays the citadel to his foes. They may glory in the multitudes that flock to their expanded gates, and exult in their brightening prospects; but the joy and the triumph will be alike transient. They have mistaken a device of the enemy for the work of God. They hailed, as they thought, an angel of light; they have received Satan. I admire and love the many sincere and zealous Christians that are found in such [pedobaptist] Churches; but I fear that this Trojan horse will finally prove their ruin. On the subject

When the lives of those in the church lie about Jesus, the church has lost its purpose and the surrounding world its light. The recovery of a biblical understanding of membership is a task that is both urgent and important. In the remainder of this chapter, we will consider an understanding of membership that must be taught and some practical steps to implement meaningful membership in a local congregation.

MAKING MEMBERSHIP MEANINGFUL AS COMMITTED LOVE

Pastors today cannot assume that Christians understand either church membership or its importance. In fact, many pastors seem to have forgotten anything more than the most pragmatic arguments for it. But in Baptist history, pastors have recognized the vigorous practice of membership, not only as a matter of prudence but also of principle. It would not merely be unwise to neglect it; such neglect itself would be sin and would lead others into sin. How can we again make membership meaningful to ourselves and to our congregations? I suggest that we speak of it as a matter of love and teach it as the manifestation of love in various ways. Let me simply give five ways as examples.

THE WITNESS OF LOVE

Jesus said in John 13:34–35 that the world will know that we are his disciples by the love we have for one another. The church is Jesus' evangelism plan. Our love for each other is to be the compelling witness to the non-Christians around us that the life and society they desire so much can exist. Even in this fallen world, we can know lives lived in the context of unconditional, inconvenient, and inconveniencing self-sacrificial love for one another. The Christian gospel necessarily includes a message about sin that is convicting; but the Christian gospel is also to be illustrated by lives of love that are compelling.

---

of infant baptism, and what seem to me to be its legitimate tendencies, I have recorded my sentiments without reserve, and, I trust, without offence. I impeach no man's motives; nor do I question the piety and sincerity of those my Christian brethren who believe that this practice is sanctioned by the divine command. Many pedobaptists are among the lights and ornaments of the age; their ministry has been blessed of God to the extension of the Redeemer's kingdom, and their Churches present numerous examples of pure and unaffected piety. Such men would not, knowingly, contravene the law of Christ. They would welcome the obloquy of the world, and even the agonies of martyrdom, in obedience to the command of their Lord and King, and rejoice that they were counted worthy to suffer for Christ's sake. It is impossible not to admire and love men whose faith and practice associate them with Baxter, Leighton, Edwards, and Martyn, and who breathe their heavenly spirit. While I think I see and regret their errors, I would extend to them the same indulgence which I ask for my own. ("Church Polity [1849]," in Dever, *Polity*, 327–28)

The equivalent "Trojan horse" today is the retention of merely nominal, uninvolved, non-attending Christians as members in Baptist churches.

This God of justice is a God of mercy. This God of holiness is a God who has himself borne the weight of his own opposition to evil. The love of Christ on the cross is displayed in the lives of Christians in the church. Our lives are to back up the witness of our lips. We were made in the image of God, and we long to live again in that image, even while we are in rebellion against God. God uses the local church to bring those longings to the surface, to testify to the truth of them, and to hold out a foretaste of their ultimate fulfillment someday in the visible presence of God himself. Membership witnesses to Christ's love.

THE ASSURANCE OF LOVE

In 1 Corinthians 5 Paul told the Corinthian congregation to wake up to the truth and realize that they had someone in their number who was living as an enemy to the gospel that he professed. A man was committing adultery with his father's wife (a serious crime even in pagan Corinth)! But the man is not the direct object of Paul's rebuke; that is reserved for the congregation. Why? Because it was the congregation who was allowing the man to continue thinking of himself as a follower of Jesus, when he was in open and unrepentant sin. His sin was as leaven in the loaf (as Paul goes on to say); or, it was infection in the body. The infection itself was serious but not nearly as serious as the congregation's toleration of it. To be welcoming and tolerant at this point was not simply an individual infection; it was a failure of the body's entire immune system. It showed that something essential to the body's life and continuance was missing. And it would quickly lead to the death of that local body if not immediately addressed. A body that could not resist such an intrusion would soon succumb to it.

Considered from the point of the individual disciplined, such an action as Paul was calling them to implement was an act of love. Given that this man was obviously continuing to regard himself as, and was being regarded by others as, a Christian, he was clearly self-deceived. We know that professing Christians can deceive themselves. Paul wrote later to the Corinthians, "Examine yourselves to see whether you are in the faith; test yourselves" (2 Cor. 13:5; cf. 2 Peter 1:10–11). We should realize that our immediate assurance to someone else of that person's salvation, based merely upon a past profession of faith in Christ, may not be the most loving thing we can do. And if that's true for us as individuals, it is doubly true of our congregations. Joining a church is joining an assurance-of-salvation cooperative. We are to observe evidences of God's grace in each other's lives and to encourage one another. And we are to correct one another when occasion requires. Paul was urgent in 1 Corinthians 6 that the church not be deceived about who would inherit the kingdom of God. That warning sprang from love. Membership functions to assure us that we have known God's love truly and are truly loving God in response.

THE NATURE OF LOVE

This is especially important because we are so confused about what true love is. John said, "This is how we know who the children of God are and who the children of the devil are: Anyone who does not do what is right is not a child of God; nor is anyone who does not love his brother" (1 John 3:10). Love is a necessary attribute of a Christian. It is not merely mature Christians who give themselves to loving other Christians; love is what *real* Christians do. The commitment of church membership begins to give a shape and appearance to our love. Membership tests its claims and calls for particular obediences.

"But surely we know God," one might say, "because our hearts are moved, and tears roll down our cheeks when we sing this hymn or that chorus!" "No," says John. "We know that we have passed from death to life, because we love our brothers. Anyone who does not love remains in death. . . . This is how we know what love is: Jesus Christ laid down his life for us. And we ought to lay down our lives for our brothers" (1 John 3:14, 16). Our lives are the pictures that illustrate the text of our words. "If anyone says, 'I love God,' yet hates his brother, he is a liar. For anyone who does not love his brother, whom he has seen, cannot love God, whom he has not seen" (1 John 4:20).

I sometimes say to young theologues in my own congregation "If you love to read Wayne Grudem and John Piper but won't inconvenience yourself to go pick up an older person and give that person a ride to church, I don't know if you are a Christian." It is in the nature of loving real people that it will at times be difficult and inconvenient. That is why we covenant together with a flock of imperfect sheep. The lack of commitment fostered by a lack of formal membership is a temptation to our flesh and an opportunity for self-deception. Homogeneous congregations are filled with the more natural empathy for those who are like us. The inconveniences of love are minimized. In such a situation, the worth of our love is therefore less compelling evidence of its divine nature. Membership functions to instruct us in the very nature of Christian love and to encourage its expression.

THE OBEDIENCE OF LOVE

The writer to the Hebrews said, "Obey your leaders and submit to their authority. They keep watch over you as men who must give an account. Obey them so that their work will be a joy, not a burden, for that would be of no advantage to you" (Heb. 13:17). Church membership is showing a committed love to particular leaders. Ephesians 4:11 teaches us that pastors are gifts that Christ gives to his church. Christians are to accept that gift by obeying those pastors.

"Obedience" is an awkward word for sinners. By nature, we don't like it. We immediately think of abuses of authority. Abuse is widespread and at times terrible in its consequences. But such abuses do not delegitimize authority itself. Satan's attack on God from the very beginning has been to tell humans that authority and love cannot go together. And his great proof is God's call for us to deny ourselves when our own desires contradict his commands (e.g., in the garden of Eden). And yet, God has shown himself unbelievably loving, as he has in Christ's sacrificing his comfort for our good (e.g., in the garden of Gethsemane). God is worthy of trust. Throughout creation, authority is to be an expression of God's own character (see Eph. 3:14–15). David's final words are a beautiful reflection of authority's divine nature: "When one rules over men in righteousness, when he rules in the fear of God, he is like the light of morning at sunrise on a cloudless morning, like the brightness after rain that brings the grass from the earth" (2 Sam. 23:3–4). Authority exercised well blesses those under it. This is as true in the home as it is in the nation, and as true in church as it is in marriage.

Practically, pastors need to know for which Christians they'll be giving an account to God. In our own congregation, we may have six or seven hundred attending, but only four or five hundred of those have made themselves known to me. Only they, the members, have told me their understanding of the gospel and their experience of God's grace. Only they have pledged themselves to me and other members of the congregation to pray for us, to support us, to care for us, and to love us. Some of the other attenders may in fact do those things, but for some reason they have not told us that they will, and so we do not know how to pray for them, to count on them, and to care for them. Practically, membership functions to facilitate loving obedience to the pastors God has placed there and to facilitate loving care among all the members.

THE GLORY OF LOVE

When Saul was going to persecute the Christians in Damascus, "he fell to the ground and heard a voice say to him, 'Saul, Saul, why do you persecute me?'" (Acts 9:4). The risen Christ did not ask Saul why he was going to persecute Christians, or the church; he asked Saul, "Why do you persecute me?" Christ so identifies with the church he founded (in Matt. 16) and purchased (Acts 20:28) that he takes an attack upon the church as an attack upon himself.

The local church was not the idea of a preachers' union trying to create jobs; it is the idea, the creation, of Christ himself. It is the expression of his own nature and character. Its acts reflect on him. Its evident goodness brings him glory. So we read the words of Jesus in Matthew 5:16, "Let your light shine before men, that they may see your good deeds and praise your Father in heaven." Or, as Peter later wrote, "Live such good lives among the pagans that, though they accuse you of doing wrong, they may see your good deeds and glorify God on the day he visits us" (1 Peter 2:12). Note the connection between our actions and God's glory. Somehow, he is praised and glorified by our good actions. This is the work of the church, to bring such glory to God from his creation as we display his character in our lives.

If Jesus is the image of the invisible God, how do we see Jesus today? Jesus is not to be worshipped through physical icons, or images. We have no account of him teaching his disciples to draw or sketch or sculpt. We have books they wrote, but no images they made remaining for our adoration. In fact, the earliest image we have found of Christ was made in derision. It was found on the wall of a Roman catacomb. It is a cross, with a stick figure, and an ass's head, with a mocking inscription scrawled beneath, "Aleximenos worships his god."

John of Damascus said that to deny icons is to deny the Incarnation. It may be in his day that some who opposed the use of icons did deny the Incarnation, but those who went before him neither denied the Incarnation nor used icons. The point of the Incarnation was never the mere physical appearance of Christ. It was the life of flesh and blood that he lived out. Christ probably couldn't be identified in a photograph of him with the twelve disciples. There was nothing distinctive in his appearance (Isa. 53:2). But let that become a moving picture, and I think by his loving interaction with others, his glory would begin to appear.

Do not misunderstand me. I do not mean to deride our desire for the visible. People say this is a visual age. Every age is a visual age. We are made to crave the immediacy of sight. We naturally desire to see God immediately, but that blessing was taken from us at the fall. We live in salvation history in the era, not of the eye, but of the ear. One day that glorious immediacy of seeing God will be restored to us—that is the climax of the Bible! That is the consummation we find in Revelation 22:4—we shall see God! Until then, God is made most visible, it seems, not in two-dimensional paintings, but in lives lived out in the local church. That is his plan: for church membership to display the glory of his nature of goodness and love and so bring him praise.

Twelve Steps to Regain Meaningful Membership

In conclusion, here is a suggested twelve-step recovery plan for pastors to regain meaningful church membership.

1. Regularly proclaim the gospel in your preaching. Be certain to include clear statements of the nature of God, of human sin, of God's provision in Christ, of his substitutionary death and bodily resurrection. Be clear in calling for repentance and faith. Even in the way you explain what repentance looks like, you can make it clear that people who do not give themselves in loving

commitment to each other have no reason to think that they have given themselves in loving commitment to God. Repeatedly define what it means to be a Christian in provocative ways that cause complacent evangelicals to obey Paul's exhortation to "examine yourselves" (2 Cor. 13:5).

2. Have and use a congregationally agreed-upon statement of faith and a church covenant. Congregations are best served by documents shorter than those that Presbyterian elders must agree on but longer than a mere profession of faith. With membership in the congregation comes responsibility. The statements of what the congregation together believes and how together they will live are important. They are a clear ground of unity, a tool of teaching, and a fence from the worldly, who would erase such distinctions, or the divisive, who would narrow them.

3. Require attendance at membership classes before admitting individuals into membership in a congregation. It is a loving thing to present carefully the expectations others will have of new members and what they, in turn, can expect from the congregation. Teach carefully through the statement of faith and the church covenant before asking prospective members to sign them. You also can explain membership and something of the history of Christianity, of your denomination, and even of your own particular congregation. It is a good time, too, to introduce the practical nuts and bolts of how your own local church works.

4. Require an interview after individuals have been through the membership classes but before they've been recommended to the congregation for membership. This interview can be the occasion for the actual signing of the two documents they have studied in the membership class. In the past, Christians have conducted such membership interviews by a committee of members, deacons, or elders, or even in front of the entire congregation. It is the practice of our own congregation to do this with an elder and one or two others present (usually staff or an intern). Ask the interviewee to share the gospel with you and to give you a detailed account of their own conversion and their discipleship since then. Reiterate the expectations the congregation has for them to be present at gatherings on the Lord's Day, at the Lord's Table, and at members' meetings. Also, remind them of their obligation to build relationships as they get to know others and allow themselves to be known, to pray for the other members, and to give financially.

5. Do not baptize babies, and be careful about baptizing young children into formal local church membership. Here is what a former Baptist pastor and

professor of evangelism at Southwestern Seminary said a few decades ago, as he noted the trend to younger and younger baptisms.

> At a time when he is too young to choose his clothes for himself, at a time when he is too young to choose a life's vocation, at a time when he is too young to serve on a church committee, at a time when he is really too young to vote intelligently on business matters in the church, at a time when he is not considered legally responsible by any agency in the community, there has been a tendency to feel that he is sufficiently responsible to make a life-binding, permanent-type decision concerning his relationship to Christ and his church. If we are unwilling to feel that the child is capable of making lesser decisions, how can we justify our confidence in the efficacy of this greater decision at this age?[6]

The question is not whether a five-year-old or a ten-year-old can savingly confess Christ. The question is one of the congregation's ability to discern. The large number of nominal Christians and rebaptisms in Southern Baptist churches seems to answer the question clearly in the negative. We are not *meant* to be able to fully distinguish a child's love and trust in God, from their love and trust in adults, especially their own parents. That grows up over time, as the distinct outlines of the young adult's life comes into place as he or she feels the pull of the world, the flesh, and the Devil and yet follows Christ. Baptists around the world know this; Baptists here in America used to know this. We can again.

6. Realize that admission into church membership is an act of the congregation. This is clearly implied in 2 Corinthians 2:6. Whether that is done in the most direct manner (by a congregational vote) or in a less direct method (by publicizing the names for a set period of time and asking for feedback), the congregation should be taught that it acts to admit someone into its membership and that (apart from death) it acts to release someone from its membership.

7. Publish a membership directory in which the members of the church are represented by name, picture, physical address, e-mail, and work and home telephone numbers. Publish it regularly so that it is accurate. Teach the members to update their information regularly. Cultivate using this directory as a prayer list for the pastors and members of the church. In our congregation, we ask members to try to pray through a page each day in their own personal prayer time.

---

6. Kenneth L. Chafin, "Evangelism and the Child," *Review and Expositor* 60, no. 2 (1963): 166.

8. Give active pastoral oversight to the members. Try to make sure that every member is in regular conversation with some elder or some mature Christian in the congregation. Take initiative in trying to know what's going on in the members' lives. Lunches, telephone calls, and e-mails, as well as book recommendations and conversations after church gatherings, are obvious tools. The pastors also can make more structured efforts at member visitation.

9. Work to create a culture of discipleship in the church. Rather than basically relying on programs of small groups or shared interests, encourage members to deliberately give themselves in love to each other. Encourage them in their responsibilities to care for each other. Use the staff to facilitate relationships, with the goal that everyone in the congregation would have multiple natural relationships with others in the congregation in which they are being built up as Christians. Help them to understand that their welfare is the business of their brothers and sisters.

10. Limit some activities, events, and areas of service to members. For example, there should be meetings that only members attend. These could be on Sunday night or Saturday, but they would need to be separate from the public services to which all are welcome. A biblical practice of church membership requires discussions that are churchwide but only of the church. (Matthew 18:17 seems to imply something like this.) Make sure that only members can hold offices in the church, lead in various kinds of service, and take public roles that would imply the congregation's knowledge and consent. In our congregation, except for evangelistic small groups, we have small groups available for members only. As part of our congregation's discipleship plan, we take responsibility for them, and so we need to be able to approve the leaders and settle any difficulties that occur. (Of course, our members are free themselves to arrange Bible studies with whomever they would like, from however many different churches. We as a staff simply do not take responsibility for training those leaders and filling those groups. We do not rely on them for our own congregation's life.)

11. Only after membership is recovered, consider reviving the practice of corrective church discipline (including excommunication or exclusion). Too many pastors attempt to recover meaningful church membership by first recovering the practice of corrective church discipline, but this is normally a jarring transition in congregational life. One must first take steps to recover a positive understanding and experience of membership, before one begins to exclude members for demonstrable unrepentant sins of nonattendance, adultery, and so on.

12.   Finally, we must recover something of the grandness of God's plan. Pray for God's blessings on other local evangelical congregations by name in your Sunday morning services. Remind the congregation that the story we're involved in is greater than our local congregation.

Pastors again must meditate on Hebrews 13:17 and consider the seriousness of the accounting to God we are to give for those to whom we have given assurance of their salvation. Continued membership in our congregation is giving such assurance. If there are no signs of a sinner being repentant and reconciled with God, we do not love them by simply adding their name to our church's role and counting them among our number. And remind yourself of the one who finally determines the meaning of church membership. I love this quotation of the Scottish pastor John Brown in a letter of paternal counsels to one of his pupils newly ordained over a small congregation: "I know the vanity of your heart, and that you will feel mortified that your congregation is very small, in comparison with those of your brethren around you; but assure yourself on the word of an old man, that when you come to give an account of them to the Lord Christ, at his judgment-seat, you will think you have had enough."[7] Ultimately that is the meaning of church membership.

---

7. Cited in Richard Sibbes, *The Works of Richard Sibbes*, ed. Alexander Grosart (1862; reprint, Edinburgh: Banner of Truth, 1973), 1:294.

3

The Meaning of Baptism

DANIEL L. AKIN

Few doctrines are more central to the life and identity of the people of God than baptism. Baptism inaugurated the public ministry of the Lord Jesus (Matt. 3:13–17) and is at the heart of the Great Commission (Matt. 28:16–20).[1] In the book of Acts believers in the Lord Jesus Christ were baptized immediately (Acts 2:38, 41; 8:12–13, 36, 38; 9:18; 10:47–48; 11:16; 16:15, 33; 18:8; 22:16), even if a church was not gathered (Acts 8:36, 38; 9:18; 16:33).[2] The New Testament has no category for a believer in Jesus Christ who has not been baptized. As G. R. Beasley-Murray asserts, "From references to baptism in Paul's letters it is apparent that he assumes all believers in Christ have been baptized. . . . Since baptism existed prior to Paul's conversion, it is reasonable to view it as coexistent with the inception of the church."[3]

Historically, believer's baptism appears in the very first confessions of our forefathers, the evangelical wing of the Anabaptists. Balthasar Hubmaier spoke to it in 1524 in *Eighteen Dissertations Concerning the Entire Christian Life and of What It Consists*, proposition 8, and Michael Sattler listed it as the first of the seven articles

---

1. It is clear from the Scriptures that the baptism of Jesus is unique and should not be equated with New Testament believer's baptism.
2. Thomas R. Schreiner, *Paul, Apostle of God's Glory in Christ: A Pauline Theology* (Downers Grove, IL: InterVarsity Press, 2001), 371.
3. George R. Beasley-Murray, "baptism," in *Dictionary of Paul and His Letters*, ed. Gerald Hawthorne, Ralph Martin, and Daniel Reid (Downers Grove, IL: InterVarsity Press, 1993), 60. Beasley-Murray's work *Baptism in the New Testament* (Grand Rapids: Eerdmans, 1962) still stands as the classic treatment on the subject of baptism. The thief on the cross (Luke 23:39–43) is an exception that proves the rule. He was incapable of being baptized. He also lived and died prior to Acts 2 and the birth of the church. However, Mark Dever makes the point that "based upon Acts and the letters, it seems this [baptism] was the universal practice of the New Testament Christians." "The Doctrine of the Church," in *A Theology for the Church*, ed. Daniel L. Akin (Nashville: B & H Publishing Group, 2007), 782.

of the Schleitheim Confession of 1527.[4] In fact, one will look in vain to find a major Baptist confession that does not include the doctrine of baptism.[5] It is interesting to note, however, that the discussion most often revolves around the proper candidate (a believer) and the proper mode (immersion). The meaning of baptism does not garner nearly as much ink, which may contribute to confusion and to some strange ideas being bantered about at the present.

Consider, for example, the discussion taking place at the International Mission Board of the Southern Baptist Convention over the proper administrator and the relationship, if any, of the doctrine of baptism to the doctrine of the eternal security of the believer.[6] Likewise, there have been discussions, now on hold, at Bethlehem Baptist Church in Minneapolis, Minnesota, and at Henderson Hills Baptist Church in Edmond, Oklahoma, that considered allowing persons not baptized as believers by immersion to become members of their local church, something taught by John Bunyan and D. Martyn Lloyd-Jones and also practiced for some time by a number of liberal churches in North Carolina.[7] Former Southern Baptist Andy Stanley espouses the view that all that matters is the "time" of one's baptism, that one was a believer. Neither mode, nor administrator, nor location is of any consequence.[8] It simply needs to be public and identify one with Jesus.

---

4. William L. Lumpkin, *Baptist Confessions of Faith*, rev. ed. (Valley Forge, PA: Judson Press, 1969), 18–31. On the import of baptism in the Schleitheim Confession, see Daniel L. Akin, "An Expositional Analysis of the Schleitheim Confession," *Criswell Theological Review* 2, no. 2 (1988): 354–56.

5. Lumpkin, *Baptist Confessions of Faith*.

6. The policy requiring baptism to be administered by a "like faith and practice" church that affirms the doctrine of eternal security was approved by the trustees of the International Mission Board of the Southern Baptist Convention in November 2005.

7. See John Bunyan, *Differences in Water-Baptism, No Bar to Communion* (1673); Mark Dever, "On Believers Baptism by Immersion as Essential for New Testament Churches" (The Southern Baptist Theological Seminary Gheens Lectures, February 2002); Nathan Finn, "Baptism, Church Membership, and the Baptist State Convention of North Carolina" (June 29, 2006), at http://nathanafinn.wordpress.com/2006/06/ (accessed February 11, 2007). The Web sites at both Bethlehem Baptist Church and Henderson Hills Baptist Church have extensive documentation concerning their rationale for considering a change in their baptism policy.

8. See Andy Stanley's sermon, "Baptism: What's the Big Deal?" February 26, 2006, http://www.northpoint.org/messages (accessed June 22, 2007). Stanley at one point misrepresents *baptizō* as meaning "washed." The word is universally recognized as having "immersion" as its primary meaning. This may explain why, in part, he is not worried about how and where but when you are baptized. Hence, "I don't think [immersion] is such a big deal," he says. It should be noted that the idea of a "washing" is not completely foreign to baptism biblically and historically. Both Ephesians 5:26 and Titus 3:5 convey the concept. Historically, the catechisms of both James Boyce and John Broadus speak of a washing or purifying significance in baptism. The following is from J. P. Boyce, *A Brief Catechism of Bible Doctrine* (1874), questions 4–6:

Q. What does the use of water in Baptism represent?
A. The washing away of our sins by the cleansing influences of the Holy Spirit.

Rick Warren has even written a treatise on "How to Increase Baptisms at Your Church," with the theme of "Nike baptisms," which means "we just do it."[9]

There is actually no systematic treatment of baptism in the Bible. There is no central or definitive text(s) as we have, for example, with the doctrine of Christology.[10] However, all is not lost. In Romans 6:1–14 the apostle Paul continues his development of the doctrine of justification, which he began in 3:21. Responding to a number of questions, real or created as a rhetorical device, Paul gives attention to the relationship of justification to sanctification beginning at 6:1 and extending through 8:39. It is in Romans 6 that Paul expounds upon our identification and union with Christ. In developing his argument, he brings to the discussion the doctrine of baptism. It is the evidence of, or perhaps better, the signification, of (1) identification and (2) union with Christ.

John Stott correctly asserts, "The essential point Paul is making is that being a Christian involves a personal, vital identification with Jesus Christ, and that this union with him is dramatically set forth in our baptism."[11] James Boyce believed

---

Q. What does the act of immersion represent?
A. The union of the believer with Christ in His death.
Q. Do the Scriptures assign this union as a reason why we are to profess Christ by immersion?
A. They do; they tell us that it is on this account that we are buried with Christ by baptism unto death.

The following is from John Broadus, A Catechism of Bible Teaching (1892), lesson 11, question 4:

Q. What does this signify?
A. The water signifies purification from sin, and the immersion signifies that we are dead to sin, and like Christ we have been buried and risen again.

According to Broadus, the word baptizein means "to immerse, immerge, submerge, to dip, to plunge, to inbathe, to whelm" (ibid., xiii). The classic treatment of this subject remains Thomas Jefferson Conant, The Meaning and Use of Baptizein (1864; reprint, Grand Rapids: Kregel 1977). Conant's conclusion on the matter is worth noting: "The word baptizein, during the whole existence of the Greek as a spoken language, has a perfectly defined and unvarying import. In its literal use it meant, as has been shown, to put entirely into or under a liquid, or other penetrable substance, generally water, so that the object was wholly covered by the inclosing element. By analogy, it expressed the coming into a new state of life or experience, in which one was as it were inclosed and swallowed up, so that, temporarily or permanently, he belonged wholly to it" (p. 188).

9. *Rick Warren Ministry Tool Box*, no. 267 (July 12, 2006). Pastor Warren also notes in this issue another article titled, "40 Ways to Increase Baptisms in Your Church."
10. There are four foundational texts for building a biblical Christology. They are John 1:1–18; Philippians 2:6–11; Colossians 1:15–20; and Hebrews 1:1–3. This approach is reflected in the chapter "The Person of Christ" in Daniel Akin, *A Theology for the Church*, (Nashville: B & H Publishing Group, 2007) 480–594.
11. John Stott, *Romans* (Downers Grove, IL: InterVarsity Press, 1994), 174.

the rite also contained a doctrinal component of confession. He spoke of baptism as, "the initiative rite of His [Christ's] Church . . . an act which involves the very formulary which accompanies it, profession of doctrinal belief."[12] Mark Dever asserts, "Such testimony should occur in the context of a believing community, whose responsibility it is to test the credibility of the profession."[13] Spurgeon saw a similar connection but drew attention to the witness or testimony aspect of our public immersion in water. He said,

> What connection has this baptism with faith? I think it has just this, *baptism is the avowal of faith*; the man was Christ's soldier, but now in baptism he puts on his regimentals. The man believed in Christ, but his faith remained between God and his own soul. In baptism he says to the baptizer, "I believe in Jesus Christ;" he says to the Church, "I unite with you as a believer in the common truths of Christianity;" he saith to the onlooker, "Whatever you may do, as for me, I will serve the Lord." It is the avowal of his faith . . . baptism is also to the believer a *testimony of his faith*; he does in baptism tell the world what he believes. "I am about," saith he, "to be buried in water. I believe that the Son of God was metaphorically baptized in suffering: I believe he was literally dead and buried." To rise again out of the water sets forth to all men that he believes in the resurrection of Christ.[14]

Believing there are vital and even necessary implications for a Bible doctrine of baptism orbiting about Romans 6, I will highlight and briefly discuss seven implications for this doctrine that can be drawn from a careful examination of this passage. It is my hope that a greater appreciation for the meaning of this wonderful ordinance and doctrine will be the outcome.

BAPTISM SIGNIFIES THAT WE ARE NOW IDENTIFIED WITH THE MAN OF LIFE, NOT THE MAN OF DEATH (ROM. 5:12–21)

The context of Romans 6 is important for a proper understanding of baptism. Paul has just drawn the remarkable contrast between the Man of Life, Jesus Christ, and the man of death, Adam. The one to whom you belong counts for everything.

---

12. James P. Boyce, *Three Changes in Theological Institutions: An Inaugural Address* (Greenville, SC: C. J. Elford's Book and Job Press, 1856). Available online at http://www.BaptistTheology.org.
13. Dever, "Doctrine of the Church," 787.
14. C. H. Spurgeon, "Baptismal Regeneration," preached June 5, 1864, in *Metropolitan Tabernacle Pulpit*, http://www. spurgeon.org/sermons/-573.htm (accessed June 22, 2007).

Beasley-Murray notes that in Romans 5 we see Christ as our substitute; in Romans 6 we see Christ as our representative.[15] From the man named Adam flows sin, death to all humanity (vv. 12, 14, 17), judgment, and condemnation (vv. 16, 18). From the man called Jesus Christ one receives the free gift of justification (vv. 15, 16, 18), righteousness (vv. 17, 19), life (v. 17), and grace through righteousness to eternal life (v. 21). It is to this transfer of identification that our baptism gives witness. Douglas Moo summarizes well this aspect of the soteriological transaction: "Paul has shown how God's gracious act in Christ, when appropriated by faith [5:1–2], puts people into a new relationship with God and assures them that they will be saved from wrath in the last day. What has this to do with life in this present age? Anything? Everything."[16]

Romans 5, therefore, paves the way for Romans 6. Identification with the Man of Life is transformative. It alters one's identification, practice, and destiny. Such a radical break with our past requires a bold declaration of our transfer of allegiance. It demands a public declaration that we are now united with the Man of Life and done with the man of death. Baptism appropriately serves to highlight this new reality and realm of existence. John Piper notes, "There is something about this open ritual of new-found faith that makes clear where a person stands and what he is doing. . . . One of the great things about this text [Rom. 5:20–6:4] is that it shows that, if you understand what baptism portrays, you understand what really happened to you when you became a Christian."[17] Baptism testifies to our new identity. We are now identified with the Man of Life.

BAPTISM MEANS WE CAN NO LONGER CONTINUE DELIGHTING IN SIN, BECAUSE WE ARE NOW DEAD TO SIN (ROM. 6:1–2)

Michael Green, in commenting on baptism, says, "Baptism means death to the person I once was, self-centered, unforgiven, alienated from the life of God. Goodbye to all that."[18] But is that true? Is that what God intends? Paul addresses the issue by raising three questions, real or hypothetical, in verses 1 and 2 of Romans 6. Affirming that "where sin abounded, grace abounded much more" (5:20),[19] he recognizes it is possible to argue that "more sin means more grace." Thus he responds, "What shall we say then? Shall we continue in sin that grace

---

15. Beasley-Murray, "baptism," 62.
16. Douglas Moo, *The Epistle to the Romans*, New International Commentary on the New Testament (Grand Rapids: Eerdmans, 1996), 350.
17. John Piper, "What Baptism Portrays," (sermon preached at Bethlehem Baptist Church in Minneapolis, MN, May 25, 1997).
18. Michael Green, *Baptism* (Downers Grove, IL: InterVarsity Press, 1987), 49.
19. All Scripture quotations in this chapter are from the New King James Version (NKJV).

may abound?" (6:1). His response is quick and clear, "Certainly not! How shall we who died to sin live any longer in it?" (6:2). The gospel of grace does not empower sin, it executes sin.

"Eternal life through Jesus Christ our Lord" (5:21) has as one of its results a death, a termination with the previous life, the life of sin. Thomas Schreiner points out, "The grace that believers receive is so powerful that it breaks the dominion of sin. Grace does not simply involve forgiveness of sins; it also involves a transfer of lordship [signified by baptism], so that believers are no longer under the tyranny of sin . . . believers cannot continue in sin, because they have died to sin (v. 2). Dead people cannot continue to practice sin."[20] Bruce Corley and Curtis Vaughn add, "Justified people are of such a nature that continuance of sin is excluded. They are people who have died to sin. Therefore, their relation to sin has been broken. They have been released from its power and influence, and it is morally impossible for them to continue in it. . . . Believers baptism is a symbolic representation of this death to sin."[21]

Baptism means a new and different relationship concerning my affections for sin. The "old me" loved sin, but the "new me" hates sin. The old me has been executed in baptism, never to live again. Though once alive to sin, I am now dead to sin. Baptism declares I am new in identification with the Man of Life and, therefore, I am dead in my affection for sin. I love the former (the Man of Life), and I am repulsed by the latter (sin). Baptism is my declaration of this new allegiance. In repentance I have turned from sin and am now dead to its penalty and its passions. I have turned to the Man of Life in faith. He is now my life, my passion. Baptism again witnesses to this decisive break with what I was. It testifies now and eschatologically to what I am and to what I will become.

BAPTISM MOST CLEARLY IDENTIFIES US WITH CHRIST IN HIS DEATH (ROM. 6:3)

We now come to the heart of Paul's argument concerning the blessings of baptism. Beasley-Murray notes that the structure of Romans 6:3–4, "is reminiscent of the terms of the primitive *kerygma* cited by Paul in 1 Cor. 15:3ff., 'Christ *died* for our sins . . . was *buried* . . . has been *raised* . . .'"[22] He goes on to state that baptism by immersion is "the *kerygma* in action."[23]

Arguments over whether Paul has in mind Spirit baptism or water baptism are unnecessary. Paul never would have thought to separate the two. Moo sees water

---

20. Thomas R. Schreiner, *Romans*, Baker Exegetical Commentary on the New Testament (Grand Rapids: Baker, 1998), 298–99.
21. Bruce Corley and Curtis Vaughn, *Romans* (Grand Rapids: Zondervan, 1976), 74–75.
22. Beasley-Murray, *Baptism in the New Testament*, 127.
23. Ibid., 133.

baptism being taught, and he is correct in what he affirms. He says, "It seems clear that Paul alludes in vv. 3–4 to water baptism, but baptism is not the theme of the paragraph nor is it Paul's purpose to exposit his theology of baptism. Baptism, rather, functions as shorthand for the conversion experience as a whole."[24] This is accurate but not adequate to capture all that Paul is saying.

I believe a more fully accurate assessment is that of Schreiner, who argues,

> The reference to baptism is introduced as a designation for those who are believers in Christ. Since unbaptized Christians were virtually nonexistent, to refer to those who were baptized is another way of describing those who are Christians, those who have put their faith in Christ. Thus Paul is saying here that *all Christians* have participated in the death and burial of Christ, for all Christians had received baptism. To posit that the baptism mentioned here is simply metaphorical or baptism in the Spirit rather than water baptism is incorrect. Moo observes rightly that Paul normally uses the verb βαπτίζειν (*baptizein*, to baptize) to refer to water baptism (1 Cor. 1:13, 14, 15, 16 [twice], 17; 12:13; 15:29; Gal. 3:27). Roman Christians would have inevitably thought of water baptism since it was the universal initiation rite for believers in Christ. Moreover Paul probably loosely associated baptism with water and baptism by the Spirit (1 Cor. 12:13), since both of these occurred at conversion. Thus any attempt to distinguish between Spirit baptism and water baptism in Pauline writings goes beyond what Paul himself wrote . . . it would never have occurred to Paul that baptism in water could be separated from baptism in the Spirit.[25]

Bob Stein makes a similar and compelling case, when he says,

> In the New Testament conversion involves five integrally related components or aspects, all of which took place at the same time, usually on the same day. These five components are repentance, faith, and confession by the individual, regeneration, or the giving of the Holy Spirit by God, and baptism by representatives of the Christian community.[26]

24. Douglas Moo, *Romans 1–8* (Chicago: Moody, 1991), 371.
25. Schreiner, *Romans*, 306–7; cf. idem, *Paul*, 376.
26. Robert H. Stein, "Baptism and Becoming a Christian in the New Testament," *Southern Baptist Journal of Theology* 2, no. 1 (1998): 6.

Baptism as a shorthand for conversion? In certain contexts, yes. Baptism as only this shorthand? Clearly, no. Baptism as vital union with Christ? Yes. Baptism exhausted by this meaning? Again, clearly, no.

In verse 3 Paul raises a fourth question, "Or do you not know that as many of us as were baptized into Christ Jesus were baptized into His death?" Several observations can be made here that impact a number of aspects of biblical baptism. I note five. First, there is a knowledge component to the doctrine. There is doctrinal content that we should both know and understand about our baptism. This is problematic for those who baptize infants and especially for the infant. This is probably problematic for the baptizing of children as well, at least in a number of instances.

Second, Paul takes for granted that the Romans to whom he is writing have been baptized. As Moo says, "Paul signifies that what he is saying has a basis in what the Roman Christians already know about baptism and Christian experience."[27] That there might be an unbaptized believer in Jesus Christ would be an oxymoron to Paul.

Third, "baptized into Christ Jesus" means immersion into Christ. It affirms my full union and identification with the one in whom I now exist and have my very being. Galatians 3:27 beautifully complements this truth when Paul writes, "For as many of you as were baptized into Christ have put on Christ." Such language is an additional argument for immersion as the proper mode of baptism.

Fourth, our immersion into Christ Jesus is an immersion "into His death." Jesus Christ died to sin "once for all," as verse 10 makes clear. This death to sin was decisive and climactic. It is never to be repeated. There is no need. Karl Barth wonderfully grasps the magnitude of this truth in his *The Epistle to the Romans*.

> To be baptized means to be immersed, to be sunk in a foreign element, to be covered by a tide of purification. The man who emerges from the water is not the same man who entered it. One man dies and another is born. The baptized person is no longer to be identified with the man who died. Baptism bears witness to us of the death of Christ, where the radical and inexorable claim of God upon men triumphed. He that is baptized is drawn into the sphere of this event. Overwhelmed and hidden by the claim of God, he disappears and is lost in this death. The death of Christ dissolves the Fall by bringing into being the void in which the usurped independence of men can breathe no longer. It digs up the invisible roots of visible sin, and makes Adam, the man of

---

27. Moo, *Romans 1–8*, 375–76.

the "No-God", a thing decayed and gone. Beyond this death the man who asks that he may continue in sin (vi. 2) and be like God lives no longer. He is dissolved by the claim of which God makes upon him.[28]

Barth then draws on Luther, whose insight and rhetoric is simply too priceless to pass by.

Your baptism is nothing less than grace clutching you by the throat: a grace-full throttling, by which your sin is submerged in order that ye may remain under grace. Come thus to thy baptism. Give thyself up to be drowned in baptism and killed by the mercy of thy dear God, saying: "Drown me and throttle me, dear Lord, for henceforth I will gladly die to sin with Thy Son."

Barth simply concludes, "This death is grace."[29] Baptism as an immersion most clearly identifies the believer with Christ in his death, his once and for all death to sin. Michael Green, an Anglican, does not neglect the self-evident meaning: "[Baptism] is not only incorporation in Christ. It is union with him in his death and resurrection. Baptism plunges us into the dying and the rising of the Lord Jesus, and this aspect is particularly clearly emphasized by full immersion."[30]

Fifth, baptism into Christ has implications for where I am baptized and by whom I am baptized. First Corinthians 12:13 teaches that "by one Spirit we were all baptized into one body—whether Jews or Greeks, whether slaves or free." Those who are baptized into Christ Jesus now identify with Christ in two ways: he is their head, and they are his body. Such identification is to be public, and it should be witnessed by the body of Christ, that is, a local, visible body of believers. As Schreiner comments on 1 Corinthians 12:12–13, "Those who belong to Christ (v. 12) are baptized into his body (v. 13)." Now, this is not to ignore the fact that in Romans 6, "the focus of the text is on incorporation into Christ, not into the church."[31] We should be clear and acknowledge this to be the main thrust of Paul's argument. Still, the trajectory of the text would point to baptism being administered by the visible body of Christ as normative. Missionary expansion and accompanying baptisms, like those found in the book of Acts, should not be viewed as the pattern once local churches are established. To follow any model other than that which is normative is to introduce a disconnect of the believer from the Head

---

28. Karl Barth, *The Epistle to the Romans*, trans. Edwyn C. Hoskyns (reprint, London: Oxford University, 1980), 193.
29. Ibid., 194.
30. Green, *Baptism*, 49.
31. Schreiner, *Romans*, 308.

and body with whom he or she now identifies. Green sees this aspect of baptism and notes,

> It is important to stress this corporate side of baptism. Nobody is meant to be a Christian on their own. We belong to one another, and the mark of belonging is baptism. That has an important message for us in our local churches. Baptism is not a solitary thing, marking me out as a Christian on my own. It is a corporate thing, making us part of the Body of Christ, with all the privileges, partnerships and responsibility which that entails.[32]

To this R. Albert Mohler Jr. adds,

> The common experience of believer's baptism is central to the unity and identity of the church. In Ephesians 4:5, Paul writes of the church as constituted by "one Lord, one faith, one baptism." In 1 Corinthians 12:13, Paul reminds us, "For by one Spirit we were all baptized into one body, whether Jews or Greeks, whether slaves or free, and we were all made to drink of one Spirit." Thus baptism is presented as a necessary act of obedience to Christ that marks the believer's incorporation into the church as the Body of Christ. Put simply, the New Testament has no concept of an unbaptized Christian, much less an unbaptized church member.[33]

Stan Norman amplifies this truth further by saying, "To identify with Christ is to identify with his people. Our union with Christ also brings union with his body, the church. A believer cannot be united with the Head of the body without simultaneously being united with the body. . . . Baptism thus signifies the inclusion and union of the candidate into the body of Christ."[34]

However, the most persuasive argument in this context may be that of Mark Dever, who ties the issue both to the fidelity of Scripture and to the issue of obedience. He writes,

> This brings us to the . . . more important matter, which must not be overlooked—fidelity to Scripture. If baptism is not essential for Communion and church membership, it effectively becomes a

---

32.   Green, *Baptism*, 52.
33.   R. Albert Mohler Jr., "Biblical Perspective on Church Membership and Baptism," *The Baptist Messenger*, July 20, 2006 (special insert between pp. 8 and 9).
34.   Stan Norman, *The Baptist Way* (Nashville: Broadman & Holman, 2005), 134.

matter of individual judgment. The desire for doctrinal inclusiveness and unity in the Spirit ironically reduces obedience to a matter of subjective preference. Some, like John Bunyan, have argued that disobedience to a command of Christ, especially when done in ignorance, represents a mere lack of light to be borne with more than it represents a disciplinable offense, or a sin.

A sin can consist of either an action or an intention. Certainly the intention to disobey God is sin. But a disobedient action toward God is also a sin even if the individual does not intend to sin. The Bible teaches clearly that there are unintentional sins. Intentions are an important consideration in the nature and gravity of a sin, but they are not the only consideration. One of the effects of sin is to stupefy the sinner, to dull and darken the faculties. So those dwelling in sin are said to dwell in the darkness, but that darkness does not ameliorate one's guilt. In the parable of the sheep and the goats in Matthew 25, Jesus teaches with stark clarity that obedience to God does not lie in the eye of the beholder, unless the beholder is God himself. Many goats thought they had lived righteous lives, but Jesus says they have not.

How then do we know what God considers obedience? By his own self-revelation. There is no other sure and certain guide! If Christ has commanded Christians to be baptized, then countermanding that instruction, or substituting mere intention, even sincere intention, does not serve him best. His glory is most displayed in the church when baptism guards both the regeneracy of church membership and the consistency of the church's corporate witness. If we understand that Christ commands the church to baptize only those who repent and believe, then it seems clear that a biblically faithful church is a Baptist church.[35]

Beasley-Murray would wisely, and pastorally, add:

The question not infrequently has been raised, "To which church does baptism give entry: to the local or universal church, to the visible or the invisible church?" The question is essentially modern. It would have been inconceivable to Paul. The church is the visible manifestation of the people of God, whose life is "hidden with Christ in God" (Col 3:3). Baptism is a visible act with a spiritual meaning; it is therefore well adapted to be the means

35. Dever, "Doctrine of the Church," 844.

of entry into a visible community of God's people *and* the body which transcends any one place or time. How to give satisfactory expression to the outward and inward elements, alike of baptism and of the church, is a perpetual pastoral problem; that dilemma, however, challenges believers to reform themselves according to the Word of God rather than to accept laxity of doctrine and practice.[36]

BAPTISM FURTHER IDENTIFIES US WITH CHRIST IN HIS RESURRECTED LIFE (ROM. 6:4–5)

Going down into the water, being submerged in a watery grave, beautifully depicts our death to sin and union with Christ in his death. However, there is a wonderful corollary to our death because of our union with the Man of Life. He was buried in death and gloriously raised in resurrection life. Because we are in him, we too are raised unto resurrected life. Indeed our text affirms:

1. Just as Christ was raised from the dead by the glory of the Father, so are we (v. 4a).
2. We should, like our head, walk in newness of life (v. 4b).
3. United together in the likeness of his death, certainly we also shall be in the likeness of his resurrection (v. 5).

Emerging from the waters of death, I now testify and give witness publicly of the resurrection life I now share in union with Christ. E. Y. Mullins, in "Why I Am a Baptist," points to this aspect when he writes, "Submersion is a symbol of spiritual death and burial. Emergence from the water is a symbol of resurrection from the dead. Thus the form of the ordinance, immersion, is necessary to express the spiritual meaning. To destroy the form is to destroy the meaning."[37] The two predominate Baptist confessions of our day both emphasize this important truth as well. *The Abstract of Principles* (1859), Article XV states, "Baptism is an ordinance of the Lord Jesus, obligatory upon every believer, wherein he is immersed in water in the name of the Father, and of the Son, and of the Holy Spirit, as a sign of his fellowship with the death and resurrection of Christ, of remission of sins, and of his giving himself up to God, to live and walk in newness of life."

The Baptist Faith and Message (2000), Article VII, likewise affirms, "Christian baptism is the immersion of a believer in water in the name of the Father, the Son, and the Holy Spirit. It is an act of obedience symbolizing the believer's faith in a

---

36. Beasley-Murray, "baptism," 64.
37. E. Y. Mullins, "Why I Am a Baptist," in *The Axioms of Religion* (Nashville: Broadman & Holman, 1997), 274.

crucified, buried, and risen Savior, the believer's death to sin, the burial of the old life, and the resurrection to walk in newness of life in Christ Jesus. It is a testimony to his faith in the final resurrection of the dead."

And hear also *The Baptist Catechism*, written by Benjamin Keach in 1693, Question 97:

> Q. What is baptism?
>
> A. Baptism is an ordinance of the New Testament instituted by Jesus Christ, to be unto the party baptized a sign of his fellowship with him, in his death, burial, and resurrection; of his being ingrafted into him (Rom. 6:3, 4, 5; Col. 2:12; Gal. 3:27); of remission of sins (Mk. 1:4; Acts 2:38, and 22:16); and of his giving up himself unto God through Jesus Christ, to live and walk in newness of life (Rom. 6:3, 4).

John Murray is correct when he affirms, "Death to sin is not itself an adequate characterization of the believer's identity; it is basic and it is the fundamental premise of the argument. But death to sin is but the precondition of that life which is the final issue of grace (cf. 5:15, 17, 18, 21). And baptism as signifying union with Christ (vs. 3) must mean also union with Christ in his resurrection and therefore in his resurrection life."[38]

BAPTISM AFFIRMS THAT WE ARE NO LONGER ENSLAVED TO SIN FOR THAT MAN IS NOW DEAD (ROM. 6:6–7)

Paul now develops the doctrine of sanctification as the normal and expected result of union with Christ through baptism. Again the knowledge component of our union, practice, and destiny is noted. We know that the old man was crucified, put to death, "that the body of sin might be done away with." And why? It is so that we should no longer be slaves, captives, of sin. My former self is dead and gone by virtue of my immersion into Christ. Again, Schreiner states well our new status:

> Those baptized into Christ, by virtue of sharing his death and the promise of his resurrection, have died to the power of sin (6:2). The "old person" (*palaios anthropos*), the person we are in Adam, "has been crucified together" with Christ (Rom 6:6; cf. Gal 2:20). Thus, the body dominated by sin has been stripped of its power (*katargeo* in Rom 6:6), and believers are now freed

---

38. John Murray, *Romans*, New International Commentary on the New Testament (Grand Rapids: Eerdmans, 1968), 216.

from the dominion that sin exercised over them when they were
in Adam.[39]

Stott understands this similarly, stating, "*Our old self* denotes, not our lower self
but our former self, 'the man we once were' (NEB), 'our old humanity' (REB), the
person we used to be in Adam. So what was crucified with Christ was not a part
of us called our old nature, but the whole of us as we were in our pre-conversion
state."[40]

Having then died to sin by virtue of my baptism into Christ, I am no longer
a slave to sin but a son under grace (Rom. 6:14). Baptism signals and signifies my
new Master, who is Christ. Having died to sin in baptism, I, the new man in Christ
(2 Cor. 5:17), am now freed from sin. This freedom is immediate as to sin's penalty,
progressive as to sin's power, and eschatological with respect to sin's very presence.
Kent Hughes notes simply but correctly, "As Christ did not serve sin, neither must
we . . . if one's life has not changed and if there is no impulse for further change
toward Christ, he or she is very probably not a Christian."[41]

Baptism declares that I can serve sin no longer, for that "I" is dead. Formerly I
was a slave to an evil and wicked master, but death by baptism unto resurrection
life has freed me from that tyranny. This I also confess in my baptism.

BAPTISM REFLECTS AN ESCHATOLOGICAL CONFIDENCE THAT THE LIFE I HAVE IN CHRIST IS A LIFE THAT WILL NEVER END (ROM. 6:8–10)

Verses 8–10 are eschatological in focus, revealing that there is an important
connection between the doctrine of baptism and the doctrine of eschatology.
Debate exists over whether Paul has in view our resurrection at the parousia or our
present experience of new life in Christ. The language seems to point to the future
and the parousia, and yet as Moo notes, "This future life of resurrection casts its
shadow into the believer's present experience."[42] What I will become in the future
has already begun in the present.

United with Christ in his death and resurrection, I confess in baptism my confidence of a future resurrection, the kind of life I already have begun to enjoy. Verse
9 amplifies this truth. Again, there is an emphasis on the knowledge I should have
concerning this aspect of my union with Christ. Christ has been raised once and

---

39. Schreiner, *Paul*, 258.
40. Stott, *Romans*, 176.
41. R. Kent Hughes, *Romans* (Wheaton: Crossway, 1991), 124–25.
42. Moo, *Romans*, 395. *The London Confession* of 1644, Article 40, notes the eschatological dimen-
    sion when it states, "So certainly shall the bodies of the saints be raised by the power of Christ,
    in the day of resurrection, to reign with Christ."

for all. He will never die again. Death's dominion was crushed by his resurrection from the dead. Verse 10 further reiterates the climactic nature of this event. "He died to sin once for all." In stark contrast, "the life that He lives, He lives to God." Robert Mounce beautifully captures the victory note of the text: "Christ's resurrection broke forever the tyranny of death. That cruel master can no longer exercise any power over him. The cross was sin's final move; the resurrection was God's checkmate. The game is over. Sin is forever in defeat. Christ the victor died to sin 'once for all' and now lives in unbroken fellowship with God."[43] This life then is perpetual, never ending. As Corley and Vaughan point out, "The believer's confidence that he shares in Christ's resurrection life rests on the knowledge that Christ is alive forevermore."[44] The implication of this is significant in my judgment. Because I am as united with Christ in his life as I am in his death, I have the security and certainty of a life that will never end.

Murray says it well: "There can be suspension or interruption of participation in Christ's resurrection life or reversion to death in sin no more than can the fact of Jesus' resurrection be negated or repeated. . . . Because of union with Christ in his resurrection the newness of life which this union involves for the believer is as definitively abiding as is the resurrection of Christ."[45] In other words, is there within the act of baptism, a declaration of my eternal security, of my preservation in this resurrection life? I believe the answer is yes. United with Christ in baptism, I too died to sin once for all. United with Christ in baptism, I too emerge from the realm of death unto a new life both in quality and quantity, a new life that will not and cannot end! This is decisively driven home in verse 11 and following, which leads to our seventh and final implication.

BAPTISM IS THE BASIS FOR MY DAILY MORTIFICATION OF THE FLESH (ROM. 6:11–14)

The "likewise" of verse 11 draws attention to an additional connection between Christ and the Christian. As Christ has died to sin, we who are united to him in baptism must reckon, or consider (present imperative), ourselves likewise dead to sin. Again, in Paul the indicative is the basis for the imperative. We are truly new in Christ through baptism, but we are not totally and completely new just yet. John MacArthur states it well when he says, "New birth in Christ brings death to the sinful self, but it does not bring death to the temporal flesh and its corrupted inclinations until the future glorification."[46] We must daily appropriate and live

---

43. Robert Mounce, *Romans* (Nashville: Broadman & Holman, 1995), 152.
44. Corley and Vaughn, *Romans*, 76.
45. Murray, *Romans*, 223.
46. John MacArthur, *Romans 1–8* (Chicago: Moody, 1991), 325.

in the reality of the truth that we have died to sin. Dead to sin, I am now alive to God in Christ Jesus our Lord. Believing this to be who I truly am as witnessed by my baptism, I will not let sin reign (present imperative) in my body by obeying its lusts, its passions, its desires. Further, I will not present (present imperative) the members of my body as instruments of unrighteousness to sin, but I will present them to God as instruments of righteousness. My baptism will serve as a reminder, a memorial if you like, to inspire and motivate me in my pursuit of this righteous life. This is how it must be, for sin shall not have dominion over me; indeed, it cannot, for I am not under the law, which kills and enslaves, but under grace, which gives life and freedom.

Spurgeon saw the beauty of this truth and captured it superbly in his sermon, "Baptism—A Burial."

> If God has given to you and to me an entirely new life in Christ, how can that new life spend itself after the fashion of the old life? Shall the spiritual live as the carnal? How can you that were the servants of sin, but have been made free by precious blood, go back to your old slavery? When you were in the old Adam life, you lived in sin, and loved it; but now you have been dead and buried, and have come forth into newness of life: can it be that you can go back to the beggarly elements from which the Lord has brought you out? If you live in sin, you will be false to your profession, for you profess to be alive unto God? [sic] If you walk in lust, you will tread under foot the blessed doctrines of the Word of God, for these lead to holiness and purity. You would make Christianity to be a by-word and a proverb, if, after all, you who were quickened from your spiritual death should exhibit a conduct no better than the life of ordinary men, and little superior to what your former life used to be. As many of you as have been baptized have said to the world, We are dead to the world, and we have come forth into a new life. Our fleshly desires are henceforth to be viewed as dead, for now we live after a fresh order of things. The Holy Spirit has wrought in us a new nature, and though we are in the world, we are not of it, but are new made men.[47]

Beasley-Murray notes that in the act of baptism "the actions of stripping off clothes for baptism and putting on clothes after baptism affords a symbol of 'putting off' the old life without Christ and 'putting on' the new life in Christ, and

---

47. C. H. Spurgeon, "Baptism—A Burial," *Metropolitan Tabernacle Pulpit,* preached October 30, 1881, http://www.spurgeon.org/sermons/1627.htm (accessed June 22, 2007).

even putting on Christ himself (Gal. 3:27; Col. 3:9, 12). . . . In baptism, therefore, the Lord appropriates the baptized for his own and the baptized owns Jesus Christ as Lord and submits to his lordship."[48]

CONCLUSION

In speaking of our union with Christ, John Stott talks of "the logic of baptism." Following a methodology similar to the one followed in this paper, he identifies "eight steps or stages" in Paul's argument in Romans 6. I believe they are right on target and provide a fitting summation of our study of this text and its implications for biblical baptism.

1. We died to sin. This is the foundation of Paul's thesis. How can we live in what we have died to (v. 2)?
2. The way in which we have died to sin is that our baptism united us with Christ in his death (v. 3).
3. Having shared in Christ's death, God wants us also to share in his resurrection life (vv. 4–5).
4. Our former self was crucified with Christ in order that we might be freed from sin's slavery (vv. 6–7).
5. Both the death and the resurrection of Jesus were decisive events: he dies to sin once for all, but he lives continuously unto God (vv. 8–10).
6. We must realize that we are now what Christ is, namely, "dead to sin but alive to God" (v. 11)
7. Being alive from death, we must offer our bodies to God as instruments of righteousness (vv. 12–13).
8. Sin shall not be our master, because our position has radically changed from being "under law" to being "under grace." Grace does not encourage sin; it outlaws it (v. 14).[49]

Baptism, then, as Erickson notes, "is a powerful form of proclamation of the truth of what Christ has done; it is a "word in water" testifying to the believer's participation in the death and resurrection of Christ (Rom. 6:3–5). It is a symbol rather than merely a sign, for it is a graphic picture of the truth it conveys."[50] This truth is our union with Christ. This is our existence by virtue of our immersion in the Man of Life. This is what the right doctrine of baptism will rightly convey. This is the doctrine we must teach and proclaim.[51]

---

48. Beasley-Murray, "baptism," 61.
49. Stott, *Romans*, 168–69.
50. Millard Erickson, *Christian Theology*, 2nd ed. (Grand Rapids: Baker, 1998), 1110.
51. Let me also commend a very fine overview of the doctrine of baptism by Thomas White, "What Makes Baptism Valid?" in chapter 5 of this book. *An Address on Baptism* by James H.

SUGGESTED SERMON OUTLINE FOR PREACHING ON
BAPTISM FROM ROMANS

The Meaning and Purpose of Baptism
Romans 6:1–14

I.   Baptism declares our separation from sin (vv. 1–2)
    1. I will not continue in sin (v. 1)
    2. I will not live in sin (v. 2)

II. Baptism declares our identification with our Savior (vv. 3–5)
    1. I identify with his death (vv. 3–4)
    2. I identify with his life (vv. 4–5)

III. Baptism declares our mortification of the old self (vv. 6–14)
    1. I am loosed from slavery to sin (vv. 6–9)
    2. I am alive for slavery to the Savior (vv. 10–14)

Cuthbert, delivered June 11, 1854, also can be consulted with much profit (Charleston, SC: James, Williams & Gitsinger, 1854). Cuthbert's successor as pastor of Wentworth-Street Baptist Church was Basil Manly Sr. Cuthbert said baptism was "that ordinance which constituted the initiatory step of your public entrance into the Christian life" (p. 7). He is spirited in his criticism of infant baptism and his affirmation of immersion. He notes the mode, appointed and sanctioned by Christ, "cannot be a point of *indifferency*" (p. 21, emphasis added).

4

"Dipped for Dead"
THE PROPER MODE OF BAPTISM

DAVID ALLEN

When it comes to Baptists and baptism, twin pillars of truth are evident: (1) immersion is the only biblical and thus proper mode of baptism, and (2) without immersion there is no biblical baptism.[1]

It is the height of irony that while some within pedobaptist churches are pushing for a recognition and renewal of baptism by immersion,[2] some Baptists are questioning whether baptism by immersion really should be required of all believers.[3] The Baptist Union of England's ecumenical embrace has opened the door for a liberalizing of traditional Baptist theology concerning baptism.[4] Among Baptists in the United States, it is surprising to see some churches giving consideration to relaxing their views on the necessity of baptism by immersion for church membership. Consider the celebrated case of Bethlehem Baptist Church in Minneapolis, Minnesota, which surprised the Baptist world when the elders of the church

---

W. T. Whitley, "Baptized—Dipped for Dead," *Baptist Quarterly* 11 (1943): 175–77, showed from manuscript evidence that the original edition of Leonard Busher's *Religious Peace, or, A Plea for Liberty of Conscience* published in 1614 contained the words, "And such as shall willingly and gladly receive it [the preached gospel], he hath commanded to be baptized in the water; that is, dipped for dead in the water."

1. See Thomas White, "What Makes Baptism Valid?" chapter 5 in this book.
2. C. Owen, ed., *Reforming Infant Baptism* (London: Hodder & Stoughton, 1990).
3. See Bill J. Leonard, "At the River," in *Proclaiming the Baptist Vision: Baptism and the Lord's Supper*, ed. Walter B. Shurden (Macon, GA: Smyth & Helwys, 1999), 13–20. Also in that work, G. Todd Wilson, "Why Baptists Should Not Rebaptize Christians from Other Denominations," 41–48, who questions whether those baptized by a mode other than immersion should be rebaptized. See also John Tyler, *Baptism: We've Got It Right . . . and Wrong* (Macon, GA: Smyth & Helwys, 2003).
4. Many British Baptists have an open membership policy with respect to baptism in that they do not require baptism by immersion for those seeking to join the church from other denominational backgrounds. See George R. Beasley-Murray, *Baptism Today and Tomorrow* (London: Macmillan, 1966), 86; and Anthony R. Cross, *Baptism and the Baptists: Theology and Practice in Twentieth Century Britain* (Carlisle, England: Paternoster, 2000).

expressed a desire to drop baptism by immersion as a requirement for church membership.[5] As surprising as this announcement was, some are shocked to discover that within the conservative Southern Baptist Convention, a few churches have broadened their baptismal policies to allow for membership without baptism by immersion.[6] The recent reaction to the Southern Baptist Convention's International Mission Board's baptismal policy for missionary candidates has drawn the ire of some critics, who have accused the board of trustees of unnecessarily narrowing the doctrinal parameters stated in the SBC's doctrinal statement, the Baptist Faith and Message (2000).[7] The spate of articles that have appeared recently on the subject of baptism within Southern Baptist Convention literature testifies to a heightened awareness of the ordinance. The time is ripe to revisit the theology of baptism. Although this chapter is written with all Baptists in mind, its central focus is on the proper mode of baptism and the implications of such for the Southern Baptist Convention in its theology and practice.

The past sixty years has witnessed quite an upsurge of interest in the subject of baptism among Protestant denominations.[8] When it comes to Baptists and their treatment of baptism, both doctrinally and in practice, the twentieth century was a period of significant change, even schizophrenia. For example, H. Wheeler Robinson rightly championed the necessity of believer's baptism as the foundation of a

---

5. The pertinent section of the proposed constitutional revision (which is now on hold for further study) states: "Since we believe that the New Testament teaches and demonstrates that the mode of baptism is only the immersion of a believer in water, we therefore regard all other practices of baptism as misguided, defective, and illegitimate. Yet, while not taking these differences lightly, we would not elevate them to the level of what is essential. Thus, we will welcome into membership candidates who, after a time of study, discussion, and prayer, prescribed by the Elders, retain a conviction that it would be a *violation* of their conscience to be baptized by immersion as believers. This conviction of conscience must be based on a plausible, intelligible, Scripturally based argument rather than on mere adherence to a tradition or family expectations." John Piper, "Baptism and Church Membership," Bethlehem Baptist Church (August 9, 2005), at http://www.desiringgod .org/media/pdf/baptism_and_membership.pdf (accessed February 2, 2007).
6. Lake Pointe Church in Rockwall, Texas, practices what it calls "alternative baptism," acceptance into membership of a person who has been baptized by sprinkling or pouring if it occurred after salvation and was done for the right reasons. Henderson Hills Baptist Church in Edmond, Oklahoma, recently contemplated a similar change.
7. Article 7—Baptism, in the Baptist Faith and Message, states, "Christian baptism is the immersion of a believer in water in the name of the Father, the Son, and the Holy Spirit. It is an act of obedience symbolizing the believer's faith in a crucified, buried, and risen Savior; the believer's death to sin; the burial of the old life; and the resurrection to walk in the newness of life in Christ Jesus. It is a testimony to his faith in the final resurrection of the dead. Being a church ordinance, it is prerequisite to the privileges of church membership and to the Lord's Supper." The Baptist Faith and Message can be found online at http://www.sbc.net/bfm/bfm2000.asp.
8. For a helpful survey, consult Stanley Porter, "Introduction: Baptism in Recent Debate," in *Baptism, the New Testament and the Church: Historical and Contemporary Studies in Honor of R. E. O. White,* JSNTSS 171, ed. R. E. O. White, Stanley E. Porter, and Anthony R. Cross (Sheffield: Sheffield Academic, 1999), 33–39. Some of the pertinent works include Alec Gilmore, *Christian*

biblical ecclesiology, stating, "The Baptist stands or falls by his conception of what the Church is; his plea for believer's baptism becomes a mere archaeology idiosyncrasy, if it be not the expression of the fundamental constitution of the Church."[9] Yet it was Robinson who first challenged the symbolic nature of baptism by arguing for a sacramental dimension as well.

G. R. Beasley-Murray's pilgrimage toward a more liberal understanding of baptism is evidenced when one compares what he wrote in his *Baptism in the New Testament* (1962), his *Baptism Today and Tomorrow* (1966), his "The Authority and Justification for Believer's Baptism" at the Consultation on Believer's Baptism held at the Southern Baptist Theological Seminary in Louisville in 1979, and then his "The Problem of Infant Baptism: An Exercise in Possibilities," in the *Festschrift* for Günther Wagner in 1994.

In *Baptism in the New Testament*, after an eighty-page discussion and rejection of infant baptism, Beasley-Murray penned these strong words:

> It seems that a small amount of water is bestowed on a small infant with a very small result. And this, it is alleged, is *baptism!* Can it be wondered at that Baptists should be strengthened in their determination to strive for the retention of the fullness of

---

Baptism: A Fresh Attempt to Understand the Rite in Terms of Scripture, History, and Theology (Chicago: Judson Press, 1959); R. E. O. White, *The Biblical Doctrine of Initiation* (London: Hodder & Stoughton, 1960); George R. Beasley-Murray, *Baptism in the New Testament* (Grand Rapids: Eerdmans, 1962); and idem, *Baptism Today and Tomorrow*.

A significant and often overlooked study (it is not mentioned by Porter in his "Introduction: Baptism in Recent Debate") is that of J. Ysebaert, *Greek Baptismal Terminology: Its Origins and Early Development*, Graecitas Christianorum Primaeva, fasc. 1 (Nijmegen, Netherlands: Dekker & Van De Vegt, 1962). See also Alec Gilmore, *Baptism and Christian Unity* (Valley Forge, PA: Judson Press, 1966); a series of articles in *Review and Expositor* 77, no. 1 (Winter 1980) on the Consultation on Believer's Baptism held at Southern Baptist Theological Seminary in Louisville in 1979; Paul Fiddes, ed., *Reflections on the Water: Understanding God and the World Through the Baptism of Believers* (Oxford: Regents Park College, 1996); R. Wayne Stacy, "Baptism," in *A Baptist's Theology*, ed. R. Wayne Stacy (Macon, GA: Smyth & Helwys, 1999); and Cross, *Baptism and the Baptists*.

Two recent significant studies covering a wide range of issues concerning baptism are White, Porter, and Cross, *Baptism, the New Testament and the Church*; and Stanley E. Porter and Anthony R. Cross, eds., *Dimensions of Baptism: Biblical and Theological Studies*, JSNTSS 234 (Sheffield: Sheffield Academic, 2002). Among more recent Southern Baptist treatments, consult James Leo Garrett's massive *Systematic Theology: Biblical, Historical and Evangelical* (Grand Rapids: Eerdmans, 1995), 2:502–36, esp. 529–31, on the mode of baptism. See also R. Stanton Norman, *More Than Just a Name* (Nashville: Broadman & Holman, 2001); idem, *The Baptist Way: Distinctives of a Baptist Church* (Nashville: Broadman & Holman, 2005), 129–45; Fred Malone, *The Baptism of Disciples Alone* (Cape Coral, FL: Founders Press, 2003); and Brian Russell, *Baptism: Sign and Seal of God's Grace* (London: Grace Publications Trust, 2001).

9. H. Wheeler Robinson, *The Life and Faith of the Baptists*, rev. ed. (London: Kingsgate, 1946), 73.

baptism, ordained of the Lord and continued in the Apostolic Communities, and that they should continue to lift up their voices among the Churches to plead for a return to this baptism.[10]

Four years later, in *Baptism Today and Tomorrow*, he was beginning to call on Baptists: (1) to opt for a moderate position that holds together the sacramentalist and symbolic views of baptism (pp. 23–24); (2) to view conversion and baptism as inseparable (p. 37); and (3) to yield to a more open membership stance (which was already the norm in England).[11] In his "The Problem of Infant Baptism," he explored the possibilities of a rapprochement between believer's baptism and infant baptism, where one views infant baptism as "the commencement of the work of grace within the baptized with a view to its blossoming into fullness of life in Christ and in his Body the Church as the individual's life progressively opens to Christ." He also stated, "Churches which practice believer's baptism should consider acknowledging the legitimacy of infant baptism."[12]

Whereas once in English Baptist life the question of open membership in Bunyanesque fashion was a minority viewpoint, today it is the norm in the Baptist Union of England. Yet, in spite of this, in that very Baptist Union, infant baptism continues to be rejected as a valid form of baptism.[13] Roger Hayden correctly noted with respect to English Baptists in the twenty-first century that a "common understanding of the meaning and practice of baptism has remained elusive."[14]

Even with respect to the mode of baptism by immersion, troubling signs were on the horizon in H. Wheeler Robinson's *Life and Faith*. After championing believer's baptism as the hallmark of Baptist baptism, Robinson says of the mode, "As a quite subsidiary point, they practice the most ancient form of baptism, because they find this the most eloquent expression of the essentials of that faith—the death and resurrection of their Lord." He goes on to say that neither the General nor the Particular Baptists first practiced baptism by immersion, "so that the mode was historically, as well as logically, an afterthought."[15] No mention here of the clear meaning of the word in the Greek New Testament, nor of the necessity of obedience to the command of Christ, nor even of the theological inadequacy of sprinkling or pouring.

---

10. Beasley-Murray, *Baptism in the New Testament*, 385–86.
11. Robinson began this trend in his *Life and Faith of the Baptists*, 146.
12. "The Problem of Infant Baptism," in *Festschrift Günther Wagner*, ed. The Faculty of the Baptist Theological Seminary, Rüschlikon (New York: Peter Lang, 1994), 13–14.
13. Anthony R. Cross, "Baptists and Baptism: A British Perspective," *Baptist History and Heritage* (2000): 116. His entire article, along with his *Baptism and the Baptists*, is a helpful summary of the present state of affairs in Britain.
14. Roger Hayden, *English Baptist History and Heritage*, 2nd ed. (Oxfordshire, UK: Nigel Lynn Publishing & Marketing Ltd. on behalf of the Baptist Union of Great Britain, 2005), 224.
15. Robinson, *Life and Faith of the Baptists*, 70–71. This last statement leaves the reader to infer that the mode of immersion, while practiced in the New Testament, and even desirable as the best

One of the clearest facts of church history is that from shortly after the founding of the first Baptist church on English soil to the present time, Baptists have affirmed immersion as the only biblical mode of baptism.[16] From the seventeenth century until today, Baptist authors have produced a plethora of books and pamphlets on baptism. Many of these were called forth in answer to pedobaptist objections to believer's baptism by immersion. English Baptists wasted no time in engaging their pedobaptist counterparts in baptismal debates. Numerous records cataloging these debates exist.[17] One of the earliest and most famous was the debate between Daniel Featley and William Kiffin. Featley's 1645 book titled *The Dippers dipt: or, the Anabaptists Duck'd and Plung'd over Head and Eares, at a Disputation in Southwark* chronicled the debate. Featley, age sixty-two and a veteran debater, took on Kiffin, who was thirty-six at the time. Featley castigated his opponents with the charge that Anabaptism was a heresy long ago condemned and then proceeded to denigrate Kiffin and the other three Baptists accompanying him by insulting their scholarly capacity since they were rudely dressed and chiding them for their lack of knowledge of Greek and Hebrew. Early into the debate, Kiffin asked Featley the question, "What is the nature of a visible church?" This question was prophetic since the single most distinctive contribution Baptists make to church history is our ecclesiology. The statement also illustrates the important theological conviction that the baptism question cannot be separated from the question of the nature of the church. Any discussion about baptism presupposes ecclesiology.

The conflicts between Anabaptists and pedobaptists in the sixteenth century and beyond were primarily over the question of the nature of a New Testament church.[18] Michael Jinkins correctly distinguished between two different understandings of the church: the church as voluntary association, which reflects an emphasis on conversion as the necessary condition for full participation in the

expression of baptism's meaning, is not crucial to the meaning of the ordinance. Hence, the door is opened in Baptist churches for "alien immersion" and "open membership."

16. As demonstrated from Baptist histories as well as Baptist confessions of faith. See W. L. Lumpkin, *Baptist Confessions of Faith*, rev. ed. (Valley Forge, PA: Judson Press, 1969). Article 40 of the 1644 London Confession prescribes immersion, as do all subsequent revisions of this confession. All other Baptist confessions, English, American, and other nationalities to the present time affirm immersion as the only scriptural mode of baptism. See James Leo Garrett, "The Theology and Practice of Baptism: A Southern Baptist View," *Southwestern Journal of Theology* 28 (Spring 1986): 66, for a listing of eight Baptist confessions with their specific wording on the mode of baptism.

17. For a summary discussion of this debate, along with some of the more controversial debates conducted between the outbreak of the English civil war and the Restoration of Charles II, consult J. G. Goadby, *Bye-Paths in Baptist History* (London: Elliot Stock, 1871), 139–79. On the Featley-Kiffin debate, see also H. Leon McBeth, *The Baptist Heritage: Four Centuries of Baptist Witness* (Nashville: Broadman Press, 1987), 80.

18. "The question of baptism cannot be separated from the question of the Church. It is

community of believers, and church as a gathered body, emphasizing the inclusion of children who have not yet made the gospel their own by faith. He rightly noted that these two perspectives "inevitably compete," and "there is an undeniable and irresolvable conflict between them."[19] The fountainhead of this conflict began with the Reformation. William Estep perceptively noted, *"A most important fact often overlooked is that the very concept of the gathered church, which is the heart of Separatism, was Anabaptist in origin and not a conscious product of the Magisterial Reform."*[20] From the perspective of the magisterial Reformers, if believer's baptism were initiated, the unity of the church would be jeopardized. As Johannes Warns noted, "Baptism is the issue whereby the State church stands or falls,"[21] a fact that goes a long way toward explaining the vitriolic opposition of Luther, Calvin, and Zwingli to the Anabaptists. "If the rightfulness of infant baptism is called into question, the rightfulness of a state church in general is called into question."[22] What Baptists have always desired was a return to biblical ecclesiology, which includes a return to believer's baptism by immersion.

With respect to baptism, three central issues have been at the heart of the debate since the Reformation: meaning, subject, and mode. As to meaning, is it a sacrament, or is it symbolic? As to subject, is it an infant or a believer? As to mode, is it immersion or sprinkling/pouring? Baptists have universally held that immersion is

---

indissolubly bound up with it. Indeed one has to say that the question of the Church has precedence over the question of Baptism." Johannes Schneider, *Baptism and Church in the New Testament*, trans. Ernest Payne (London: Carey Kingsgate, 1957), 50.

19. Michael Jinkins, "The Gift of the Church: Ecclesia Crucis, Peccatrix Maxima, and the Missio Dei," in *Evangelical Ecclesiology*, ed. John Stackhouse (Grand Rapids: Baker, 2003), 185. Leonard Vander Zee states, "If we don't really know what baptism is we don't really know what the church is either." *Christ, Baptism and the Lord's Supper* (Downers Grove, IL: InterVarsity Press, 2004), 112.

20. William Estep, "A Believing People: Historical Background," in *The Concept of the Believers' Church: Addresses from the 1968 Louisville Conference*, ed. James Leo Garrett (Scottdale, PA: Herald, 1969), 47 (author's italics).

21. Johannes Warns, *Baptism: Studies in the Original Christian Baptism, Its History and Conflicts, Its Relation to a State or National Church and Its Significance for the Present Time*, trans. G. H. Lang (London: Paternoster, 1957; reprint, Minneapolis: Klock and Klock, 1976), 240.

22. Ibid., 251. "There can be no biblical solution to the question of baptism as long as one holds fast the conception of a State Church" (ibid., 264). The Magisterial Reformers thought that without infant baptism, which was so ingrained in the populace, the whole fabric of the church might be torn asunder. Surprisingly, Baptists found a strange ally when Karl Barth wrote, "There can be no doubt that in all Zwingli's baptismal works one seeks in vain a true elucidation of what takes place in baptism. . . . His will and purpose in relation to the Anabaptists is quite plain. Infant baptism must be accepted at all costs as the shibboleth of the people of God." *Church Dogmatics* 4.1 (Edinburgh: T & T Clark, 1956), 129. The last sentence of the quote applies to Luther and Calvin as well. Barth's *The Teaching of the Church Regarding Baptism* was published in German in 1943 and was translated into English by Ernest Payne, a Baptist, in 1948. See Karl Barth, *The Teaching of the Church Regarding Baptism*, trans. Ernest A. Payne (London: SCM Press, 1948).

the only biblical and hence proper mode of baptism. Southern Baptists, along with most other Baptists, consider baptism by any mode other than immersion to be invalid baptism.[23] The major question to be answered is, does the New Testament know of any kind of baptism other than immersion?

Linguistic Evidence

"Philology is the eye of the needle through which every theological camel must enter the heaven of theology."[24] A theology of baptism must begin with the meaning and usage of *baptizō* in the LXX and Greek New Testament and then expand into the broader context of contemporary usage both sacred and secular. When it comes to word studies, one must tread very carefully in order to avoid semantic fallacies.[25]

Tabal in the Old Testament

Koehler and Baumgartner designate the meaning of the Hebrew *tabal* as "to dip something into; to dive or plunge." Elmer Martens assigns it the meaning of "immerse."[26] From the usage of this word in the Hebrew Old Testament, and especially from its use in 2 Kings 5:14, of Naaman immersing himself in the Jordan, it is evident that the word is never used for anything other than immersion. The LXX usually translates this word with *baptō* (thirteen times), while *baptizō* is used only twice in the LXX: metaphorically in Isaiah 21:4, where the Hebrew *tabal* is not present, and literally of Naaman immersing in water in 2 Kings 5:14. This is the only place in the LXX where *baptizō* is used to translate *tabal*. Naaman is told by the prophet Elisha to bathe (*rachats*) seven times in the Jordan River, and he will be cleansed of his leprosy. Naaman at first resists this but finally, upon the

---

23. Although Baptists affirm immersion as baptism's only proper mode, they allow for a variety of means to immerse, including laying the candidate backward under water, as practiced by the early English Baptists, or bowing the candidate forward under water, as practiced by the Greek, Armenian, and Oriental churches. See Adoniram Judson, "An Address on the Mode of Baptism," *Fundamentalist Journal* 6, no. 4 (April 1987): 49–50, which he gave June 7, 1846, describing this posture of immersion on the mission field as being congruent with the early church. One Baptist preacher said in 1643 that all were "to be rebaptized stark naked, and diped as well head as tayle." Henry Dexter, *The True Story of John Smyth* (Boston: Lee and Shepard, 1818), 56, as quoted in McBeth, *The Baptist Heritage: Four Centuries of Baptist Witness* (Nashville: B & H Publishing Group, 1987), 48.

24. Nathan Söderblom, cited by D. A. Carson in *Exegetical Fallacies*, 2nd ed. (Grand Rapids: Baker, 2004), 27.

25. D. A. Carson has helpfully identified and illustrated these fallacies in the first chapter of his *Exegetical Fallacies*. See also the important work by Moisé Silva, *Biblical Words and Their Meaning: An Introduction to Lexical Semantics* (Grand Rapids: Zondervan, 1983).

26. L. Koehler and W. Baumgartner, *The Hebrew and Aramaic Lexicon of the Old Testament*, trans. and ed. M. E. J. Richardson (Leiden: Brill, 2001), 368; Elmer Martens, "Tabal" in *New International Dictionary of Old Testament Theology and Exegesis*, ed. Willem VanGemeren (Grand Rapids: Zondervan, 1997), 2:337.

urging of his servants, relents and immerses himself in the Jordan. Three times the Hebrew text uses the verb *rachats*, "to bathe or wash," and each time it is translated by *louein* in the LXX. But when the action of Naaman in the Jordan is described, the Hebrew *tabal* is used, translated by *baptizō* in the LXX.

In his significant but often overlooked study, *Greek Baptismal Terminology*, Ysebaert explains how *tabal*, along with *baptizein*, as used for Jewish ritual washing as an immersion may be traced back to the story of Naaman in 2 Kings 5. The words indicate purification in its outward aspect as an immersion and do not carry the meaning of washing (except when that washing is done by immersion) or sprinkling.[27] This leads to the question of the nature of Jewish ablutions in the Old Testament and in Second Temple Judaism and their bearing on New Testament baptism. Due to the constraints of space, we will speak of these only in a general summary fashion.

JEWISH ABLUTIONS IN THE OLD TESTAMENT AND SECOND TEMPLE PERIOD

The primary purpose of ablutions in the Old Testament is cleansing. For example, prior to the Levites performing their duty, they were sprinkled with water (Num. 8:7). The red heifer ritual likewise involved the sprinkling of water (Num. 19:18). Washing parts of the body is almost exclusively a priestly regulation (Exod. 30:18–21). Robert Webb has stated, "In most other cases, cleansing from uncleanness required an immersion. . . . Only in the cases of the high priest on the Day of Atonement and the example of Naaman are immersions performed without other requirements."[28] Webb concluded that in the Second Temple period the metaphorical use of ablution language in the Old Testament to express cleansing from sin is being linked to the actual use of ablutions as cleansing from uncleanness. "Ritual immersions expanded during this period to express repentance and conversion, and perhaps in symbolizing cleansing from sin."[29]

As noted by Ysebaert, in Mark 7:4 and Hebrews 9:10, *baptismos* follows the Jewish usage of the verb form and indicates the cleansing of both the body and vessels by immersion. When *baptizein* and *baptismos* are used for the cleansing of vessels (e.g., Mark 7:4; Luke 11:38), one might draw the erroneous conclusion that the idea of immersion has been lost. Much is made of this in pedobaptist arguments against immersion. However, this overlooks the common household practice of cleaning

---

27. Ysebaert, *Greek Baptismal Terminology*, 27–39.
28. Robert Webb, *John the Baptizer and Prophet: A Socio-Historical Study*, JSNTSS 62 (Sheffield: JSOT Press, 1991), 106.
29. Ibid., 132.

vessels by immersing them in water, a procedure not uncommon in both the Old Testament (Lev. 11:32) and the Mishna.[30]

JEWISH PROSELYTE BAPTISM

This subject has received considerable attention from scholars. Some have sought for the antecedents of Christian baptism in the rite of Jewish proselyte baptism. Although the question of exactly when Jewish proselyte baptism began is a matter of ongoing debate, what is now generally agreed upon is that Jewish proselyte baptism was done by immersion.[31] Daube refers to the Tannaitic provision on proselyte baptism, which states, "'When he has undergone baptism and come up, *tabhal we'ala*, he is like an Israelite in all respects.'" The statement "come up," Daube noted, "is a detail of the highest importance," because of its symbolic meaning. It is even conceivable that, among other reasons, John the Baptist baptized in the Jordan, "because he saw in the 'coming up' a new entry into the Promised Land." *'Ala* is used four times in Joshua 4 to describe the priests and the people crossing over Jordan. Both Matthew and Mark speak of Jesus "coming up" from his baptism in the Jordan (Matt. 3:16; Mark 1:10).[32]

Oskar Skarsaune, in commenting on Daube's discussion, also finds parallels in *Barnabas* 11.11 and in Shepherd of Hermas, *Similitude* 9.16.3–4.[33] It is interesting that I. Howard Marshall, in an attempt to argue that *baptizō* can mean "pouring," refers to Skarsaune's citations in *Barnabas* and the *Similitudes* of the Shepherd of Hermas and uses the above statements about "going down" and "coming up" as evidence that "candidates were either immersed in water or perhaps stood in water

---

30. Ysebaert, *Greek Baptismal Terminology*, 28. Also see G. R. Beasley-Murray, "Βαπτιζω," in *New International Dictionary of New Testament Theology*, ed. Colin Brown (Grand Rapids: Zondervan, 1975), 1:144.

31. Emil Schürer, *A History of the Jewish People in the Time of Jesus Christ*, trans. Sophia Taylor and Peter Christie, 2nd division (1890; reprint, Hendrickson, 1994), 2:319–24; F. Gavin, *The Jewish Antecedents of the Christian Sacraments* (London: Society for Promoting Christian Knowledge, 1928), 26–58; G. Foote Moore, *Judaism in the First Centuries of the Christian Era* (Cambridge: Harvard University Press, 1932), 1:331–35; Hermann L. Strack and Paul Billerbeck, *Kommentar zum Neuen Testament aus Talmud und Midrash*, München: Beck, 1922) 1:102–13; W. Michaelis, "Zum judischen Hintergrund der Johannes taufe," *Judaica* 7 (1951): 81–120; D. Daube, *The New Testament and Rabbinic Judaism* (London: Athlone, 1956), 111–12; T. F. Torrance, "Proselyte Baptism," *New Testament Studies* 1, no. 2 (November 1954): 150–54; T. M. Taylor, "The Beginnings of Jewish Proselyte Baptism," *New Testament Studies* 2, no. 3 (February 1956): 193–98; W. F. Farmington, *The New Testament Doctrine of Baptism* (London: S.P.C.K., 1957), 8; and Webb, *John the Baptizer and Prophet*, 122–30.

32. Daube, *New Testament and Rabbinic Judaism*, 111–12. Daube views all this as "conclusive evidence" that Christian baptism originated in Jewish proselyte baptism. While hardly conclusive, at the very least it confirms that proselyte baptism and John's baptism were antecedents to Christian baptism.

33. Oskar Skarsaune, *In the Shadow of the Temple* (Downers Grove, IL: InterVarsity Press, 2002), 366–67.

while they were affused with water." Of course, he offers no evidence for affusion but follows up by saying the terminology is "ambiguous," and when used for proselyte baptism, "has been interpreted as referring to immersion."[34]

THE BAPTISM OF JOHN THE BAPTIST

Jewish purification rites were called *baptismoi*, whereas John's baptism and Christian baptism in the New Testament are referred to by the noun *baptisma*. What was the nature of John's baptism, and what relationship did it have to Christian baptism? Two significant studies on John the Baptist have appeared in the last fifteen years: Robert Webb's *John the Baptizer and Prophet* (1991) and Joan Taylor, *The Immerser: John the Baptist within Second Temple Judaism* (1997). Webb demonstrated that both Josephus and the New Testament are reliable historical sources concerning John's baptism. With respect to the mode of baptism, he concluded "John's baptism was an immersion."[35] Taylor traced what she considered to be the influence of John on Jesus with respect to baptism. John immersed Jesus in the Jordan, and after John's death Jesus continued John's teaching on immersion based on repentance. After the death of Jesus, the disciples furthered Jesus' teaching on baptism.[36] Without commenting on the merits of Taylor's understanding of Jesus' relationship to John, what is important to note is that the evidence is clear that John's baptism was by immersion, John immersed Jesus in the Jordan, and Jesus, along with his disciples, taught baptism by immersion.

In John's baptism, repentance indicated a real change of heart symbolized by complete immersion. Interestingly, Ysebaert considered the possibility that John may have understood his baptizing against the backdrop of the Jewish concept that the realm of the dead is the sea into which one "descends" and from which one can "emerge" again. He cites Jonah 2:3 and following; Psalm 17:5 and following; and Job 26:5 and following as examples of this concept. If John gave his baptism this meaning, it could explain why he baptized by immersion, why he performed it in the Jordan River and why he did not refer to his own rite of baptism as "cleansing" from sin.[37] It is interesting that Jesus called his own death a baptism. Whether Ysebaert's suggestion has merit or not, one thing is clear: John's baptism was by immersion.

We learn from Acts 18:25 and 19:3 that following the resurrection of Jesus and Pentecost, John's baptism was inadequate for a follower of Jesus, although it cor-

---

34. I. Howard Marshall, "The Meaning of the Verb 'Baptize,'" in Porter and Cross, *Dimensions of Baptism*, 18–19.
35. Robert Webb, *John the Baptizer and Prophet*, 214.
36. Joan Taylor, *The Immerser: John the Baptist within Second Temple Judaism* (Grand Rapids: Eerdmans, 1997), 49–58, 318–22.
37. Ysebaert, *Greek Baptismal Terminology*, 38–39.

responded to the mode of baptism employed by the early Christians. Apollos knew only the baptism of John (Acts 18:25). His preaching of Jesus did not overcome his defective baptism. The same was true of John's disciples in Ephesus in Acts 19:3. Only when they were baptized in the name of Jesus had they received baptism valid for membership in the church.[38]

MEANING AND USE OF BAPTIZŌ IN THE NEW TESTAMENT

Bauer, Arndt, Gingrich, and Danker list the following meanings for *baptizō*: "dip, immerse, dip oneself, wash."[39] The word is used in non-Christian literature to mean "plunge, sink, drench, overwhelm." Three major uses are listed: (1) of Jewish ritual washings (Mark 7:4; Luke 11:38. Both of these usages indicate washing by immersing in water.); (2) in the special sense of "baptize" used of John's baptism and of Christian baptism; (3) in the figurative sense related to the idea of Christian baptism. There are at least ten metaphorical uses of *baptizein* in the New Testament. Six times the word is used for the pouring out of the Spirit and fire (Matt. 3:11; Mark 1:8; Luke 3:16; John 1:33ff.; Acts 1:5; 11:16). Once it is used for the crossing of the Red Sea by the Israelites (1 Cor. 10:2). Three times it is used for the concept of death; once for Christ (Mark 10:38), once for James and John (Luke 12:50), and for the Corinthians (1 Cor. 15:29). The following uses of *baptisma* (translated "baptism") occur: (1) thirteen times of John's baptism (Matt. 3:7, etc.), (2) four times of Christian baptism (Rom. 6:4; Col. 2:12; Eph. 4:5; 1 Peter 3:21), and (3) three times of baptism figuratively for Jesus' death (Mark 10:38, etc.). The following uses of *baptismos* (translated "dipping" or "baptism") occur: (1) of washing of dishes (Mark 7:4, 8); and (2) of ritual washings (Heb. 6:2; 9:10).[40]

Louw and Nida recognize three major semantic categories for the word *baptizō*:

38. A point well made by Schneider, *Baptism and Church in the New Testament*, 25–26.

39. Walter Bauer, William F. Arndt, F. Wilbur Gingrich, and Frederick W. Danker, "baptizō," in *A Greek-English Lexicon of the New Testament*, 3rd ed. (Chicago: University of Chicago Press, 2001), 131.

40. Ibid., 131–32. See also H. G. Liddell and Robert Scott, *An Intermediate Greek-English Lexicon* (Oxford: Clarendon, 1995), 146. For the usage of *baptizein* among Greek papyri, see James Hope Moulton and George Milligan, *Vocabulary of the Greek Testament: Illustrated from the Papyri and Other Non-literary Sources* (Grand Rapids: Eerdmans, 1930), 102–3; George Milligan, *Selections from the Greek Papyri* (Cambridge: Cambridge University Press, 1910), 22, where the metaphorical use of *baptizein* in the "Letter of Apollonius" ("we are immersed in trouble") is similar to the language of Mark 10:38. *Baptizein* is used seventy-seven times in the Greek New Testament; *baptisma* is used nineteen times; *baptismos* is used four times and *baptisēs* occurs twelve times. See Philip Clapp, Barbara Friberg, and Timothy Friberg, eds., *Analytical Concordance of the Greek New Testament*, Lexical Focus (Grand Rapids: Baker, 1991), 1:327–28. See also George R. Beasley-Murray, "baptism, wash," *New International Dictionary of New Testament Theology*, 1:144–50; J. H. Moulton and W. F. Howard, *A Grammar of New Testament Greek* (n.p., 1929), 2:408; and Ysebaert, *Greek Baptismal Terminology*, 40–63.

(1) to wash (possibly in some contexts by dipping into water) with the purpose of purification; (2) to baptize in the sense of "to employ water in a religious ceremony designed to symbolize purification and initiation;" and (3) to cause religious experience, a figurative extension of the term.

After noting most translators employ a transliterated form of the Greek word (which they themselves have done), they state in some languages this would be "inappropriate, especially if another term or expression has already been employed and is widely accepted by groups practicing various types or forms of baptism."[41] This is an egregious example of lexical prejudice that ignores the clear evidence that *baptizō* means "to immerse" in terms of mode. Liddell and Scott give the meaning "to dip in or under water." In the first edition of Liddell and Scott's lexicon, the seventh meaning of *baptizō* was listed as "to pour upon" but with no example in Classical Greek cited in support. It is significant to note that this meaning was deleted in the second edition and has been absent in each subsequent edition. Furthermore, Liddell and Scott's lexicon contains no example of *baptizō* being used for sprinkling or pouring. In fact, in ancient Greek, Septuagint Greek, and first-century A.D. Greek, the word consistently meant "to dip, dunk, or immerse." It is a simple linguistic fact that *rantizō* ("to sprinkle") and *eccheō* ("to pour") both occur in the New Testament but never in connection with baptism.

From a linguistic perspective, an inadequate diachronic analysis of *baptizein* has contributed to the confusion surrounding the meaning and use of this word. If, as established by Ysebaert, *baptizein* originally carried its Jewish meaning of "to immerse," did the word ever come to mean "to sprinkle" or "to wash"? Since vessels were washed by being immersed, Mark 7:4 cannot be used as a proof-text to support the meaning of "wash." Nor can help be sought from Luke 11:38, since Jewish ritual washing meant dipping the hands in water, and, as Ysebeart argued, this "merely indicates that the verb was becoming more technical."[42] The cognates *apoluein* and *loutron* are used only in rare cases for the concept of cleansing from sin and are not synonymous with *baptizein*.[43] Thus, the word *baptizein* retains its Jewish meaning of "immerse" in the New Testament and there is no evidence that its meaning ever changed into that of "wash."

The question of whether *baptizein* has become a technical term in the New Testament without reference to mode need not detain us here. If the mode is inher-

---

41. Johannes P. Louw and Eugene A. Nida, eds., *Greek-English Lexicon of the New Testament Based on Semantic Domains*, 2nd ed. (New York: United Bible Societies, 1988), 2:536–38.

42. Ysebaert, *Greek Baptismal Terminology*, 41.

43. Ibid., 42, 62–63.

ently bound up in the meaning and usage of the term, as demonstrated above, then the chronology of when the term became a technical term for baptism is moot.[44]

Etymologically, *baptizō* clearly means "immerse." However, meaning cannot be determined by etymology alone. The usage of a term must be carefully studied to determine its meaning. When this is done with *baptizein*, the term unquestionably means "immerse."[45] Pedobaptists argue that the secular usage of *baptizō* cannot determine its meaning in the New Testament. While it is certainly true that lexicography alone cannot determine meaning or usage, the lexicon cannot be ignored or minimized, as is often the case with pedobaptists.

OTHER LINGUISTIC CONSIDERATIONS

The use of *baptizein* in the passive voice illustrates why, from a semantic standpoint, the meaning must be "immerse." Take Mark 1:9 as an example. Jesus, not the water, was baptized by John in the Jordan River. When it comes to *baptizō*, the passive form grammaticalizes the mode as immersion. Never is water the subject of the passive use of the verb *baptizō*. The subjects of the ordinance are baptized; the water is not. Sprinkling or pouring simply do not make sense. Nor is the pedobaptist case helped by appeal to the use of the Greek preposition *en* or *eis* here or elsewhere, since the verb, in this case the passive verb, dictates the usage of the preposition. When either of these prepositions is used with the verb *baptizō*, the focus is on being baptized "in" or "with" water, specifying location. In fact, Carson noted the "absurdity" of translating *baptizō* in Mark 1:9 as "sprinkle" or "pour." "You can dip someone in the water but you cannot sprinkle them into the water unless you have used a mincer beforehand!"[46] Oliver studied the use of the preposition *en* with *baptizō*, with the noun *hudati* "water" as well as the use of *hudati* without the preposition and concluded, "According to the strict sense of *baptizō*, it would seem impossible to make *hudati* or *en hudati* out as instrumental."[47] Semantically, *baptizō* necessitates the locative use of the preposition *en*.

---

44. A. Oepke, "*baptō*," in *Theological Dictionary of the New Testament*, ed. Gerhard Kittel (Grand Rapids: Eerdmans, 1964), 1:529, considers the term to have reached technical status in the New Testament. Ysebaert, *Greek Baptismal Terminology*, 37, disagrees. See discussion in Carson, *Exegetical Fallacies*, 45–46, in relation to the phrase "baptism in the Spirit" in 1 Corinthians 12:13.

45. Significant works proving this from both secular and sacred usage of the term in Classical and Koine Greek include Alexander Carson, *Baptism in Its Mode and Subjects* (Philadelphia: American Baptist Publication Society, 1848); and Thomas J. Conant, *The Meaning and Use of Baptizein* (1860; reprint, Grand Rapids: Kregel, 1977). J. L. Dagg, *Church Order: A Treatise* (Philadelphia: American Baptist Publication Society, 1871), 21–37, collates these according to semantic domains in tables for ease of study.

46. Herbert Carson, "The Mode of Baptism," in *The Ideal Church*, 2nd Carey Conference, 1971, in Nottinghamshire, England (Haywards Heath: Carey Publications, 1972), 25.

47. A. Ben Oliver, "Is *Baptizō* Used with *en* and the Instrumental?" *Review and Expositor* 35, no. 2 (April 1938): 195.

It has been suggested that when the preposition *eis* means "into" it is used before the noun as well as the verb. Since *eis* is used only once in Acts 8:38, it is sometimes surmised that Philip and the eunuch did not go *into*, but only *to*, the water, and the conclusion is drawn that the eunuch was not immersed.[48] However, James Pendleton pointed out, correctly, that in numerous places *eis* is used only once to express the same idea of entrance. Pedobaptists admit *eis* means "into" in all other places except where baptismal waters are referred to. Pendleton's sarcasm is pointed:

> This little word *eis* is a strange word indeed if all said of it is true. It will take a man *into* a country, *into* a city, *into* a house, *into* a ship, *into* heaven, *into* hell,—*into* any place in the universe except the water. Poor word! Afflicted, it seems, with hydrophobia, it will allow a person to go *to* the water, but not *into* it.[49]

Other indications in Acts 8:36–39 support a baptism of the eunuch by immersion. The use of *katabainō* and *anabainō*, "to go down" into the water and "to come up" out of the water, certainly suggests immersion.[50]

I. Howard Marshall has attempted to modify the meaning of *baptizō* from the root idea of immersion by a consideration of its metaphorical uses, specifically the notion of the baptism of the Spirit and of fire.

> We must conclude that when John spoke of baptism with the Spirit he had in mind the descent of the Spirit from above like a stream of water pouring over a person. . . . But if this is how the verb "baptize" is to be understood in relation to the Spirit, then the same can also be true when it is used in relation to water.[51]

Marshall suggests that the idea of immersion is not the best to employ with the Spirit; therefore, our understanding of baptism "may stand in need of revision."[52] Paul's theological case in Romans 6:4 is not drawn from the literal act of baptism,

---

48. Thomas Summers, *Baptism: A Treatise on the Nature, Perpetuity, Subjects, Administration, Mode, and Use of the Initiating Ordinance of the Christian Church* (Richmond, VA: John Early for the Methodist Episcopal Church, South, 1852), 100.

49. J. M. Pendleton, *Distinctive Principles of Baptists* (Philadelphia: American Baptist Publication Society, 1882), 131. For a thorough analysis of J. M. Pendleton's views on baptism, consult Thomas White, "James Madison Pendleton and His Contributions to Baptist Ecclesiology," in *Selected Works of James Madison Pendleton*, ed. Thomas White (Paris, AR: Baptist Standard Bearer, 2006), see esp. 62–117.

50. Everett Ferguson, "Christian and Jewish Baptism According to the Epistle of Barnabas," in Porter and Cross, *Dimensions of Baptism*, 222–23. Ferguson noted, "The express statement that 'we go down into the water' and 'we come up' (11.8.11) is sufficient to indicate immersion" (ibid.).

51. Marshall, "Meaning of the Verb 'Baptize,'" 22.

52. Ibid., 17.

according to Marshall; hence, it is not tied to a particular mode of baptism. Immersion fails to offer a fitting symbolism for the concept of sprinkling and pouring, which is associated with the baptism of the Spirit in the New Testament.

Marshall concludes that in the case of literal baptism involving water and metaphorical baptism involving the Spirit, the reference is not so much to the mode as to the result. He makes the linguistic mistake of deriving the literal usage of a term from its metaphorical usage. This is linguistically backward. The metaphorical meaning of a word is dependent upon its literal meaning, not the other way around. For a metaphor to work, there must be something that by analogy is compared to baptism. How could Paul's use of the phrase "all were baptized . . . in the cloud and in the sea" (NKJV) in 1 Corinthians 10:2 be effective for the readers unless the literal meaning of the term was a part of the common vocabulary of the people? Expressions such as "baptized in the Spirit" in Acts and "baptized in the Spirit and fire" in the Gospels depend on the literal meaning of immersion to provide sense to the metaphorical meaning. When Jesus referred to his death as a "baptism," again the notion of immersion looms in the background. James Dunn, wrongly in my view, asserts that Paul in Romans 6:3–5 is speaking metaphorically and not about literal baptism, yet his article "'Baptized' as Metaphor," makes it clear that the meaning of "immersion" for *baptizō* is foundational for the metaphorical use of the term. He notes, "The imagery of being submerged in a river of spirit (*ruah*) and fire may strike modern readers as odd and repellent . . . but it would have been by no means surprising for John or his hearers."[53]

ADDITIONAL BIBLICAL EVIDENCE

Consider the following biblical references:

- Matthew 3:16—"Jesus, when he was baptized, went up straightway out of the water" (KJV)
- Mark 1:5—"and were all baptized by him in the Jordan River" (NKJV)
- Mark 1:10—"coming up out of the water" (KJV)
- John 3:23—"John also was baptizing in Aenon near Salim, because there was much water there" (NKJV)
- Acts 8:38–39—"and they went down both into the water, . . . and he baptized him. And when they were come up out of the water . . ." (KJV)

In each of these cases, the Greek language used, contextual considerations, and logic itself dictate that immersion is intended. It often has been argued against immersion that there was insufficient water in Jerusalem on the Day of Pentecost

---

53. James D. G. Dunn, "'Baptized' as Metaphor," in White, Porter, and Cross, *Baptism, the New Testament and the Church*, 304.

to baptize three thousand in one day. Likewise, no mention is made of available water for the Philippian jailer's baptism. We shall see below that the former argument is refuted by archaeological discoveries and the latter is an argument from silence. When Baptists point to John 3:23 and the reference to "much water," we are told by pedobaptists that an abundance of water does not indicate immersion. To such pedobaptist unreasonableness, J. M. Pendleton responded sardonically:

> We cannot please them at all. . . . If there is no mention of a "river" in a baptismal narrative, the cry is "No immersion" and "scarcity of water." If the river Jordan is named, the same cry of "No immersion" is heard; so that, according to Pedobaptist logic, scarcity of water and abundance of water prove the same thing.[54]

CONCLUSION

In the New Testament, the obvious meaning of *baptizō* is immersion. While the KJV translators may have been under constraint from King James I to follow his rules of translation and thus transliterate rather than translate *baptizō*, modern translators are under no such restriction. The word means what it means, and nothing short of bias, cowardice, or even misrepresentation can explain why the word is not translated "immerse." It is tragic to see pedobaptists searching in vain for some linguistic bypath far from the interstate of standard usage that will provide a scintilla of evidence to support their notion of baptism as pouring or sprinkling. When the Greek dictionary of the first century was loaded with words for sprinkling and pouring, it would have been all too easy for the New Testament authors to have made use of these words had that been their intended meaning.[55]

As the dean of the School of Theology at Southwestern Baptist Theological Seminary, I have a master key that fits all the locks in Scarborough and Fleming Halls. By analogy, word definitions are like master keys. When a word is properly defined, the definition becomes the key that unlocks the meaning. If the definition is incorrect, it may fit some contexts, but in many others its substitution leads to ambiguity, error, or nonsense.[56]

---

54. Pendleton, *Distinctive Principles of Baptists*, 132.
55. Typical of the present-day misrepresentation of the meaning of *baptize* in the Greek New Testament is Vander Zee, *Christ, Baptism and the Lord's Supper*, 99: "While some insist that the word *baptize* means 'to immerse,' scholars point out that it is clearly used to describe other modes in Greek." He offers no supporting evidence. He does, however, note that baptism's "sacramental nature is best highlighted by using as much water as possible. . . . There is an exciting return to immersion among non-Baptist churches, even for the baptism of infants and young children" (ibid., 100).
56. I am indebted to John Broadus, famed homiletician and president of Southern Seminary, for this analogy. Broadus tried the key of immersion in many of the baptismal locks in the New Testament and found that in every case the door was opened! Jeremiah Jeter, "Only Immersion Is Baptism," in *Baptist Principles Reset*, new ed. (Richmond: Religious Herald, 1902), 72.

Philip Schaff, famed church historian who was professor of church history at Union Theological Seminary, said, "The baptism of Christ in the river of Jordan, and the illustrations of baptism used in the New Testament, are all in favor of immersion rather than sprinkling, as is freely admitted by the best exegetes, Catholic and Protestant, English and German. *Nothing can be gained by unnatural exegesis. The aggressiveness of the Baptists has driven Pedobaptists to the opposite extreme.*"[57]

HISTORICAL EVIDENCE

Space does not permit an extensive evaluation of what the church fathers, pedobaptists, and Baptists have said about the mode of baptism, nor is such necessary since their views have been well documented.[58] The older Baptist works defending baptism by immersion are laced with references to pedobaptists who have acknowledged that immersion was the mode practiced in the apostolic church. We will attempt a mere summary of the later evidence.

Perhaps the earliest work from the patristic era to address baptism is the *Didache* (early to mid-second century). It instructs that baptism should be in "living water," but if this is not possible, "baptize in other water." If neither is available, "pour water upon the head thrice."[59] It is evident from this statement that baptism by immersion was the standard practice. In the *Epistle of Barnabas*, we read, "We go down into the water full of sins and pollutions, and come up again bringing forth fruit."[60] Likewise, the Shepherd of Hermas speaks of the "water of Baptism in which men go down bound to death, but come up appointed to life."[61] These latter two statements clearly indicate baptism by immersion. In the Middle Ages,

---

57. Philip Schaff, *Teaching of the Twelve Apostles* (Edinburgh: T & T Clark, 1887), 55–56. See also J. Taylor, *The Immerser*, 49–58, 318–22.

58. See, for example, Robert Sanders, *The Ante-Nicene Fathers on Baptism* (Louisville: Baptist Book Concern, 1891), who demonstrated clearly that the ante-Nicene fathers rejected infant baptism and practiced baptism by immersion. See also Robert Robinson, *The History of Baptism* (Boston: Lincoln and Edmands, 1817); James Chrystal, *A History of the Modes of Christian Baptism* (Philadelphia: Lindsay and Blakistan, 1861); Isaac Hinton, *History of Baptism from the Inspired and Uninspired Writings*, rev. John Hinton (London: J. Heaton and Son, 1864), 131–35; R. Ingham, *Christian Baptism: Its Subjects* (London: E. Stock, 1871), 393–510, who provides one of the most comprehensive surveys of the historical testimony; idem, *A Handbook on Christian Baptism* (London: Simpkin, Marshall, and Co., 1865); Henry Burrage, *The Act of Baptism in the History of the Christian Church* (Philadelphia: American Baptist Publication Society, 1879), a work that covers the history from the New Testament until 1879; Edward Hiscox, *Principles and Practices for Baptist Churches* (Grand Rapids: Kregel, 1980), 386–444; Alec Gilmore, *Christian Baptism*, 187–220; and William Lumpkin, *A History of Immersion* (Nashville: Broadman Press, 1962).

59. Didache, chapter 7, available at http://www.ccel.org/ccel/richardson/fathers.viii.i.iii.html, or Philip Schaff, *History of the Christian Church*, vol. 2, 5th ed. (Peabody: Hendrickson, 2006), 247.

60. *Epistle of Barnabas* (100.11); or see Alexander Roberts and James Donaldson, eds., "The Epistle of Barnabas," in *The Ante-Nicene Fathers: The Writings of the Fathers Down to A.D. 325* (Edinburgh: T & T Clark, 2001), 1:144.

61. Shepherd of Hermas (Similtude 9.100.16); or see Alexander Roberts and James Donaldson, eds., "The Pastor of Hermas," in *The Ante-Nicene Fathers*, 2:49.

Thomas Aquinas stated, "The symbol of Christ's burial is more expressively represented by immersion, and for that reason this mode of baptizing is more common
and more commendable."[62] Aquinas argued, however, that the mode was theologically indifferent.

In the Reformation era, Martin Luther spoke of baptism in his *The Babylonian
Captivity of the Church*. After noting baptism is a symbol of death and resurrection,
Luther said,

> For this reason I would have those who are to be baptized com-
> pletely immersed in the water, as the word says and as the mystery
> indicates. Not because I deem this necessary, but because it would
> be well to give to a thing so perfect and complete a sign that is
> also complete and perfect. And this is doubtless the way in which
> it was instituted by Christ. The sinner does not so much need to
> be washed as he needs to die, in order to be wholly renewed and
> made another creature, and to be conformed to the death and res-
> urrection of Christ, with whom he dies and rises again through
> baptism.[63]

In Luther's *Order of Baptism*, we read, "Then he shall take the child and dip
him in the font."[64] In *The Holy and Blessed Sacrament of Baptism*, penned in 1519,
Luther noted both the Greek and Latin words for "baptism" indicate immersion.
Although he noted that it was no longer "customary" to immerse in "many places,"
Luther contended that immersion "is what should be done" because the "old man"
must be "wholly drowned by the grace of God." "We should therefore do justice to
its meaning and make baptism a true and complete sign of the thing it signifies."[65]
Charles Krauth analyzed Luther's views on baptism as immersion, pouring, and
sprinkling. He confirmed Luther's preference for immersion but correctly noted
that Luther expresses no doubt as to the validity of baptism by other modes.[66]

John Calvin spoke of the mode of baptism in his *Institutes*: "Yet the word 'baptize' means to immerse, and it is clear that the rite of immersion was observed
in the ancient church."[67] John Wesley likewise confirmed the apostolic church

62. Thomas Aquinas, *Summa* 3.66.7; or see *The Summa Theologica of St. Thomas Aquinas* (London:
     Burns, Oates & Washburne, 1923), 17:109–10.
63. Martin Luther, *Three Treatises* (Philadelphia: Fortress, 1960), 191.
64. Martin Luther, *Luther's Works: Liturgies and Hymns*, ed. Ulrich S. Leupold (Philadelphia: For-
     tress, 1965), 53:100.
65. Martin Luther, *Luther's Works: Word and Sacrament 1*, ed. E. Theodore Bachman (Philadelphia:
     Fortress, 1960), 35:29.
66. Charles P. Krauth, *The Conservative Reformation and Its Theology* (Minneapolis: Augsburg, 1963),
     519–40.
67. John Calvin, *Institutes of the Christian Religion*, in Library of Christian Classics, chapter xv, vol.

baptized by immersion: "Mary Welsh, aged eleven days, was baptized, according to the custom of the first church and the rule of the Church of England, *by immersion*."[68] Moses Stuart, a Congregationalist who taught at Andover Seminary, wrote a significant work on the mode of baptism. He stated, "*Bapto* and *baptize* mean to dip, plunge, or immerse, into anything liquid. All lexicographers and critics of any note are agreed in this."[69]

The remarkable book by W. A. Jarrell, *Baptizo-Dip-Only: The World's Pedobaptist Greek Scholarship*, contains a sizeable collection of quotations from hundreds of pedobaptist scholars around the world, *all of whom affirm that baptizō means "to dip, to immerse,"* and most of whom affirm that it means nothing else in the Greek New Testament.[70]

Finally, we may note that Karl Barth, in his *The Teaching of the Church Regarding Baptism*, affirmed immersion as the apostolic practice, criticized infant baptism severely, and urged further theological reflection on baptism.[71] Most recently, Methodist I. Howard Marshall, in an article attempting to defend paedobaptism, acknowledged, "The most that can (and must) be said is that both modes of baptism, immersion (certainly) and affusion (at least from the third century) were practiced, depending on local circumstances."[72] This statement is remarkable in that it asserts two "certainties": immersion was practiced in the apostolic church and affusion was practiced, along with immersion, from the third century onward. This is a statement with which virtually every Baptist could agree.

Since even pedobaptists are agreed that the apostolic practice was immersion, how and why did a change take place in the early church? Affusion was first permitted as early as the second century A.D., but even then only under extraordinary circumstances when immersion could not be used. During the third and fourth centuries, the false doctrine of baptism of infants to remove the stain of original sin brought about a change in the significance of baptism, giving rise to the practice of infant baptism. This change in doctrine resulted in a modification of the practice of baptism to forms such as affusion or aspersion. As orthodoxy gave way to heterodoxy, orthopraxy likewise gave way to heteropraxy. In spite of this,

2, book iv, trans. F. L. Battles, ed. John T. McNeill (Louisville: Westminster John Knox Press, 1960), 1320.

68. John Wesley, *The Journal of John Wesley*, ed. Nehemiah Curnock (London: Epworth, 1938), 1:166 (emphasis added).

69. Moses Stuart, *Is the Mode of Christian Baptism Prescribed in the New Testament?* (Nashville: Graves, Mark & Rutland, 1856), 41.

70. W. A. Jarrell, *Baptizo-Dip-Only: The World's Pedobaptist Greek Scholarship*, 2nd ed., reissued by V. C. Mayes (1910; reprint, Splendora, TX: Splendora Sales, 1978).

71. Barth, *Teaching of the Church Regarding Baptism*.

72. Marshall, "Meaning of the Verb 'Baptize,'" 20.

immersion continued to be the official mode of baptism in both the Western Latin church and in the Greek Orthodox church.

Immersion is the only mode of baptism practiced since earliest times. During the thirteenth century, Aquinas noted that immersion was even more common than sprinkling.[73] It was not until A.D. 1311, in Ravenna, that the first law was passed to recognize sprinkling as an authoritative baptism.[74] This is supported by historian Philip Schaff, who wrote, "River baptism gradually ceased when baptisteries began to be built in the age of Constantine in or near the churches with all of the conveniences for the performance of the rite. They [immersion baptisteries] are very numerous, especially in Italy. They went out of use when immersion ceased in the West. The last is said to have been built in Pistoria, in Italy, A.D. 1337."[75]

What of the Reformation era? William Wall's celebrated explanation of the rise of affusion and aspersion in his widely heralded *History of Infant Baptism* tells the story.

> Now, *Calvin* had not only given his Dictate, in his Institutions, that *the difference is of no moment, whether thrice or once; or whether he be only wetted with the water poured on him*: But he had also drawn up for the use of his church at *Geneva* (and afterward published to the world) *a form of administering the sacraments*, where, when he comes to the order of baptizing, he words it thus: *Then the minister of baptism pours water on the infant; saying, I baptize thee*, etc. There had been, as I said, some Synods in the Dioceses of France that had spoken of affusion without mentioning immersion at all; that being the common practice; but for an Office or Liturgy of any church; this is, I believe the first in the world that prescribes affusion absolutely.[76]

Hughes Old chronicles the transition from immersion to sprinkling in the sixteenth century. The Reformers were agreed that immersion, pouring, and sprinkling were all acceptable modes of baptism. They regarded the mode of baptism as *adiaphorous* (theologically indifferent).[77] The Constance Latin Ritual of Baptism (1510) clearly reveals the following about baptism at that time: (1) the church

---

73. Aquinas, *Summa* 3.66.7.
74. William Wall, *The History of Infant Baptism* (Oxford: Oxford University Press, 1862), 1:583.
75. Schaff, *Teaching of the Twelve Apostles*, 41.
76. Wall, *History of Infant Baptism*, 1:580–81.
77. Hughes O. Old, *The Shaping of the Reformed Baptismal Rite in the Sixteenth Century* (Grand Rapids: Eerdmans, 1992), 264ff. See also John Calvin, *Institutes* 4.15.19. Jules Corblet, *Historie dogmatique, liturgique et archeologique du sacrament de bapteme*, 2 vols. (Brussels, Paris, and Geneva, 1881–82), 1:235ff., gives a listing of documents chronicling this transition.

accepted both immersion and pouring; (2) four conditions are given that make it unsuitable for immersion—an elderly priest, a weak infant, a cold winter, and an elderly adult candidate; (3) appeal is made to Acts 2 and 3 as well as the historical records of Saint Lawrence (third century) and Remigius (sixth century), who baptized by pouring.[78]

First, we may note that by implication immersion is the preferred mode of baptism, since conditions are given for diverging from immersion to pouring. The very fact that these conditions are given indicates sprinkling had, in the words of Olds, "only recently become the normal procedure."[79] Second, that the baptism of the 3,000 and the 5,000 in Acts 2 and 4 was by pouring is an unjustified inference and an argument from silence based on the assumption that so large a number could not be baptized in a single day.

The Reformers decided that "on the basis of Scripture they could not insist on immersion." Reformed-minded priests discovered that their change to immersion was "undermining their introduction of the use of German" for the baptismal liturgy. Since the use of a common language was crucial to the reform movement, immersion was discarded.[80] Theologically, the Reformers concluded that the central action in baptism was not the sign of the death and resurrection of Christ but rather the action of washing, and sprinkling best illustrates washing.[81]

Space permits only a short survey of the mode of baptism during the English Reformation of the sixteenth century. The first liturgy of King Edward VI required baptism by trine immersion. Edward VI and Elizabeth were both immersed. King James I, who came to the throne from Scotland early in the seventeenth century, had been taught sprinkling from the Scottish divines, who themselves had imported it from Geneva,[82] and he favored this mode over immersion. It was during the Protectorate, when Presbyterianism was in vogue, that the Westminster Assembly of Divines voted by a majority of one (25–24) that sprinkling and immersion were both valid modes of baptism and that sprinkling should be mentioned in the church directives without immersion. During the Restoration, when the Anglican church regained ascendancy, immersion continued to be the official church position, but in practice most churches practiced sprinkling.[83] But of course, by this

---

78. Old, *Shaping of the Reformed Baptismal Rite*, 266.
79. Ibid., 267.
80. Ibid., 277.
81. Ibid., 278–80.
82. Under the persecution of Mary, many fled England and Scotland to Geneva. Having renounced the authority of the pope, they straightway fell under the spell of Calvin. One such reformer was John Knox, who upon his return to Scotland, brought Calvin's mode of baptism with him. Scotland's James VI became England's King James I, and with him he brought sprinkling as his favored mode of baptism.
83. See Hinton, *History of Baptism*, 156–61.

time, a growing group of dissenters called "Baptists" were pressing their claims for believer's baptism by immersion as the only valid biblical position.

ARCHAEOLOGICAL EVIDENCE

While in England this past summer, I came across a book titled *Baptismal Fonts Classified and Illustrated*. This work by pedobaptist E. Tyrrell-Green is one of the most significant archaeological studies of baptismal fonts. I was struck by his candor regarding the mode of baptism in the introduction: "In the earliest times it was natural that the ceremony of Baptism should be performed in running water by immersion, after the example of Christ's own baptism in the Jordan. . . . References to the spiritual significance of Baptism also imply this method of administration, for the full force of St. Paul's words, 'We are buried with Him by Baptism into death,' could only be realized if the candidate were wholly immersed in the water." He further stated that a study of the early church fathers confirmed that the mode of baptism was "complete submersion."[84]

An interesting appendix, "Modern Fonts Constructed for Immersion," catalogs ten fonts in England designed for the "total immersion of adults" and twenty such fonts in Wales and Monmouthshire. The explanation for so many such immersionist fonts in South Wales "lies in the fact that the Baptists are very strong there, and in face of Baptist opposition it is thought desirable to emphasise the Church's normal rule for Baptism by 'dipping,' as expressed in the rubrics of the Prayer Book."[85] By "Church" Tyrrell-Green means the Anglican Church.

One of the most significant books published on the archeology of baptism is W. N. Cote's *Baptism and Baptisteries*. Cote was a nineteenth-century missionary to Rome and spent considerable time researching the writings of the church fathers and the art and archaeology of baptism in the Biblioteca Casanatense, a library adjacent to the Dominican convent containing over 120,000 volumes and ancient manuscripts. The book is divided into two sections, the first treating baptism from the writings of the Fathers, the second covering the archaeology of baptisteries in Italy. Cote demonstrated clearly that immersion was the mode of baptism during the first three centuries of Christian history and that the baptisteries of Italy were immersionist baptisteries. Cote dedicated his book to The Southern Baptist Convention.[86] Philip Schaff confirmed this finding, writing, "The baptisteries of the Nicene age, of which many remain in Asia, Africa, and Southern Europe, were

---

84. E. Tyrrell-Green, *Baptismal Fonts Classified and Illustrated* (London: Society for Promoting Christian Knowledge, 1928), 1–2.

85. Ibid., 167.

86. W. N. Cote, *Baptism and Baptisteries* (Philadelphia: The Bible and Publication Society, 1864). A complete list of sixty-six Italian baptisteries is given on pages 110–12.

built for immersion, and all Oriental churches still adhere to this mode."[87] The remains of several early churches in North Africa have been discovered and studied, and most have immersionist baptisteries, usually located at the entrance to the church building.[88]

John Christian's *The Form of Baptism in Sculpture and Art* decisively proves that the evidence from both sculpture and art in early Christian Italy and beyond confirms immersion as the mode of baptism. Published in 1907, this was the first book in English to study the sculpture and art of baptism.[89] In the last quarter of the twentieth century, over 300 *miqva²ot*, or immersion pools, have been discovered in Israel and date from the first century B.C. to A.D. 70. "Of these about 150 have been found in Jerusalem—about 60 in the Upper City (Avigad's excavations), about 40 from the excavations near the southern gates of the Temple Mount and the rest in various locations."[90] Jewish ritual baths involving the *miqva²ot* were used for purification of the entire body by immersion since, according to the *Mishna*, no part of the body's surface could be untouched by water.[91] Grasham stated, "All of the pre-A.D. 70 synagogues that have been discovered—at the Herodium, Masada, and Gamla—had immersion pools in close proximity for the purificatory washings of those who attended their services."[92] This discovery puts to bed once and for all the old argument put forth by pedobaptists that there was not enough water in Jerusalem to baptize 3000 and 5000 people in a single day.

Walter Bedard argued that the church fathers derived from Romans 6:3–5 the concept of baptism as "tomb" and from John 3:3–5 the concept of baptism as the "womb" of the church. He demonstrated this from the archaeological remains of

---

87. Philip Schaff, *History of the Christian Church*, 5th ed. (Peabody, MA: Hendrickson, 2006), 2:248.

88. Lloyd A. Harsch, "The Architecture of Baptisteries in North Africa," (paper presented to the Evangelical Theological Society Valley Forge, PA, November 17, 2005); *contra* Marshall, "Meaning of the Verb 'Baptize,'" 18: "Discoveries of early baptisteries shows [sic] that they were incapable of being used for immersion." Wharton Marriott's article on "Baptism" in William Smith and Samuel Cheetham, *A Dictionary of Christian Antiquities* (London: John Murray, 1875), 1:161, 168, 177, concurred with Harsch: "Triple immersion . . . was the all but universal rule of the Church in early times. Of this we find proof in Africa . . . , in Palestine . . . , in Egypt . . . , at Antioch and Constantinople . . . , in Cappadocia."

89. John Christian, *The Form of Baptism in Sculpture and Art* (Louisville: Baptist Book Concern, 1907). See especially his final conclusions on pages 225–35.

90. Ronny Reich, "The Great Mikveh Debate," *Biblical Archaeology Review* (March–April 1993): 52–53. See also Jerome Murphy-O'Connor, *The Holy Land: An Archaeological Guide from Earliest Times to 1700* (Oxford: Oxford University Press, 1992), 108.

91. H. Danby, *The Mishna*, pp. 732, 742. *Yoma* 3:3 states, "None may enter the temple court [an act of the temple] Service, even though he is clean, until he has immersed himself" (fn. on 164).

92. Bill Grasham, "Archaeology and Christian Baptism," *Restoration Quarterly* 43, no. 2 (2001): 115. See also William LaSor, "Discovering What Jewish *Miqva²ot* Can Tell Us About Christian Baptism," *Biblical Archaeology Review* 13, no. 1 (January–February 1987): 57. LaSor believed that the Jewish *miqva²ot* provided the background for Christian baptism.

baptisteries and baptistery inscriptions.[93] The significance of this study is three-fold. First, Bedard is a Catholic, yet he affirms immersion as the earliest form of baptism. Second, he demonstrates that the archaeological evidence confirms immersion as a mode of baptism used by the Catholic Church throughout the Middle Ages. Third, he grounds the church fathers' theology of baptism as a symbol of dying and rising with Christ in Romans 6.

It is clear that the archaeological evidence indicates baptism was performed by immersion at the very earliest time of Christian history, and evidence of this mode has been discovered in churches, sculpture, and art from the earliest days to the end of the Middle Ages.

THEOLOGICAL EVIDENCE

The two bedrock passages concerning the theology of baptism are Romans 6:3–5 and Colossians 2:12. In Romans 6:4 baptism not only symbolizes identification with Christ in his death, burial, and resurrection; it also declares our burial with him. It is precisely here that the true significance of the mode of baptism comes into play. Baptism is more than a bath; it is a burial, and only immersion can symbolize burial. John Gill rightly said, "A corpse cannot be said to be buried when only a little earth or dust is sprinkled or poured on it."[94] The focus of the New Testament authors is on baptism as immersion, and only rarely on baptism as an ablution. The reason for this, according to Ysebaert, is articulated by Paul in Romans 6:3–4 and Colossians 2:12, where the use of the Greek preposition *eis* in the final sense shows that Paul views immersion as being performed "with a view to Christ's death, and for the purpose of the Christian's participation in it." The Christian's descending into the tomb (buried with Christ) requires a corresponding act of ascending (rising with Christ).[95]

If baptism has to do with death, burial, and resurrection, does it not logically follow that immersion of a believer is an essential component of the rite of baptism? In fact, without immersion and without a believer, is there really any baptism in the New Testament sense of the term? Even if it is argued that Romans 6:3–4 has not a drop of water in it and is symbolic of spiritual baptism, we realize that the outward sign must correspond to the inner experience. Baptism commemorates the burial and resurrection of Christ, hence immersion. If it commemorates the believer's death to sin and resurrection to new life, again immersion is the

---

93. Walter Bedard, "The Symbolism of the Baptismal Font in Early Christian Thought," in *The Catholic University of America Studies in Sacred Theology*, 2nd series (Washington, DC: Catholic University of America Press, 1951), 45.

94. John Gill, *A Complete Body of Doctrinal and Practical Divinity* (1839; reprint, Paris, AR: Baptist Standard Bearer, 1984), 911.

95. Ysebaert, *Greek Baptismal Terminology*, 50.

only mode that pictures this. If it symbolizes the washing away of sin, the symbol requires immersion since the thoroughness with which we are interpenetrated by sin calls for a washing that is potent enough to affect the whole body.

J. M. Pendleton was right on target: if baptism has to do with death, burial, and resurrection, "it follows inevitably that the immersion in water of a believer in Christ is essential to baptism—so essential that without it there is no baptism."[96] For Pendleton, sprinkling and pouring are as unlike a resurrection as they are a burial; immersion alone captures the symbol. Baptism is the instrument (note *dia*) of burial. It is by means of baptism that burial is effected. Paul does not say, "We have been crucified with him by baptism," but "We have been buried with him by baptism." It is not the manner of dying in view but the finality of it.[97]

Baptism symbolizes cleansing, but it is far more than a cleansing. To substitute sprinkling or pouring for immersion focuses on the cleansing only; it lacks the symbolism of the method of cleansing that is the cross of Christ. The tragedy of sprinkling or pouring leads, in the words of A. J. Gordon, to a "bloodless moralism where the act of baptism is viewed as a kind of Christian circumcision, marking the sanctifying of human nature, and bringing it into covenant with God. How easily the idea of mystical efficacy becomes attached to the element of water, unless the form of its use be such as to carry the thought immediately and certainly to Christ crucified and dead."[98] As Romans 6:3–5 makes clear, baptism is a symbol that we are raised with Christ spiritually (justification) and that we will rise bodily at the last day (glorification). We are clothed with righteousness now; we will be clothed with immortality then.

CONCLUSION

Our Anabaptist and Baptist forefathers were mistreated, imprisoned, tortured, and murdered by Catholic and Protestant alike over their commitment to a New Testament ecclesiology centered on believer's baptism by immersion. I wonder if we modern-day Southern Baptists will follow our forefathers to so radical a conclusion. It does not seem likely that we will have the stomach for it. Indeed, today some Baptist pastors, contrary to the New Testament, are willing to lead their churches to relax the necessity of baptism by immersion for membership in the local church. Such a move is based on misguided reasons, such as appeasing pedobaptist friends, fostering church growth by making it easier for some people to join Baptist churches, or allowing Reformed soteriology to blur Baptist ecclesiology.

96. Pendleton, *Distinctive Principles of Baptists*, 119.
97. Ibid., 120–21.
98. A. J. Gordon, *In Christ* (New York: Revell, 1880), 74.

The indications that many Southern Baptists have lost touch with what it means to be Baptists is evident. Under no circumstances and for no reasons should Southern Baptists abandon their convictions about what the Scriptures teach on the subject of baptism. The "Prince of Preachers," Charles Haddon Spurgeon knew this all too well.

> If I thought it wrong to be a Baptist, I should give it up and become what I believed to be right . . . if we could find infant baptism in the word of God, we should adopt it. It would help us out of a great difficulty, for it would take away from us that reproach which is attached to us—that we are odd and do not as other people do. But we have looked well through the Bible and cannot find it, and do not believe it is there; nor do we believe that others can find infant baptism in the Scriptures, unless they themselves first put it there.[99]

The distinctive principle of Baptists is that *"the immersion in water of a believer in Christ is essential to baptism—so essential that without it there is no baptism."*[100]

99. Charles Haddon Spurgeon, *C. H. Spurgeon's Autobiography* (London: Passmore & Alabaster, 1897), 1:155.
100. Pendleton, *Distinctive Principles of Baptists*, 158 (emphasis in original).

5

What Makes Baptism Valid?

Thomas White

ractically every church in the world requires their members to be baptized. Thus, a large portion of the world's population believes they have experienced proper baptism; however, Baptist churches do not accept all of these baptisms. In fact, much confusion exists over what constitutes valid baptism. Some believe in the validity of infant baptism, while others accept only believer's baptism. Some practice baptism by sprinkling or pouring, while others only immerse. Some divide over the doctrine of baptism, while others consider it a minor doctrine of little importance.

Perhaps some categories may help us embark upon an investigation of this issue. A Christian baptism could be validated by the historical tradition of the "Christian church." If valid baptism is based on the foundation of Christian tradition, then Catholic, Presbyterian, Methodist, and other Protestant groups that make up the "Christian tradition" possess valid baptism. The Baptists are part of the Christian tradition yet do not accept as valid the baptism of these other groups. Baptists generally look to Scripture alone to determine what baptism is. Based on their understanding of Scripture, Baptists have denied the validity of infant and nonimmersion baptisms. This essay will focus primarily on what Scripture has to say about baptism but secondarily will discuss the view of the Baptist tradition regarding baptism as the author deems it relevant.

In order to discuss completely the ordinance of baptism, this chapter will address six overlapping categories. Some of these categories have been emphasized by Baptists more than others, and some have been at the center of controversies. Nevertheless, one must examine and determine the importance of these six aspects in order to understand baptism. I will list these categories with a brief sentence explaining how they relate to the issue. The remainder of the chapter will explain in more detail the importance of each category, attempting to focus attention on the more problematic elements and providing historical illumination where beneficial. As always, the Bible is the final source of authority.

SIX CATEGORIES OF BAPTISM

1. *Subject.* The subject of baptism must be a believer. Any other subject cannot make a profession of faith or identify with Christ or his church.
2. *Mode.* Immersion is the proper mode of baptism. No other mode is supported by Scripture.
3. *Meaning.* Baptism is not essential for salvation and does not grant an elevated status of sinlessness. Baptism is the profession of the believer placing his or her allegiance with Christ and the initiatory ordinance into the local church. Baptism symbolizes the death, burial, and resurrection of Jesus Christ.
4. *Place.* Proper baptism must be performed in connection with a true church. Baptism is a church ordinance, not a Christian ordinance. Since this view is so little understood, discussion of the definition of a true church also must occur.
5. *Administrator.* The administrator should be someone selected by the local church. Overemphasis on this can lead to problems, as it did with the Donatists.
6. *Formula.* The traditional formula is baptism in the name of the Father, the Son, and the Holy Spirit (or Holy Ghost in older times). Valid baptism must at the very least be in Jesus' name.

THE SUBJECT OF BAPTISM

Historically Baptists have understood baptism in its most basic definition to have a believer as the subject and immersion as the mode. Many New Testament examples could be discussed to lay the foundation for believers as the proper subjects of baptism; however, only a few will be mentioned here. For a more complete discussion, this author has written another article dedicated to this topic that should be consulted.[1] First, the Great Commission of Christ states that we are to "make disciples of all nations, baptizing them. . . ." (NIV). People must first be made disciples, or become believers, before baptism. Peter states in Acts 2:38, "Repent and be baptized" (NIV). Repentance leads one to become a believer before baptism. Philip preached the gospel to the Ethiopian eunuch, and the eunuch then requested baptism. While many pedobaptists appeal to the household baptisms in Acts as

1. Thomas White, "The Proper Subject of Baptism," White Paper (The Center for Theological Research, Southwestern Baptist Theological Seminary, Ft. Worth, TX, March 2006) at http://www.baptistheology.org/documents/ProperSubjectofBaptism_001.pdf.

precedent for infant baptism, careful study demonstrates no foundation anywhere in the Scriptures for infant baptism. The Scriptures know of only believers as the subjects of baptism. Infant baptism did not begin until a few hundred years after Christ, based upon a misconception of original sin. The Council of Carthage in A.D. 258 discussed how infants should be baptized, thus demonstrating the newness of infant baptism and an improper theological view of the practice.[2]

THE MODE OF BAPTISM

Baptists have universally held that immersion is the only proper mode of baptism, and without immersion there is no true baptism. The New Testament consistently uses the word *baptizō* to describe the act of baptism. This Greek word has been brought directly into the English language as the word "baptize." Properly translated, instead of transliterated, this word means "immerse." One may consult any number of Greek lexicons and even pedobaptist scholars to support this definition.[3] Perhaps the writing of John Calvin himself should be read. In the *Institutes of the Christian Religion*, Calvin wrote, "But whether the person being baptized should be wholly immersed, and whether thrice or once, whether he should only be sprinkled with poured water—these details are of no importance, but ought to be optional to churches according to the diversity of countries. Yet the word 'baptize' means to immerse, and it is clear that the rite of immersion was observed in the ancient church."[4] For additional evidence from history, one need only visit the

2. This view resulted from a belief in "original guilt" or "infant guilt" by which infants had to be baptized in order to remove their original guilt in order for them to go to heaven should they die in infancy. Richard P. McBrien, *Catholicism* (San Francisco: HarperCollins, 1989), 188, said, "Cyprian of Carthage was the first to argue that infants are baptized because of the 'contagion of death' inherited from Adam." Cyprian also addressed this at the council of Carthage in A.D. 253. See "The Epistles of Cyprian," in *Ante-Nicene Fathers*, ed. Alexander Roberts and James Donaldson (Peabody, MA: Hendrickson, 1999), 5:353–55. This belief also can be traced to Augustine. Neville Clark, "Theology of Baptism," in *Christian Baptism*, ed. Alec Gilmore (Chicago: Judson Press, 1959), 320, states, "Upon the basis provided by Tertullian and Cyprian in their doctrine of original sin, Ambrose and Augustine superimposed a theology of original guilt. From such guilt infant baptism guaranteed deliverance." Augustine's thoughts on the relationship between infant baptism and original sin can be seen in Augustine, "On Original Sin," in *Nicene and Post-Nicene Fathers*, ed. Philip Schaff (Peabody, MA: Hendrickson, 1999), 5:237–57.
3. For a more detailed treatment of this subject, consult David Allen's essay on the proper mode of baptism in chapter 4 of this book. One also may consult John Wesley, who said, "Mary Welsh, aged eleven days, was baptized, according to the custom of the first church and the rule of the Church of England, by immersion." *The Journal of John Wesley*, ed. Nehemiah Curnock (London: Epworth Press, 1938), 1:166. See also Moses Stuart, *Is the Mode of Christian Baptism Prescribed in the New Testament?* (Nashville: Graves, Mark & Rutland, 1856), 41; and Thomas Chalmers, *Lectures on the Epistles of Paul the Apostle to the Romans* (New York: Carter, 1845), 152.
4. John Calvin, *Institutes of the Christian Religion*, in Library of Christian Classics, chapter xv, vol. 2, book iv, trans. F. L. Battles, ed. John T. McNeill (Louisville: Westminster John Knox Press, 1960), 1320.

ruins of ancient churches, noticing the variety of immersion baptisteries in those churches.[5]

The question may arise, How did sprinkling become a common practice? William Wall, a pedobaptist, explains in his *History of Infant Baptism.*

> Now, *Calvin* had not only given his Dictate, in his Institutions, that *the difference is of no moment, whether thrice or once; or whether he be only wetted with the water poured on him*: But he had also drawn up for the use of his church at *Geneva* (and afterward published to the world) *a form of administering the sacraments*, where, when he comes to the order of baptizing, he words it thus: *Then the minister of baptism pours water on the infant; saying, I baptize thee,* etc. There had been, as I said, some Synods in the Dioceses of France that had spoken of affusion without mentioning immersion at all; that being the common practice; but for an Office or Liturgy of any church; this is, I believe the first in the world that prescribes affusion absolutely.[6]

It quickly becomes obvious that church history and not Scripture forms the basis for any mode other than immersion.

Finally, the symbolic representation of the ordinance—the death, burial, and resurrection of Christ—can be fulfilled only by immersion. Immersion is so central to baptism that without it the ordinance is nullified.

THE MEANING OF BAPTISM

The vast majority of Baptists have always believed that baptism is a symbolic ordinance that identifies the believer with the death, burial, and resurrection of Jesus Christ. Baptists also have identified the ordinance of baptism as the following: (1) the believer's public profession of faith, (2) the believer's identification with Christ, and (3) the initiatory ordinance into the local church. All of these meanings of baptism have scriptural foundation. The identification of baptism as symbolic of the death, burial, and resurrection of Christ and the Christian comes from Romans 6:3–4, "Or do you not know that all of us who have been baptized into Christ Jesus have been baptized into His death? Therefore we have been buried with Him through baptism into death, so that as Christ was raised from the dead through the glory of the Father, so we too might walk in newness of life" (NASB).

---

5. Lloyd A. Harsch, "The Architecture of Baptisteries in North Africa," (paper presented to the Evangelical Theological Society, Valley Forge, PA, November 17, 2005).
6. William Wall, *The History of Infant Baptism* (Oxford: Oxford University Press, 1862), 1:580–81.

Baptism as the believer's public profession of faith comes from Acts 2:38, where Peter states, "Repent, and each of you be baptized in the name of Jesus Christ for the forgiveness of your sins" (NASB). This close association with salvation also indicates the importance of baptism. When presenting the gospel to the Ethiopian eunuch, Philip did so in such a way that the eunuch responded not with a prayer or by signing a card but by asking to be baptized.

Baptism also served as the initiatory ordinance into the local church. Matthew 28:19–20 states, "Go therefore and make disciples of all the nations, baptizing them in the name of the Father and the Son and the Holy Spirit, teaching them to observe all that I commanded you" (NASB). The commission is to make disciples. The acceptance of Christ is an inward decision of faith and repentance. This decision is made public by baptizing the believer in the name of the Father and the Son and the Holy Spirit. However, in order to teach them all things, they must then associate or gather for further instruction. The place for this teaching is the New Testament church. In Acts, baptisms resulted in the recipients gathering daily for additional instruction. The *ecclesia*, or local church, of the New Testament is the fulfillment of the commission of Christ. The New Testament knows nothing of baptized believers not associated with a local church.

Perhaps we also should identify what baptism is not. Along with other denominations, the Churches of Christ, formed initially by Alexander Campbell in the nineteenth century, believed that baptism is essential for salvation.[7] While many such groups no longer believe what their founders taught, Oneness Pentecostals continue to teach the doctrine of baptismal regeneration. Although many passages could be used, this author has chosen two passages to refute such claims. First, the thief on the cross did not experience baptism, and yet that very day he was in the presence of the Lord. Luke 23:42–43 states, "And he was saying, 'Jesus, remember me when You come in Your kingdom!' And He said to him, 'Truly I say to you, today you shall be with Me in Paradise'" (NASB). Second, in 1 Corinthians 1:17 Paul states, "For Christ did not send me to baptize, but to preach the gospel" (NASB). If baptism were required for salvation, Paul never would have made this claim. Thus, baptism is not essential for salvation.

---

7. Alexander Campbell believed that "three things are essential to the Christian profession—that a person must believe, and repent, and be baptized." See Alexander Campbell, *Christian Baptism with Its Antecedents and Consequents* (Bethany: published by author, 1851; reprint, Nashville: Gospel Advocate, 1951), 84. For more information on this topic, see Austin Bennett Amonette, "Alexander Campbell Among the Baptists: An Examination of the Beginning, Ambiguity, and Deterioration of Their Relationship, 1812–1830" (Ph.D. diss., New Orleans Baptist Theological Seminary, 2002). For a good history of the Campbellite movement from their perspective, see W. E. Garrison and A. T. DeGroot, *The Disciples of Christ* (St. Louis: Christian Board of Publications, 1948).

The more dangerous option for Baptists today is minimizing the ordinance to the point of irrelevance. By tacking baptism onto the end of services focused on other subjects, by neglecting to allow the recipient an opportunity to make a profession of faith, and by not investigating a new member's baptism before extending the right hand of fellowship, some Baptist churches have practically, if not intellectually, minimized the importance of this ordinance. Many pieces of evidence could be cited to note the importance of the ordinance; however, the Great Commission of Christ should suffice. Christ included many things in the commission when he told his disciples to teach new disciples to observe everything he commanded, but he specifically pointed out making disciples and baptizing. The mention of this ordinance by name and immediately following the command to make disciples should adequately place emphasis on the ordinance.

Without the proper meaning, baptism is nothing more than the dunking of the individual in water. The proper meaning is essential to proper baptism. Does the recipient have to understand everything in theology? No. However, the subject must understand that baptism is not salvific, grants no additional grace, and does not ensure sinlessness. The subject also should understand that baptism is the public profession of faith, identification with Christ, and the door to the local church. Because the subject must understand these things, the subject cannot be an infant.

THE PLACE FOR BAPTISM: THE LOCAL CHURCH

An essential part of this discussion is the definition of a true church. Thus, later in this section, that subject will be discussed. However, for now it is enough to note that the ordinances (for this discussion, baptism) separate parachurch groups, seminary classrooms, and private Bible studies from being churches. The ordinances logically are administered by the local church and more specifically by true churches. Most Christian churches reject Mormon, Hindu, Scientology, or Muslim baptisms, should they perform them, because they are not true churches and the meaning of the ordinances is irrevocably harmed. Their baptism is not into Christ but into a false religion. Valid Christian baptism is into Christ alone. For proof of this one need only look at Acts 19:1–5, where Paul required rebaptism of a group of followers who had been baptized with John's baptism but not baptized as a profession of faith in Christ. If this baptism would not do, then nothing other than baptism of a believer as a profession of faith in Christ will do.

How does one receive baptism into Christ? Can a six-year-old boy in his backyard lead a friend to Christ and baptize him? Will the local church accept that baptism as valid? Typically this strikes us as unwise. Why? Because the ordinance should be practiced by the church and not by an individual, a seminary, or a denomination. The gathered believers should see the person's baptism and accept him or her into fellowship. It is a church ordinance. Thus, baptism must be associated with a local church. Moreover, it is wisest to have the candidate actually make a profession before we baptize the person "upon his or her profession of faith." Such an important profession should occur in front of as many members of the church as possible and be taken as a serious responsibility of the local church. Proper baptism helps create the community desired by Christ for his churches.

One immediate question arises with regard to missionary baptisms.[8] The missionary is sent by the local church for the purpose of establishing more churches. Nothing could have a closer church connection than missionary baptisms. By having baptism linked to the authority given by Christ to the local church, one may safeguard baptism and regenerate church membership by ruling out all false churches. Accurate wording here clarifies all the various movements that alter the gospel message while also avoiding the problems of historical high-churchism. The problem arises when one's definition of a "true church" is incorrect. If, as the Landmark movement did, we add incorrect requirements to the "being" of a church, then local church authority can be distorted and result in many problems.[9] Thus, this discussion will now address the proper definition of a "true church."

THE DEFINITION OF A TRUE CHURCH

Being (*esse*)
- Gospel
- Ordinances
- Believers intentionally gathered

Well-being (*bene esse*)
- Offices (pastor and deacon)
- Church discipline
- Baptism by immersion of believers
- Memorial view of the Lord's Supper
- Regenerate congregation
- Missionary focus
- Text-driven preaching, etc.

---

8. The passage usually noted is Acts 8 and the baptism of the Ethiopian eunuch. However, Philip already had been commended as one of the earliest form of deacons in Acts 6 by the church at Jerusalem. In addition, this author believes he became the first evangelist/missionary when traveling to Samaria. In Acts 21:8 Philip is referred to as "the evangelist," indicating his transition to this status, which could have occurred as early as his trip to Samaria. Thus, Philip's baptism of the Ethiopian eunuch came by the authorization of the Jerusalem church with the purpose of the eunuch telling others and founding a church once he reached his destination.

9. The Landmark movement incorrectly added "rightly administering the ordinances" to the definition of the "being" of a church. This led to their denying all who baptized infants as true churches.

The above chart contains two classifications. These two classifications allow us to discuss the various marks of the true church without de-churching large majorities of the evangelical world. The first category contains what is essential for the "being" or existence of a true church. At the very minimum, a church consists of a few believers who have intentionally gathered or covenanted together for the purpose of being a church, with the gospel presented and the ordinances administered.

At a Minimum

Let us look at what happens should any one of these elements be removed. If you remove the gospel, you do not have anything Christian. It is not logical to conclude that such a gathering could constitute a Christian church. Indeed, the group could be any of a number of cults. Thus, the gospel must be present. If you remove the ordinances administered, then any Bible study group, seminary class, or parachurch ministry could be a church. As this is certainly not the case, the ordinances must exist for the "being" of a church. The purpose of the believers gathered together demonstrates the intent to be a church. A true church is intentional and does not occur by accident. Thus, a true church at a minimum has some believers who intentionally gather or covenant together for the purpose of being a church.

Adding to the Minimum

OK, so you want to move something from the "well-being" category to the "being" category? For argument's sake and for clarity, let us explore the options. If the offices (pastor and deacon) are moved into the "being" of a church, then when the pastor leaves one church for another or retires, that church ceases being a true church for a time. In addition, a church plant with no elected deacons would not be a true church until such time as it had men qualified and elected. However, these two offices are essential to the well-being of a church. While a church may continue without one or both offices temporarily, a continuance of this state will have negative consequences.

If church discipline is moved into the "being" of a church, then half the Southern Baptist Convention and most other denominations, which do not practice church discipline, have immediately been unchurched. Also, this could mean that one overlooked occurrence or improperly handled case results in the loss of being a true church. This was the contention of J. R. Graves against the First Baptist Church of Nashville and R. B. C. Howell in the middle of the 1800s.[10] Church discipline protects regenerate church membership, seeks restoration, and adds mean-

---

10. For additional information, see Kenneth Vaughn Weatherford, "The Graves-Howell Controversy" (Ph.D. diss., Baylor University, Waco, TX, 1991).

ing to membership, but it does not belong in the marks of a true church. It adds greatly, however, to the "well-being" of a church.

If the ordinances "rightly administered," as Calvin put it, are moved into the category of the "being" of a church, you have Landmarkism. In essence, you have just unchurched all pedobaptist gatherings. While baptism is properly executed by immersion of believers, and while the Lord's Supper is a symbolic, celebratory ordinance looking back at Christ's death, around in fellowship, and forward in anticipation, the proper practice of these ordinances cannot be added to the "being" of a church without repeating historical mistakes.

While Baptists and dissenting groups through history may desire to move the believers' church into a mark for the "being of the church," Augustine's arguments are well heeded. He argued against the Donatists that a truly regenerate church was not possible. While the Donatists and Baptists were and are right to seek after truly regenerate congregational membership, the requirement of such would result in constant evaluation of which churches are true and which are faulty. The effort and desire to have a regenerate church membership and the attainment of regenerate church membership adds greatly to the well-being of a church. Refusing to strive for a regenerate church is where Augustine erred. Giving up on seeking regenerate church membership harms the well-being of the church.[11] Church discipline should help maintain this mark of the "well-being" of a church once it has been achieved. If one were to move regenerate church membership to the "being" of a church, then most churches of any tradition would be unchurched.

The marks of well-being could go on indefinitely. While a missionary focus and text driven preaching add to the "well-being" of a church, neither should be required for the "being" of a church. Other marks such as the Bible as the only standard for faith and practice, a desire to fulfill the Great Commission, and a ministry to widows and orphans should be beneficial. Any number of focused ministries could be added to the "well-being" list, but the point is made. While many things add to the "well-being" of a church, the definition of the "being" of a true church should only include believers gathered together, presenting the gospel, and administering the ordinances.

---

11. Augustine and the Donatists debated the idea of a "pure church" versus a "mixed church." Robert Markus, "Donatism," in *Augustine Through the Ages*, ed. Allan Fitzgerald (Grand Rapids: Eerdmans, 1999), 286, wrote, "The issue between Augustine and the Donatists concerned, at bottom, the nature of the church and of the relation between it and the world. Central to Augustine's position was the insistence . . . that the church was a mixed body containing overt sinners." Augustine refers to the church as a mixed body in a discussion of the wheat and the tares. See Augustine, "On Baptism, Against the Donatists," in Schaff, *Nicene and Post-Nicene Fathers*, 4:452–53. Furthermore, Leonard Verduin, *The Reformers and Their Stepchildren* (Sarasota: Christian Hymnary, 2000), 40, linked the Donatists and the Anabaptists as possessing similar visions of a pure church. See also H. Leon McBeth, *The Baptist Heritage* (Nashville: Broadman Press, 1987), 75–76.

THE ADMINISTRATOR OF BAPTISM

Baptists typically have not focused upon the administrator of baptism as being essential. However, clarification of this area alleviates many problems. The Donatists sought to invalidate baptisms performed by ministers who had handed over the Scriptures during times of persecution. By holding that such traitorous ministers were not valid ministers, they placed too much authority for baptism in the administrator rather than in the ordinance and its meaning. Augustine argued against this movement, noting that if a minister were to have a moral failure late in his ministry, then that would invalidate all his previous baptisms. This places too much responsibility on the recipient to choose wisely the one who performs the baptism, and it attributes unscriptural power to the administrator.[12] The spirituality of the administrator does not give credence to baptism.

Although the administrator does not determine validity, wisdom should be used in who performs the ordinance. Since the ordinance must be connected to the local church, that church needs to appoint the administrator. While no biblical mandate exists for ordination of the administrator, the local church typically "sets apart" certain men for service to the church. Each church may appoint or set apart whomever it wishes to perform the ordinance within the bounds of Scripture. Typically, the pastor or a staff member will perform the ordinance. In their absence, a deacon also could administer the ordinance. This author sees practical problems with being too widely open with regard to who can perform the ordinance. The administrator should be an example to the congregation and not just any member in good standing, which could include a recently divorced single parent, a frequently absent father, or an eight-year-old boy. In the end, however, the validity of baptism is not derived from the administrator.

THE FORMULA FOR BAPTISM

A complete discussion of the formula throughout history would take more space than this chapter will allow. In brief, Scripture presents three possibilities concerning the formula for baptism. The most common formula can be found in Acts 2:38, where Peter states, "Repent, and each of you be baptized in the name of Jesus Christ" (NASB). In Acts 19:5, Paul mentions baptism in the name of the Lord Jesus. This is also mentioned in Acts 8:16 and 10:48. A second but related formula appears in Galatians 3:27: "As many of you as were baptized into Christ" (NKJV). The third and most popular formula can only be found in Matthew 28:19, "baptizing them in the name of the Father and the Son and the Holy Spirit" (NASB).

This author believes the different wording neither poses a problem nor represents mutually exclusive formulas. The reason for this belief comes from the

---

12. See Augustine, "The Three Books of Augustin, Bishop of Hippo, in Answer to the Letters of Petilian, the Donatist, Bishop of Cirta," in Schaff, *Nicene and Post-Nicene Fathers*, 4:515–628.

early evidence of the use of the triune formula found only once in Scripture. The *Didache* states, "Baptize in the name of the Father, and of the Son, and of the Holy Spirit."[13] Justin Martyr wrote, "For, in the name of God, the Father and Lord of the universe, and of our Savior Jesus Christ, and of the Holy Spirit, they then receive the washing with water."[14] Other early fathers could be quoted to demonstrate the use of the Trinitarian formula, but for the purposes of this essay, the previously mentioned quotes should suffice.

What is essential is that baptism occurs in the name of Jesus Christ, the second person of the Trinity. It is identification with Jesus, the incarnate Son of God, that is essential. Because some in this generation use the name Jesus but do not hold to the triune presentation of God found in the New Testament, the use of the triune formula given in Matthew 28:19 is the best choice. The formula clarifies what the baptismal candidate is doing. The candidate is identifying himself with and pledging allegiance to the Father, the Son, and the Holy Spirit.

There are some who insist upon baptism in "Jesus' name" for salvation.[15] This essay already has dealt with the fact that baptism is not salvific and has given reasons why. It is enough to dismiss any argument vying for baptism in Jesus' name alone to say that Scripture records Jesus himself as recommending the triune formula. The authority for baptism does not rest merely in the formula; otherwise the words could be, and in fact have been, construed as magical, conveying some mystical infusion.

A SPECIAL SITUATION: ALIEN IMMERSION

Throughout history there has been an ongoing discussion of what is called "alien immersion." This does not mean that one is immersed by an extraterrestrial being, but that a group not normally known to immerse has performed an immersion and a decision concerning the validity of that baptism must be adjudicated. Historically, many Baptists have rejected alien immersion based upon their definition of the church and the authority placed in proper ordination.[16] This author, however, has chosen to travel a different road. Each case must be decided on an individual basis. The determining factor is not the church since the above prescribed definition of a true church allows for pedobaptist churches to be true churches.

The determining factor is not the administrator or proper ordination. The determining factor is the ordinance itself. Was the ordinance performed with

13. "The Teaching of the Twelve Apostles," in Roberts and Donaldson, *Ante-Nicene Fathers*, 7:379.
14. Justin Martyr, "First Apology," in Roberts and Donaldson, *Ante-Nicene Fathers*, 1:183.
15. Among these are the "Oneness Pentecostal" groups. More information can be found at http://www.onenesspentecostal.com.
16. See James Madison Pendleton, *An Old Landmark Re-set: Or Ought Baptists Invite Pedobaptists to Preach in Their Pulpits?* (Nashville: Graves & Marks, 1854).

1181 of M"118118

the proper subject, in the proper mode, and with the proper meaning by a true church? If so, then it is valid. While in this age of postdenominationalism, it may be possible to find such a case, that case would be rare.

For example, any pedobaptist church performing immersions of believers would do so based upon the failure of that person to be baptized as a child and not upon conviction based on Scripture. Thus, the rare exception must be of a scripturally informed person who understands the true meaning of baptism and who requests baptism by immersion as a believer from a pedobaptist church. Logic contends that no such case would ever occur because such an informed person would not wish to unite and join with a church that held an opposing view. Thus, in the majority of instances, alien immersions have harmed the meaning of baptism enough to render the practice null and void. However, a rare valid exception may exist.

CONCLUSION

All of the six categories that have been discussed are interrelated to some degree. Offering a definition of what makes baptism valid always runs the risk of being misunderstood. I offer the following definition to encourage further thought, discussion, and research, understanding that it may yet be incomplete or inaccurate: *Valid baptism, the door to the local church, is performed by an appropriately selected administrator of a true church who immerses a believer in water for the purpose of profession of faith with and in the name of Jesus Christ, the second person of the Trinity, symbolizing the subject's identification with Christ's death, burial, and resurrection.* A shorter definition of valid baptism would be: *the immersion of a believer with the proper meaning by a true church.*

6

Baptism and Covenant

JASON K. LEE

A decade ago as I began my doctoral research, I became more acquainted with the idea of covenant in Baptist life through the writings of John Smyth. As my doctoral thesis began to take shape, Smyth's views of a covenant ecclesiology became a central aspect of my work. In this brief essay, I hope to explore further some of the ideas of a covenant ecclesiology and their application to contemporary Baptists. I intend to draw on the rich heritage of church covenants in Baptist life and to interact with the current discussions among various Baptist groups about the recovery of covenant language. The relationship between baptism and the church covenant and the latter's ability to depict the broader theological themes of covenant are fundamental issues for any recovery of church covenants in Baptist life. A practical question relates to how the recovery of a church covenant may benefit contemporary Baptist churches.

SEPARATIST VIEWS ON COVENANT

Baptist use of the church covenant finds some precedent among the English Separatists of the sixteenth century. The Separatists emphasized that the church was to be founded on a covenant. God's faithful are called to be separate from the unfaithful, as evidenced by the membership of the local church. To form a true church, Separatists agreed together on a covenant. The covenant is then requisite for membership in the church. Through this act of covenant, the people submit to the authority of Christ, becoming a true local church. The Separatist Robert Browne refers to the members' agreement to covenant together under Christ's authority as the foundation of the church. He challenges the Church of England by saying that they have not "planted the church by laying the foundacion thereof,

0

for here by is the foundacion laied, when we make & hould the couenant with the Lord to be vnder his gouerment, when we haue the power of the Lord, as it is written Cor. 1. 5. amongst vs, & the septer of Christ Iesus amongst vs."[1]

Browne describes the central role of the church covenant, saying, "The Church planted or gathered, is a companie or number of Christians or beleeuers, which by a willing couenant made with their God, are vnder the gouerment of god and Christ, and kepe his lawes in one holie communion."[2] The church is a true church endowed with the authority of God and Christ because it has joined in a pledge of obedience to God. Browne uses similar language when defining a Christian. He states, "Christians are a companie or number of beleeuers, which by a willing couenuant made with their God, are vnder the gouernement of God and Christ, and keepe his Lawes in one holie communion."[3] The interrelationship between the concepts of a true church and a true Christian is striking. A Christian's duty is to form a true church through covenanting with other believers to be faithful to God. The covenant then not only becomes central to church membership, but also is an essential mark of being a Christian.

Later Separatists such as Henry Barrow continued the practice of forming the church by means of a local church covenant. Faithfulness to the covenant was required of members to remain in communion with the church. The Puritan George Gifford charged that the necessity of faithfulness had introduced conditionality into God's covenant, thus making the stability of the covenant reliant upon human effort. Barrow responded that Gifford would never understand his reasoning, because Gifford did not perceive that he was discussing the outward covenant, not the eternal covenant.[4] Indeed, Barrow tries to make a clear distinction between the covenant of grace and the local church covenant.

> The covenant and election of God remaineth firme to the endz of the world, neither can the sinns of the parents divert or frustrate his mercies to the children. But we reason not of God's secret election whom he may or will call, but of the outward covenant

1. Robert Browne, "A True and Short Declaration," in *The Writings of Robert Harrison and Robert Browne*, ed. Albert Peel and Leland H. Carlson (London: Allen and Unwin, 1953), 421. As to his Scripture reference, Browne must have intended 1 Corinthians 5:4. See ibid., 443, 446, 456, 461, 505, 525–26, for other connections between 1 Corinthians 5 and the power of the Lord in the churches. Several words that contain the letter *w* have been emended.
2. Robert Browne, "A Book Which Sheweth the Life and Manners," in Peel and Carlson, *Writings of Robert Harrison and Robert Browne*, 253.
3. Ibid., 227.
4. Henry Barrow, "Barrow's Final Answer to Gifford," in *The Writings of John Greenwood and Henry Barrow, 1591–1593*, ed. Leland H. Carlson (London: George Allen and Unwin, 1970), 166–67.

wherin he hath called, and who may be judged within that outward covenant of us. . . . Because I hould that only such as have
made profession of the faith and continue in the same faith and
obedience are of us to be esteamed within the outward covenant.
Therfore doo I heareupon make the stablenes of God's covenant
to depend upon our righteousnes.[5]

Barrow claims that the Separatists have no intention of determining who is
within God's eternal covenant. Their concern is that if a person wants to be a part
of the visible church of Christ, then that person must covenant to be obedient. If a
person does not obey God's commands, then that one cannot be considered a part
of the local church covenant.

JOHN SMYTH'S VIEWS ON COVENANT

The writings of Browne and Barrow helped establish the Separatist milieu from
which John Smyth, the English Baptist pioneer, emerges.[6] As a Separatist, Smyth
agrees with many of Browne's and Barrow's views on covenant. Smyth continues
the Separatist distinction between the outward, or local, church covenant and the
eternal covenant of grace. While these concepts are distinct in Smyth's thought,
they are also inextricably linked.

Smyth, like Browne and Barrow, emphasizes that the faithful join with each
other in the outward covenant. They covenant together in order to be faithful to
the eternal covenant that God has offered them. Their agreement to be obedient
to God as a group allows them to continue as the covenanted community of God.
The idea of a covenanted community is important to Smyth because he sees the
covenant as the basis for God's granting his power to a church. The church has the
authority of Christ and thus the power to enact reform because it is the covenanted
community.

THE LOCAL CHURCH COVENANT AS ENTRANCE TO THE CHURCH

As Smyth became more dissatisfied with the Church of England, he led a group
of followers in Gainsborough to form a Separatist congregation. The congregation
was formed in the typical Separatist pattern by the members agreeing together to
become a church. William Bradford's description of the event states:

So many, therefore, of these proffessors as saw ye evill of these
things in thes parts, and whose harts ye Lord had touched wth

---

5. Ibid., 165–66.
6. For a more extensive treatment of John Smyth, see Jason K. Lee, *Theology of John Smyth: Puritan, Separatist, Baptist, Mennonite* (Macon: Mercer University Press, 2003).

heavenly zeale for his trueth, they shooke off this yoake of anti-
christian bondage, and as ye Lords free people, joyned them selves
(by a covenant of the Lord) into a church estate, in ye felowship of
ye gospell, to walke in all his wayes, made known, or to be made
known unto them, according to their best endeavours, whatsoever it should cost them, the Lord assisting them.[7]

Smyth's Separatist perspective that the true form of the church is a covenanted
community resembles the thought of his Separatist predecessors. Smyth alludes to
his indebtedness to other Separatists in a work from his Separatist phase, *Principles
and Inferences*. He refers to them as his "auncient brethren" in the following:

Therfore especially are those auncient brethren to be honoured,
that they have reduced the Church to the true Primitive & Apos-
tolique constitution which consisteth in these three things. 1.
The true matter which are sayntes only. 2. The true forme which
is the vniting of them together in the covenant. 3. The true prop-
ertie which is communion in all the holy things, & the powre of
the L. Iesus Christ, for the maintayning of that communion. To
this blessed work of the L. wherin those auncient brethren have
labored I know not what may more be added.[8]

These "ancient brethren" were Separatists such as Browne, Barrow, and the authors
of the "True Confession," who had led the faithful out of the Church of England
and had formed their true churches on the basis of covenant.

Smyth holds that there are two essential elements in forming a true church.
First, believers are needed. Smyth says that true membership of the church consists of "sayntes only." Second, these saints are to coalesce into a church by means
of the covenant. The covenant is then the path for membership in the church.
Anyone else wishing to join the congregation must agree to the covenant. The
covenanted community is then granted the properties of a true church, which are
participation in holy things and the authority of Christ. In a later work, Smyth
also includes the phrase, "the covenant to walke in al Gods wayes," indicating the
nature of the local church covenant.[9] At the heart of the local church covenant is
the pledge to be obedient to God.

---

7. William Bradford, *History of Plymouth Plantation*, reprinted from the original manuscript under
   the direction of the Secretary of the Commonwealth, by order of the General Court (Boston:
   Wright and Potter, 1898), 13.
8. John Smyth, "Principles and Inferences Concerning the Visible Church," in *The Works of John
   Smyth*, ed. W. T. Whitley (Cambridge: Cambridge University Press, 1915), 1:270.
9. John Smyth, *Paralleles, Censures, Observations*, ed. W. T. Whitley (Cambridge: Cambridge University Press, 1915), 2:555.

The covenant became crucial to Smyth's understanding of the church. In discussing the importance of the covenant of Smyth and his connection with earlier Separatists, B. R. White writes, "In his [Smyth's] thinking about the Church the theology of the covenant was to resume something of the central place it had once held in the thought of Robert Browne."[10] Smyth's statement of the true form being a church united in a covenant is definitely similar to Browne's. With respect to the local church, the term *covenant* is a voluntary agreement to join together to become a local body of believers.[11] Smyth says this covenanted group is empowered to become a true church.

> A visible communion of Saincts is of two, three, or moe Saincts
> joyned together by covenant with God & themselves, freely to
> vse al the holy things of God, according to the word, for their
> mutual edification, & Gods glory. . . . This visible communion of
> Saincts is a visible Church.[12]

For a congregation to be a true church, it must be formed upon a covenant. Because the covenant is with God, it can be agreed to by the faithful only. There is no acceptance of the ungodly into the covenant or church. In addition to the agreement with God, there is a second relationship in the covenant. This relationship is among the saints "themselves." A group of saints who have joined themselves to each other and to God constitute the "visible" or local church. As people agree to the covenant, they are placing themselves under the discipline and authority of that church specifically and of Christ ultimately. The covenant combines a divine element of covenant with a covenant for brotherly communion.

Why did Smyth hold the act of covenanting to be of such importance? According to Smyth, once these believers have covenanted together, they receive the kingly, priestly, and prophetic authority of Christ. Smyth writes, "But a true visible church, that is a communion of Saynts, joyned together in the true covenant, is that only communion of men wherto God hath given his covenant, his promises, his holy things, Christ for King, Priest & Prophet."[13] In practical terms, this means they can baptize, administer the Lord's Supper, elect elders, and even ordain ministers.[14] It was in the response of covenanting that the people were given the authority of Christ to become a true church. Once the covenant had been agreed to, then the people had the authority of a church. Successionism had been ruled

---

10. B. R. White, *The English Separatist Tradition* (London: Oxford University Press, 1971), 125.
11. Smyth, *Paralleles, Censures, Observations*, 2:511–12.
12. Smyth, "Principles and Inferences," 1:252.
13. Smyth, *Paralleles, Censures, Observations*, 2:350–51; "men" has been emended.
14. Smyth, *Differences of the Churches of the Seperation*, ed. W. T. Whitley (Cambridge: Cambridge University Press, 1915), 1:315; and idem, *Paralleles, Censures, Observations*, 2:511–12.

out, because authority was passed through the act of covenanting, not through history or tradition.

COVENANT THEOLOGY AND COVENANT ECCLESIOLOGY

In the English tradition, there were many Reformed theologians who stressed a conditional covenant while holding to predestination.[15] The conditional understanding of the covenant found in Fenner, Cartwright, and Perkins influenced the Puritan tradition from which Separatism sprang. The Separatists continued the idea that man was bound in obedience to God. The saints' agreement to obedience was a major element of the local church covenant. Therefore, obedience was central to the Separatist idea of the local church as the covenanted community.

Like other Separatists before him, Smyth agrees that obedience is the main aspect of man's acceptance of the covenant. As the church is formed on a covenant, it agrees to be faithful to God. In *Principles and Inferences*, Smyth states that one part of the covenant is that the faithful are "to be Gods people, that is to obey al the commandements of God."[16] The idea of obedience shows some connection between the local church covenant and the eternal covenant. The people of the local church are to be obedient because they belong to the covenanted people of God. They demonstrate their promise to obedience in their outward covenant. Like many of his Separatist predecessors, Smyth stresses the conditional nature of this covenant. If a congregation refuses to be obedient to God and remains obstinately in sin, then they cease to be a true church.[17]

In the writings of John Smyth, there are two aspects of the term *covenant*. One has to do with the theology of the covenant. The other is more akin to the Separatist idea of covenant ecclesiology. These two aspects are difficult to study in isolation from each other, because there is a close connection between the two concepts. Smyth derives his idea of covenant ecclesiology from his theology of the covenant.

---

15. John S. Coolidge, *The Pauline Renaissance in England* (Oxford: Clarendon Press, 1970), 99–140, shows the tendency among Puritans, Separatists, and Congregationalists to understand the covenant as conditional. Charles S. McCoy and J. Wayne Baker, *Fountainhead of Federalism: Heinrich Bullinger and the Covenantal Tradition* (Louisville: Westminster John Knox Press, 1991), 29–41, discuss the influence of Bullinger and the conditional covenant on the English covenant tradition, including Tyndale, Fenner, and Perkins. R. T. Kendall, *Calvinism and English Calvinism to 1649*, new ed. (Carlisle, England: Paternoster Press, 1997), 42–43, 58, mentions the conditional covenant understanding of Tyndale and Perkins, respectively. Carl R. Trueman, *Luther's Legacy: Salvation and English Reformers* (Oxford: Clarendon Press, 1994), 109–19, demonstrates Tyndale's view of the conditional nature of the covenant. These scholars have differing views on the effect that predestination had on the Reformed view of the covenant. However, the point in this context is that the understanding that there were some conditions to the covenant was present in the thought of many of the English Reformed theologians during this time period.

16. Smyth, "Principles and Inferences," 1:254.

17. Smyth, *Paralleles, Censures, Observations*, 2:451.

In Smyth's view, the person who accepts the covenant of grace offered by God should respond by agreeing to covenant with other believers to form a church. Although covenanting with other believers derives from the covenant made with God, the two ideas are not synonymous. Smyth shows the differences between the two by stressing the importance of one or the other at different times.

B. R. White says that after a certain point in Smyth's writings, ambivalence developed in his use of the term *covenant*. Occasionally, it is clear that Smyth was referring to the covenant of grace offered by God to the elect. At other times, it is clear that Smyth used the term to mean the union of the local body of believers. Then on a few occasions, Smyth seems almost to blend the concepts. White says this ambivalence points to Smyth's understanding that man's acceptance of the covenant of grace became actualized in the local congregation's covenant.[18] James Coggins rejects this connection, even to the point of suggesting that Smyth's theology of the covenant had nothing to do with his covenant ecclesiology.[19] However, there is a connection between the two. First, the Separatist background from which Smyth drew related the two concepts. Second, the fact that Smyth used the terms in close relationship and in reference to the same groups shows some connection.

Smyth is not the first in the Separatist tradition to imply that there is a relationship between the local church covenant and the eternal covenant. Robert Browne had stated that a person could respond to the gospel without being a member of the church. However, a person should not be a member of the covenanted community, or local church, without responding first to God's covenant.[20] When the covenant of grace is offered by God, the proper response is to "offer and geue vp our selues to be of the church and people of God."[21]

Smyth worked within the Separatist tradition when implying a relationship between the two concepts of covenant. One passage in Smyth's work, *Paralleles, Censures, Observations*, depicts his idea of the relationship between the two concepts. Written during the Separatist stage of Smyth's career, *Paralleles* is a debate with the Puritan, Richard Bernard. During the debate, Smyth argues that certain people who have separated from the Church of England have come together to form a true church. He makes the statement, "I hold & maintayne out of the word that a company of faithful people Seperated from al vncleanenes & joyned together by a covenant of the L. are a true Church."[22] The key here is the phrase,

18.   White, *The English Separatist Tradition*, 128.
19.   James R. Coggins, "The Theological Positions of John Smyth," *Baptist Quarterly* 30 (April 1984): 249.
20.   Browne, "A True and Short Declaration," 422, 442.
21.   Browne, "A Book Which Sheweth the Life and Manners," 256.
22.   Smyth, *Paralleles, Censures, Observations*, 2:386; "company" has been emended.

"joyned together by a covenant of the L[ord]." While the covenant is of the Lord, it also contains an aspect of the believers' joining with each other.

The local or visible church is a group that has covenanted with God and with each other. Smyth attempts to show the validity of two or three believers joining together to become a church by calling them the people "with whome God maketh his covenant to be ther God, & whome he receaveth to be his people, they are a Temple, that is a Church unto him."[23] Although he is referring to a group that has joined together, the emphasis in this use of "covenant" could be described as a theology of the covenant. Smyth continues, noting the close affinity between the covenant that God makes with his people and the covenant that is offered to the local body. When Smyth is discussing the power of excommunication in the local church, he again relates the two terms:

> Nay say we, the powre of binding & losing is given to the body of the Church, even to two or thre faithful people joyned together in covenant, & this we prove evidently in this manner. Vnto whome the covenant is given, vnto them the powre of binding & losing is given. The covenant is given to the body of the Church, that is to two or three faithful ones: For God is their God, & they are his people.[24]

In this quotation, "covenant'" is used to depict the covenanted community and the eternal covenant of grace. The phrase, "God is their God, & they are his people," alludes to the covenant of grace. Smyth sees the power of Christ given to rule the church as part of God's covenant with his people. As the church agrees together in a local covenant, then God fulfils his part of the covenant by granting that congregation the power of Christ to govern the church. Smyth says, "We say the Church or two or three faithful people Seperated from the world & joyned together in a true covenant, have both Christ, the covenant, & promises, & the ministerial powre of Christ given to them, & that they are the body that receave from Christs hand out of heaven, or rather from Christ their head this ministerial powre."[25] Those who have joined in an ecclesiological covenant are given the blessings of the theological covenant. The authority of Christ, which is given to the whole covenanted community, comes through the covenant relationship in which "God is their God, & they are his people."[26]

---

23. Ibid., 2:386.
24. Ibid., 2:388–89; "covenant" and "given" have been emended.
25. Ibid., 2:403; "from" has been emended.
26. Ibid., 2:388–89.

Once again, the covenant that the group has joined in is a covenant of the Lord, but it also has implications for its members. These implications are mentioned in the following passage from Smyth's *Principles and Inferences*:

> The outward part of the true forme of the true visible church is a vowe, promise, oath, or covenant betwixt God and the Saints. . . . This covenant hath 2 parts. 1. respecting God and the faithful. 2. respecting the faithful mutually. . . . The first part of the covenant respecting God is either from God to the faithful, or from the faithful to God. . . . The second part of the covenant respecting the faithful mutually conteyneth all the duties of love whatsoever.[27]

He states that the outward part of the true form of the church is a vow or covenant, which the people make with God. However, it is also a covenant that is between the saints mutually. Smyth's understanding of the covenant included not only a binding together with God but also the local church binding together in love. Smyth saw the importance of both uses of the term *covenant*. It also seems that he saw covenant ecclesiology as based on the eternal covenant. From these few passages, it can be determined that Smyth had no hesitation in relating the two ideas of covenant. The fact that he uses the terms with such fluidity suggests he may see them as two aspects of the same covenant. The church covenant was a human binding together under the eternal covenant. Therefore, he would agree with many of his Separatist predecessors in saying that for a group of believers the church covenant was the proper response to the eternal covenant.

In discussing the two parts of the local church covenant, Smyth says that the first part is between God and the faithful. Smyth sees this first part of the local church covenant as the acceptance of the eternal covenant of grace. After this is complete, then the Christian can agree to be obedient and demonstrate love to his fellow Christian. So, Smyth saw the church covenant as applying to the faithful who had responded to God's eternal covenant and then bonded together to be obedient to him and faithful to each other. With his understanding of the church covenant, Smyth was in theory calling for a believers' church. Therefore, Smyth's later rejection of infant baptism did not cause an immediate change to many aspects of his view of covenant.

---

27. Smyth, "Principles and Inferences," 1:254; "from" has been emended.

THE IMPORTANCE OF COVENANT AMONG LATER BAPTISTS

Contemporary secondary literature attests to the prominence of covenant in Baptist life in the centuries following Smyth.[28] Many of these sources also postulate on the reasons why the concept of covenant has at times fallen out of common practice among Baptist churches. Throughout Baptist history, there have been strong advocates of the use of church covenants. Proponents of Baptist church covenants have argued that a local church covenant captures the prominent themes of covenant in the Bible. One indication of the support church covenants have received in Baptist life is the numerous examples of church covenants that have been produced over the last four centuries.[29] While these covenants vary in form, detail, and length, they maintain a common thrust of faithfulness to God and mutual love for others in the church.

BIBLICAL IMAGERY IN BAPTIST COVENANTS

Historically, Baptists have appealed to local church covenants as an appropriate reflection of the Bible's notion of God in relationship with his people through covenant. Typical passages that have provided the background for covenant language are Genesis 12–17 (Abrahamic covenant), Exodus 19–20 (Siniatic covenant), 2 Samuel 7 (Davidic covenant), and Jeremiah 31 (new covenant). Additionally, texts such as Joshua 24 (the covenant at Shechem), 2 Chronicles 34 (Josiah's covenant), and Nehemiah 9 (Nehemiah's covenant) have been used to indicate that covenant making with God is an appropriate response on the part of people who have come together under the benefits of God's gracious actions. The New Testament is replete with covenant imagery, including the first Lord's Supper with Jesus' appeal to the "blood of a new covenant." Baptists also have cited 2 Corinthians 8:5 as indicating the dual nature of the covenant, with the Lord and with each other.[30]

Perhaps the best exemplar for Baptists of an ecclesial agreement as the fitting response to God's gracious covenant activity is found in the structure of the book

---

28. Cf. Mark Dever, ed., *Polity: Biblical Arguments on How to Conduct Church Life* (Washington, DC: Center for Church Reform, 2001); idem, *Nine Marks of a Healthy Church*, rev. and exp. ed. (Wheaton, IL: Crossway, 2000); Charles Deweese, *Baptist Church Covenants* (Nashville: Broadman Press, 1990); John S. Hammett, *Biblical Foundations for Baptist Churches: A Contemporary Ecclesiology* (Grand Rapids: Kregel, 2005); Paul Fiddes, *Tracks and Traces* (Carlisle, England: Paternoster, 2003); Nigel Wright, "Covenant and Covenanting," *Baptist Quarterly* 39, no. 6 (April 2002): 287–90; Ralph Elliott, "A Theology of the Local Congregation," *Foundations* 22 (January–March 1979): 13–27; Norman Maring and Winthrop Hudson, *A Baptist Manual of Polity and Practice*, rev. ed. (Valley Forge, PA: Judson Press, 1991); and Timothy George and Denise George, eds., *Baptist Confessions, Covenants and Catechisms* (Nashville: Broadman & Holman, 1999), hereafter abbreviated *BCCC*.

29. Deweese, *Baptist Church Covenants*, gives seventy-nine church covenants as a representative sample of the hundreds of church covenants produced in Baptist history.

30. "They first gave themselves to the Lord and to us by the will of God" (2 Cor. 8:5). Biblical citations are from the New American Standard Bible (NASB).

of Hebrews. After a prolonged exposition of God's covenant act of providing for-giveness (8:1–10:18), the writer of Hebrews alludes to the desirable response of those experiencing forgiveness from God. The believer ("full assurance of faith"), who has been forgiven ("our hearts sprinkled clean from an evil conscience") and baptized ("our bodies washed with pure water"), then has communal responsibili-ties with other believers. These communal admonitions ("let us") are to "hold fast the confession of our hope without wavering," to "consider how to stimulate one another to love and good deeds," to be consistent in "our own assembling together," to encourage "one another," and to help each other to avoid "sinning willfully."[31] Baptist covenants have tried to reflect on these goals of having baptized believers mutually consent to persevere in public testimony to faith, to encourage brotherly love and faithful piety, to gather for regular worship, to increase in reciprocal encouragement, and to guard against a lapse into habitual sin.

THE CONTENT AND USE OF BAPTIST COVENANTS

The content of Baptist covenants has varied over the years. Most church cov-enants contain five common characteristics. They intimate a confession of God's gracious work, the value of mutual care and fellowship, the concern for corporate witness, the importance of church discipline, and the practices of corporate wor-ship (often in connection with the ordinances and personal devotion). God's gra-cious work can be described in general imagery, such as "being called by the grace of God out of the iron furnace of the land of Egypt,"[32] or in specific theological terms, such as being "His people through the everlasting covenant of His free grace."[33] Other doctrinal elements, such as the Trinity, revelation, Christology, or eschatology, may be mentioned in conjunction with God's gracious work.

Expressions of mutual care and fellowship often provide the bulk of the covenant's material. The mutual care extends from their common covenant as "members one of another to promote the growth of the whole body in Christian knowledge, holiness and comfort."[34] Other phrases that encourage mutual care include, negatively, "not receiving evil reports against each other," or, positively, "waiting for all opportunity to do all kind offices to each other."[35] Maintaining the integrity of the corporate witness is another typical concern of church covenants. The Baptists of Buckinghamshire, England were encouraged to "walk in a way and manner becoming of the gospel, before them that are without."[36] Combining

---

31. References from Hebrews 10:19–26 (NASB).
32. Covenant of the Great Ellingham Baptist Church, Norfolk, England (1699), in *BCCC*, 181.
33. Covenant of Benjamin and Elias Keach (1697), in *BCCC*, 177.
34. Covenant of the New Hampshire Baptist Convention (1833), in *BCCC*, 219.
35. Covenant of the Kiokee Baptist Church (1771/1826), in *BCCC*, 206.
36. Covenant of the Baptist Church in Horse Fair, Stony Stratford, Buck, England (1790), in *BCCC*, 190.

both mutual care for members and an interest in the quality of corporate witness, Baptist covenants address the priority of church discipline. Baptists in Grassy Creek, North Carolina agreed that they were submitting to "the discipline of the church."[37] As the Baptist Association of Wales recognized, agreement to a covenant indicated willingness to provide godly rebuke or correction of others and a willingness to "receive reproof, rebuke, or advice, in humility, confessing his fault, and forsaking it."[38]

Finally, Baptist covenants express the importance of corporate worship in the lives of believers. The interest in worship often includes a reminder about the ordinances or the role of private devotions. Often Baptist covenants affirmed the importance of not neglecting the assembling for worship. The Baptists of Tulpohokin stated, "We covenant, as God shall help us, to maintain the worship of God . . . and to practice all gospel ordinances."[39] Through the widespread use of the covenant found in Newton Brown's *The Baptist Church Manual*, many Baptists committed themselves to maintaining "family and secret devotion."[40]

Baptist covenants had common characteristics, not only in terms of content, but also in usage in the church. Two prominent examples typify the use of local church covenants. Benjamin Keach and his son, Elias, exercised significant influence on Baptists both in England and in America. Additionally, the Charleston Association served a foundational role for Baptists in the American South.

Benjamin Keach, in *The Glory of a True Church, and Its Discipline Display'd* (1697), describes the church as a congregation of believers who "being first baptized upon the Profession of Faith do by mutual agreement and consent give themselves up to the Lord, and one to another, according to the Will of God."[41] Keach further describes the process by saying that, after a potential member has made public declaration of his or her faith, then that person is to agree to the church covenant. Keach writes, "before the Church they must solemnly enter into a Covenant, to walk in the Fellowship of that particular Congregation, and submit themselves to the Care and Discipline thereof."[42] Keach then explains that agreement to the covenant means participation in the ordinances, Christian fellowship, corporate worship, and pastoral care.

Similarly, *A Summary of Church Discipline* (1774), published by the Charleston Association, defines a church as consisting of "a company of saints incorporated

---

37. Covenant of the Grassy Creek Baptist Church (1757), in *BCCC*, 203.
38. Covenant of the Baptist Association in Wales (1790), in Deweese, *Baptist Church Covenants*, 130.
39. Covenant of the Tulpohokin Baptist Church, Berks County, Pennsylvania (1738), in Deweese, *Baptist Church Covenants*, 138.
40. Brown's covenant is reproduced in Deweese, *Baptist Church Covenants*, 162.
41. Benjamin Keach, *The Glory of a True Church, and Its Discipline Display'd* (1697), 5–6.
42. Ibid., 7.

by a special covenant into one distinct body, and meeting together in one place."[43] The method of forming a church echoes Keach's sentiments. The Charleston Baptists explained, "Being thus satisfied with each other's graces and qualifications, and united in the bond of love they should give up themselves to the Lord and to one another by the will of God, 2 Corinthians 8:5, by subscribing a written covenant consistent with the Word of God, Isaiah 44:5."[44] Being thus constituted, the church is now vested with the authority of the Word to perform the ordinances and to admonish and discipline one another.[45]

RECOVERING THE COVENANT IN BAPTIST LIFE

A recovery of covenant in Baptist life obviously will take on different meanings in contemporary Baptist groups. With frequent references to biblical covenants, Sam Roberts, an American Baptist, argues that in Baptist life the "vitality of worship should bespeak the vitality of covenant."[46] In line with this general admonition, the American Baptist Churches USA has made frequent use of covenant wording in their statements on polity. In their denominational documents, such as "The Covenant of Relationships," the term *covenant* is applied to both local church congregations and denominational relationships. The local church is described as "a company of believers covenanting together" in the name of Christ and endowed with the Holy Spirit.[47] The churches so assembled then cooperate with one another by a "covenant with other like-minded congregations." The intention of the covenant is "to accomplish common purposes related to the Gospel of our Lord Jesus Christ."

Some American Baptists have argued that the functional nature of the covenant resists many theological prerequisites. David Ball contends that covenant relationships among churches are by default nondoctrinal. The mutual development and voluntary acceptance of covenant cooperation among churches meant that "no doctrinal criteria" would result. "In other words, no overt commitment to avoiding doctrinal criteria for church affiliation was necessary, given our commitment

43. Dever, *Polity*, 118.
44. Ibid., 119.
45. Samuel Jones's *Treatise of Church Discipline*, produced for the Philadelphia Baptist Association, makes a similar connection between church discipline and the covenant. See Dever, *Polity*, 141.
46. Samuel K. Roberts, "A Call to Covenant," *American Baptist Quarterly* 21, no. 2 (June 2002): 171.
47. All "The Covenant of Relationships" quotations taken from the June 24, 1984, version of "The Covenant of Relationships and Its Agreements Among The General, National, and Regional Boards of the American Baptist Churches" (Valley Forge, PA: Office of the General Secretary American Baptist Churches in the USA, 1984), available at http://www.abc-usa.org/documents/ABCCovenantofRelationships.pdf.

to covenantal relationship."[48] Ball encourages theological discourse among Baptist churches in covenant. However, he urges that this discourse or "witness" not result in any attempt "to codify the content of anyone's testimony as a criterion for fellowship, in our covenant."[49]

Paul Fiddes argues for the need of a recovery of covenant language in British Baptist life. Drawing on the work of early Baptists, Fiddes values a return to the use of covenants for developing a healthy church ecclesiology. Fiddes indicates four uses of covenant in Baptist life.[50] First, "covenant" refers to the eternal covenant of grace that God makes with the elect. This covenant relationship results in the salvation of its human participants. Second, the interconnectedness between members of the Trinity can be seen in covenant language. Humans may benefit from the internal covenant of the Godhead.[51] The third use relates to corporate covenants that God makes with a church or churches. Whether with a national entity (Old Testament Israel) or a religious entity (the Church of England), God may covenant with certain bodies to accomplish his purposes. These purposes relate to his covenant of grace (mentioned above) but are not synonymous with it. The fourth usage is the local church covenant. While drawing on theological concepts from the first three usages, Baptists often have found the local church covenant a central component in their church life.

Due most likely to the ecumenical aims of Fiddes's call for renewed covenant, he does not connect the themes of believer's baptism with covenant. In describing the role of believer's baptism within Baptist tradition, Fiddes does not use covenant imagery. Nor does he argue for baptism as identifying with the eternal covenant of God. Nor does Fiddes see baptism as a means of accepting local church covenant.

COVENANT RECOVERY AMONG SOUTHERN BAPTISTS

Charles Deweese, a Southern Baptist, advocates a return to church covenants in contemporary Baptist life. In fact, he stated twenty-five years ago that Baptists needed to return to using church covenants. In spite of some publications encouraging the renewal of church covenants among Southern Baptists, it had "not attained broad implementation in local churches."[52] Deweese argues that as Baptists stress programmatic numerical growth, they often sacrifice "an essential stress on cultivating a truly regenerated membership."[53] Among other factors

---

48. David T. Ball, "Appreciating the Non-doctrinal Nature of our Covenantal Ties," *American Baptist Quarterly* 21, no. 2 (June 2002): 160.
49. Ibid., 162.
50. Fiddes, *Tracks and Traces*, 25–31.
51. Ibid., 27.
52. Deweese, *Baptist Church Covenants*, 91.
53. Ibid., 90.

contributing to the decline in covenant interest among Baptists, Deweese notes a lack of interest in the covenantal nature of the church as described in many Baptist confessions of faith.

John Hammett suggests a return to church covenants as one part of recovering a regenerate church membership. Hammett writes, "One of the major purposes for the use of church covenants is precisely to safeguard regenerate church membership."[54] Once a church has developed an acceptable form for the church covenant, they would then reconstitute around the church covenant, making signing the church covenant an essential step in becoming a member. Hammett adds that this process would be "a practical way" to deal with a large number of absentee members typical of many Baptist churches. By the individuals not signing, they would by default be removing themselves from church membership.

This comprehensive overhaul could take months in communication and education before it could be implemented. Hammett's comments could be misconstrued to say that a main reason for adopting a church covenant is that it provides an easy way to purge church membership lists. However, this cannot be the case. First, there is no easy way to accomplish such a goal, nor should a church seek one. Second, the process of establishing a church covenant, explaining its contents, and educating the congregation on its use before implementing it is hardly the easy way. As Hammett goes on to describe, former members who do not sign the covenant should be questioned regarding their lack of subscription, and they should become the immediate objects of discipleship and/or evangelism.

Both Deweese and Hammett stress originality in the form of the church covenant as a means of making the covenant meaningful to a congregation.[55] Though the value of originality may be overstated, the process of a congregation being educated in the purpose, form, and content of the covenant is essential for its overall effectiveness.

Baptism and Covenant as the Heart of a Healthy Baptist Ecclesiology

The recovery of a local church covenant actually can foster the renewal of other aspects of a healthy Baptist ecclesiology. It should be readily apparent how a church covenant adds significance to church membership. Being a member of the church means a commitment to the ideas and practices stipulated in the covenant. It also means sharing in the identity of a covenanted community. Therefore, a church covenant can serve as one measure of regaining meaningful membership. Having a church covenant in place also can facilitate the practice of church discipline. The

54. Hammett, *Biblical Foundations for Baptist Churches*, 117.
55. Deweese, *Baptist Church Covenants*, 89; Hammett, *Biblical Foundations for Baptist Churches*, 118.

church covenant provides an objective means of measuring a person's integrity to their membership commitment. Not only does a church covenant provide some criteria for evaluating a person's commitment to the Lord and to other members, but most church covenants also include a stipulation for submission to the disciplinary process. While anticipation of church discipline does not make it painless, the church covenant puts discipline in the context of mutual accountability and indicates its redemptive purposes.

In his "Epilogue" to *Baptist Church Covenants*, Charles Deweese proposes some practical ways to integrate church covenants into the typical practices of a Baptist church. Deweese connects the church covenant with baptism, the Lord's Supper, church discipline, new church plants, special covenant meetings, and "daily relationship."[56] Deweese's main purpose is to show that if the church covenant is not part of the church's regular practice, then it loses significance for the shaping of congregational life. He also implies in his conclusion that some believe that church covenants stress relationships rather than doctrine.

However, it is the theological nature of the covenant that allows it to connect the church's doctrine to its practices. Because of this interconnection, the biblical themes of covenant may be embodied in the church covenant. The value of the church covenant increases as it has clear connections with a doctrinal foundation (e.g., a confession of faith) and two essential elements of church practice, the ordinances. Since the Lord's Supper and baptism are fundamental to a healthy Baptist ecclesiology, without essential connection with them the church covenant becomes a peripheral item.[57] Connecting the Lord's Supper to the church covenant becomes straightforward for advocates of the practice of closed Communion.[58] Those who have agreed to the church covenant and are members in good standing, as reflected in their faithfulness to the church covenant, should be permitted to participate in the Supper. Church covenant as a requisite to the Lord's Supper sets a standard for confessing (and baptized) believers and provides the nexus for church discipline and the Supper.

Arguably the central trait of Baptist ecclesiology is believer's baptism. Yet, the relationship of baptism and the church covenant is rarely discussed among Baptists. When baptism and church covenant are discussed jointly, it is usually for the purpose of ordering them. Typically, when a church covenant is in place, a person

---

56. Deweese, *Baptist Church Covenants*, 207–11.
57. See other essays in this volume for further insight into the fundamental nature of the Lord's Supper and baptism for Baptist ecclesiology. Ideas such as closed Communion and believer's baptism are explicated in those essays.
58. I have in mind the version of closed Communion that restricts the Lord's Supper to the membership of that particular local church. The version of closed Communion that allows members in good standing of like-minded congregations can also reflect covenant but not as easily.

is baptized upon confession of faith and then agrees to the church covenant in order to enter into church membership.[59]

An ambiguity thus becomes apparent. Through which of these church acts does a person become a member of the church? If it is through baptism, then is the person a member if he does not affirm the church covenant? Typically, the answer is no. If it is through the church covenant that one becomes a member, then baptism no longer retains its traditional status as the means of entrance into the church. In this latter scenario, baptism may be downgraded to a Christian ordinance, by which a person merely professes his or her own faith instead of a church ordinance, by which acceptance of the church's doctrine and practice is displayed along with a profession of personal faith. In order to recover church covenants and still reiterate the corporate nature of baptism, the relationship between church covenant and baptism must be clearly defined.

Modern Baptists may need to turn to John Smyth for the way forward on this matter. Smyth seems to have realized the tension between his new position on believer's baptism and the practice of affirming the church covenant. Once Smyth accepted believer's baptism, then he no longer regarded the local church covenant as the method for entering the church. A person who desired to enter a true church had to do so by baptism that followed a profession of faith. To Smyth, baptism became the proper response to God's offer of the eternal covenant.

As a Separatist, Smyth referred to the act of covenanting as the true form of the church. As a Baptist, Smyth adjusts his thinking to replace the church covenant with baptism. In *The Character of the Beast*, he states, "the true forme of the Church is a covenant betwixt God & the Faithful made in baptisme in which Christ is visibly put on."[60] This statement marks a considerable shift in Smyth's thinking. While he still upholds the presence of a covenant, that covenant takes on a new form. The idea of covenant is included in Smyth's arguments for believer's baptism. Infants are not to be baptized because they are "vnable to enter into the New Testament by sealing back the covenant vnto the Lord, & consenting vnto the contract."[61] To enter the public body of the church, the covenant offered by God must be agreed upon by the individual. The individual makes his consent visible to fellow believers through the sign of baptism. Baptism fulfills the role of agreeing to the local church covenant for Smyth because he now sees that baptism will demonstrate a person's agreement to the eternal covenant. He says that neither he nor

---

59. Cf. Keach, *The Glory of a True Church*, 5–7.
60. Smyth, *The Character of the Beast*, ed. W. T. Whitley (Cambridge: Cambridge University Press, 1915), 2:645.
61. Ibid.

the so-called Anabaptists are bringing a new covenant; instead they are renewing the true form of the covenant, which is baptism.[62]

So, how do the thoughts of Smyth help toward establishing a meaningful relationship between baptism and church covenant? Baptism serves as an outward sign of identity with Christ but also as a visible affirmation of the believer's entrance into the body of believers.[63] Therefore, it serves as an outward acceptance of the covenant with the Lord, given by grace through faith. Baptism also marks a common confession with, and a covenantal commitment to, the believers in the church from which the person receives baptism. Baptism notes an affirmation of the two foci of covenant—it is with the Lord and with fellow believers.

With this relationship properly established, the following scenario seems most fitting. Those people who seek membership in the local church and have previously been baptized as believers should be examined by the church (or its designees), invited to affirm the church's covenant, and thereby granted membership. However, for those who seek baptism and church membership consequent to their conversion from unbelief or who come from another faith tradition,[64] the process is different. After the requisite catechesis, baptism will serve as their professions of faith in the Lord and affirmation of the church's covenant. Thus, upon their baptism they become members of the church. All members can celebrate a regular (perhaps annual) renewal of the church covenant. Because of the connection between baptism and covenant, this regular reaffirmation of covenant provides not only a reflection on the mutual covenant with fellow believers before God, but also a reminder of God's gracious offer of the eternal covenant of life.

---

62. Ibid., 2:659.
63. First Corinthians 12 indicates the spiritual reality that the baptism of the Spirit makes us a member of the body of Christ, the church. This spiritual reality is epitomized by believer's baptism, visibly indicating our membership in the local church.
64. I.e., another Christian denomination not practicing believer's baptism by immersion.

7

A Baptist's Theology of the Lord's Supper

THOMAS WHITE

lthough my concern about the Lord's Supper began many years ago, my interest intensified during the fall of 2004. I was in the process of completing my dissertation, which focused on the Lord's Supper among other things. My wife and I finished eating with relatives in Florida on Christmas Eve. At least one of these relatives does not call himself a Christian. You can imagine my surprise when they suggested we attend a Christmas Eve service at a local church. The church appeared baptistic in nature, requiring baptism by immersion for membership, but the church claimed no denominational affiliation.

After arriving, we sang several praise songs. The pastor spoke for a few minutes and then proceeded to call people to the front to distribute the Lord's Supper. Neither before, during, or after this distribution was any explanation given. There was no mention of the need to be a Christian, no time for self-examination, no discussion of baptism, and very little discussion of what the Supper means. The intrigue grew when I passed the bread without taking a piece. My conscience would not allow me to participate with this church because at this point I did not know what they believed. Meanwhile my nonprofessing relatives partook. You can imagine their surprise when the one "preacher" and "seminary employee" in the family did not participate.

I assumed that administering the Lord's Supper without any explanation rarely occurred and then only at seeker-sensitive churches. Before long, however, I found myself again in the midst of celebrating the Lord's Supper, this time in a college gathering at a very conservative church. This group contained only a portion of the church, had a female college student introduce the ordinance, and allowed each one to take individually instead of corporately. Again, no explanation was given concerning the meaning or the requirements for participation. Between these personal experiences and conversations with other believers, I became convinced that Baptists risk losing their understanding of the Lord's Supper. This chapter seeks to present this Baptist's theology of the Lord's Supper.

A presentation of the theology of the Lord's Supper in such confined limits requires brevity. The discussion will begin with an introduction to the Lord's Supper, addressing the name, the connection to the Passover, the institution of the Lord's Supper, and a defense of the Lord's Supper as a local church ordinance. After the introduction, the following will be discussed: the elements of the Lord's Supper, the meaning of the Lord's Supper, the participants in the Lord's Supper (including the partakers and the administrators), and the frequency of the Lord's Supper.

INTRODUCTION TO THE LORD'S SUPPER

THE NAME

Several biblical terms refer to the Supper: the breaking of bread (Acts 2:42), the blessing and Communion (1 Cor. 10:16), the Lord's Table (1 Cor. 10:21), the Lord's Supper (1 Cor. 11:20), and the thanksgiving, or the Eucharist (1 Cor. 11:24). Roman Catholics often refer to the Lord's Supper by the term *Eucharist*, which is the Greek word translated "thanksgiving," or "give thanks" (1 Cor. 11:24). Its celebration comes as part of Mass, and it is classified as a sacrament. The term *Mass* comes from the Latin verb *mittere*, meaning "to send." The word *sacrament* comes from the Latin translation of the Greek word *mysterion*, where it refers to divine things. This occurs in Ephesians 1:9; 3:3–4; Colossians 1:26–27; 1 Timothy 3:16, and other locations.[1] The Latin word *sacramentum* means "oath," and some believe that it was used because believers took an oath to follow Christ. This paper will refer to the ordinance as "the Lord's Supper," which accurately describes the event since the Lord instituted it during the Passover supper and Paul refers to it this way in 1 Corinthians 11:20.

THE INSTITUTION

The institution of the Lord's Supper is recorded in Matthew 26:17–30; Mark 14:12–26; and Luke 22:7–30. John also mentions the event but does not provide detailed instruction. Paul in 1 Corinthians 11 gives instructions as he received them. There are three particular areas of interest in the institution of the Lord's Supper.

First, the event occurred during the celebration of the Passover with the disciples. In addition, Paul states in 1 Corinthians 5:7, "For Christ our Passover

---

1. For a further explanation, see John Calvin, *Institutes of the Christian Religion*, in Library of Christian Classics, trans. F. L. Battles, ed. John T. McNeill (Louisville: Westminster John Knox Press, 1960), 1277–78.

also has been sacrificed."[2] After this celebration of the Passover and the institution of the Lord's Supper, the New Testament does not record the disciples celebrating the Feast of the Passover again. The Passover as the background for the Lord's Supper can enrich understanding. The Passover meal symbolized God's provision in delivering the children of Israel from bondage in Egypt. In similar fashion, the Lord's Supper symbolizes Jesus' death as the paschal lamb delivering mankind from the bondage of sin.[3]

Second, Scripture allows dispute on whether the Lord's Supper was instituted before the Passover or just after the celebration of the Passover. Common assumption and the flow of the account in the first three Gospels indicate the Lord's Supper was instituted after the Passover. However, John 13:1 states, "Now before the Feast of the Passover . . ." which seems to indicate that it was instituted before the Passover. John 19:14 says concerning the day of our Lord's death, "Now it was the day of preparation for the Passover; it was about the sixth hour." This suggests the Passover had not yet taken place when Christ had instituted the Lord's Supper. Even if Jesus celebrated the Passover early, the relationship between the Lord's Supper and the Passover cannot be denied. The timing was necessary because Christ was to be crucified as our paschal lamb.

Third, confusion has existed over whether Judas left before the institution of the Lord's Supper or after. If Judas were present, one could ask why Christ allowed an unworthy participant. Matthew mentions Judas at the paschal supper but says nothing of his presence during the Lord's Supper. Mark does not mention Judas specifically. John 13:26–30 indicates that Judas left quickly after dipping the morsel, which was part of the paschal supper but not the Lord's Supper. The difficulty arises in Luke 22:21, which implies that Judas was present after the sayings of the Lord's Supper. Although some theologians in Baptist history have sought to establish that Judas was not present during the Lord's Supper, noting Luke's chronological negligence in narratives, the issue has no enormous effect even if he was present.[4] Judas had yet to do anything publicly wrong at that point, and church

---

2. All Scripture quotations are from the New American Standard Bible (NASB).
3. The Paschal lamb comes from Exodus 12, where a lamb was killed and the blood placed on the two doorposts and on the lintel of the house. In later times, it was the lamb eaten at the Jewish Passover that celebrated this event in the escape from Egypt. Paul references Jesus as the fulfillment of the Jewish Passover in 1 Corinthians 5:7.
4. James Madison Pendleton, "Was Judas at the Lord's Supper?" *Tennessee Baptist*, April 9, 1859. Pendleton also notes an article written by Andrew Fuller on the same subject. Pendleton states in agreement with Fuller, "I am strongly inclined to believe Judas was not present at the Lord's supper." This article also notes Calvin, who believed Judas was present. Calvin said concerning Luke's account, "Though Luke hath set down this saying of Christ, *after* the celebration of the supper, yet the order of time cannot be certainly gathered thereby, which we know was often neglected by the evangelists."

discipline or exclusion from the Lord's Supper occurs because of public sin and not matters of the heart.

THE LORD'S SUPPER: A LOCAL CHURCH ORDINANCE

Much confusion over the Lord's Supper arises from an improper understanding of responsibility for the ordinance. Many overemphasize the individualistic nature of the ordinance without recognizing the local church's responsibility. A proper understanding of the Lord's Supper combines the personal self-examination with a balanced view of local church responsibility. The hidden matters of the heart must be adjudicated by the individual, but the church bears the burden of maintaining the integrity of the ordinance.

First Corinthians 11:28–30 teaches the role of individual responsibility when it states, "But a man must examine himself, and in so doing he is to eat of the bread and drink of the cup. For he who eats and drinks, eats and drinks judgment to himself, if he does not judge the body rightly. For this reason many among you are weak and sick, and a number sleep." This passage must be placed in its proper context. Many items of the heart exist of which the church cannot know. Thus, each person bears responsibility for searching the hidden things of his or her life in order to take the ordinance properly. A person must determine and make right such things as grudges, hatred, lust, covetousness, or hidden sins. Without proper self-examination, a person risks improperly taking the ordinance.

The emphasis on individual responsibility, however, cannot neglect the role of the church in maintaining the integrity of the ordinance. The first step in demonstrating church responsibility is to prove that Christ delivered the governance of the ordinances to the local church. Paul's first letter to the Corinthians was addressed, "To the church of God which is at Corinth, to those who have been sanctified in Christ Jesus" (1:2).[5] This letter, written to the local church, states in 1 Corinthians 11:23, "For I received from the Lord that which I also delivered to you." To whom was the ordinance delivered? Paul delivered it to the church at Corinth. "Now I praise you because you remember me in everything and hold firmly to the traditions, just as I delivered them to you" (1 Cor. 11:2), Paul wrote. Perhaps the clearest emphasis on church responsibility comes from 1 Corinthians 5:11: "But actually, I wrote to you not to associate with any so-called brother if he is an immoral person, or covetous, or an idolater, or a reviler, or a drunkard, or a swindler—not even to eat with such a one." This verse speaks of exclusion from the Lord's Supper. Why? Because the previous verses clearly indicate the supper

---

5. This reference to the word *church* means the local church "at Corinth" and represents the vast majority of uses of the term in the New Testament. See B. H. Carroll, *Ecclesia: The Church* (Paris, AR: Baptist Standard Bearer, 2006).

is in mind by using terminology such as "clean out the old leaven," "Christ our Passover," and "celebrate the feast." Even if one denies that this passage discusses the Lord's Supper, one could not be expected to refrain from eating in public with someone while partaking of the Lord's Supper with that same person. Thus, the church at Corinth was not to associate with such a one at the Lord's Supper.

A similar theme can be seen in 2 Thessalonians. This letter is sent to "the church of the Thessalonians" (1:1). Later in 2 Thessalonians 3:6 we see that the congregation has responsibility for discipline: "Now we command you, brethren, in the name of our Lord Jesus Christ, that you keep away from every brother who leads an unruly life and not according to the tradition which you received from us." This verse does not indicate fleeing the lost, because Christians are to evangelize the lost. Rather, Christians should avoid those who call themselves "brothers" and yet lead unruly lives. Verses 14–15 state, "If anyone does not obey our instruction in this letter, take special note of that person and do not associate with him, so that he will be put to shame. Yet do not regard him as an enemy, but admonish him as a brother." The instructions sent to the church give orders not to associate with such a person, which surely must indicate exclusion from the Lord's Supper.

If the church at Corinth and the church at Thessalonica were told not to associate with such a person at the Lord's Supper, then who bears final responsibility for the ordinances? Suppose a person who is obviously living in sin refuses to examine himself properly. The church knows that this person lives in sin. The church bears responsibility not to associate with that person. So the unrepentant person desires to partake, but the church in accordance with Scripture, denies such a person this right. Then to whom does the ordinance belong?

A man having sexual relations with his father's wife and claiming to be a Christian (1 Cor. 5:1) should not be allowed to participate in the Lord's Supper. But if the ordinance belongs to the individual, then who can stop such a person? If the church has no authority to admit or dismiss from the table, then even such a man as this must be allowed to participate. It is possible that such a man or even worse is allowed to partake of the Lord's Supper in locations where the ordinance is viewed as an individual matter. Paul, however, clearly indicates that the church at Corinth is not to even eat with such a one as this. The local church must guard the integrity of the ordinance.

While maintaining the integrity of the ordinance belongs to the church, this does not eliminate personal responsibility. A person living in open sin would in fact be guilty of partaking unworthily if he did so, but the church also would be responsible for knowingly associating with such a one. Notice that Paul admonishes the church at Corinth because they "have become arrogant" (1 Cor 5:2), and

Paul states to the church that their "boasting is not good" (1 Cor. 5:6). Thus, any person who should be placed under church discipline or excluded from church membership also must be excluded from the Lord's Supper by the church. This would include those who are not believers, those who have not been properly baptized, and those who are living in public sin.

THE ELEMENTS OF THE SUPPER

The Lord's Supper was instituted after celebrating the Passover Feast, and the elements used were unleavened bread and juice of the vine. The question emerges, Must one use wafers and grape juice to properly celebrate the Lord's Supper? The answer to that question is no. The little square wafers and plastic cups of grape juice often used during the Lord's Supper do an injustice to proper symbolism if the administrator neglects taking the proper time to discuss such matters. In addition, even unleavened bread and grape juice or wine may not be available in some cultures. Because of this, the elements used do not invalidate the Lord's Supper; however, wisdom suggests that one should seek to match the elements as closely as possible.

Concerning the bread, wisdom also suggests that unleavened bread should be used. In 1 Corinthians 5:7–8 Paul uses leaven to represent sin or ungodliness and states that leaven should be removed.[6] For the sake of proper symbolism and following the example of Christ (we know Christ used unleavened bread because of Passover requirements), unleavened bread is preferable where possible.[7] Paul also indicates that the breaking of the bread and the one loaf bears important symbolism. In today's larger churches baking a loaf large enough for all to partake is not feasible; however, the administrator of the ordinance can have one whole loaf at the front that is symbolically broken to demonstrate the breaking of Christ's body. In addition, 1 Corinthians 10:17 stresses the importance of one loaf symbolizing the one body of the church. As will be discussed later, the analogy of the one bread can be used to restrict participants to local church members only. One unleavened loaf broken in front of the congregation with an appropriate prayer of thanksgiv-

---

6. One may object that in Matthew 13:33 Jesus said, "The kingdom of heaven is like leaven, which a woman took and hid in three pecks of flour until it was all leavened." The positive use of leaven here stresses its permeating feature, but this is the exception and not the general use for leaven, which usually symbolizes sin. For example, see Exodus 12:15, 19; 13:7; Matthew 16:6, 11; Mark 8:15; Luke 12:1; 1 Corinthians 5:6; and Galatians 5:9.

7. In earliest times, the bread was baked between clay or stone bread prints containing symbols like a lamb, the cross, or the letters AO from "I am the Alpha and Omega." Around the ninth century division arose over this issue and by the eleventh century the East used leavened bread while the west used unleavened bread. For early bread prints, one may visit the Museum at the Southern Baptist Theological Seminary in Louisville, Kentucky. For more information, see Dale Moody, *A Word of Truth* (Grand Rapids: Eerdmans, 1981), 471–72.

ing and time of meditation and self-examination is the best way to celebrate the Lord's Supper.

To match the original as closely as possible, one would have to use wine as the other element.[8] However, the most important fact about the second element is that it be juice from the vine. Wisdom suggests that in American society wine should not be used because it has been the subject of strenuous debate and such debates need not occupy the mind during the celebration of the Supper.[9] In Mark 14:25 and Luke 22:18 Christ said he would not partake of the "fruit of the vine" from that time until the kingdom of God comes. Thus fruit of the vine should serve as the element. Grape juice works well for this element as the color leads the mind to reflect on the blood of Christ shed for us. For additional emphasis, the administrator could take the extra step of pouring the juice into a few of the cups explaining that this represents the pouring out of Christ's blood.

The most controversial debate concerning the ordinance has focused on the presence of Christ.[10] Many believe that Baptists have no position on the presence of Christ at the Lord's Supper. In fact, some in recent times have criticized the denomination for "mere symbolism" with regard to the ordinances.[11] This author contends that Baptists have in their past demonstrated a proper scriptural understanding of the presence of Christ at the Lord's Supper. This understanding is neither mere symbolism nor a meaningless memorial. Baptists understand that Christ is omnipresent and do not deny the spiritual presence of Christ at the Lord's Supper or anywhere else. Baptists also understand that improperly taking the ordinance results in judgment, which can affect humans physically (see 1 Cor. 11:27–30). Baptists believe that a symbolic celebration that focuses on the sacrifice

---

8. Millard Erickson comments, "If their chief concern is duplication of the original meal, they will use the unleavened bread of the traditional Passover and the wine, probably diluted with anywhere from one to twenty parts of water for every part of wine." See Millard Erickson, *Christian Doctrine* (Grand Rapids: Baker, 1998), 367.

9. Dale Moody states that "there was also one consecrated cup or chalice of wine until a rural preacher in Ohio invented the tots and trays in 1893. With the discovery of a process by which unfermented grape juice could be preserved there was a shift from the wine also. The temperance movement helped this transition" (*The Word of Truth*, 472). There is nothing sinful about the use of wine for the ordinance, but it should be avoided if its use distracts from the meaning of the Lord's Supper.

10. This debate can be traced back at least to Ratramnus and Radbertus. Radbertus wrote first supporting the view of transubstantiation. Shortly after, Ratramnus responded in A.D. 843 at the request of Charles the Bald, King of the Franks, and refuted the claim that the elements changed substantively. See Pascasius Radbertus, *De Corpore et Sanguine Domini* (Turnholti: Typographi Brepols, 1969); and Ratramnus, *De Corpore et Sanguine Domini* (London: North-Holland, 1974).

11. See, for example, Elizabeth Newman, "The Lord's Supper: Might Baptists Accept a Theory of Real Presence?" in *Baptist Sacramentalism* (Waynesboro, GA: Paternoster Press, 2003), 211–27; and Stanley Fowler, *More Than a Symbol: The British Baptist Recovery of Baptismal Sacramentalism* (Waynesboro, GA: Paternoster Press, 2002).

Christ made on the cross, the fellowship of the community, and the future coming of our Savior is meaningful to the believer and can result in spiritual maturity. However, Baptists do not believe in a physical presence of Christ. Baptists do not believe that grace is infused by the partaking of the bread or juice. Baptists do not believe that a mystical, unexplainable occurrence happens during the Lord's Supper. This section will now demonstrate that Baptists draw this position directly from Scripture. In order to systematically explain Baptist beliefs, the discussion will begin by refuting historic errors on the presence of the Lord before establishing the scriptural foundation for Baptist beliefs.

TRANSUBSTANTIATION

The doctrine known as transubstantiation simply means "the bread and wine *actually become* the body and blood of Christ. This happens at the moment the priest says, 'This is my body' during the celebration of the mass."[12] Cyril of Jerusalem (c. A.D. 315–386) in his *Catecheses* first put forth this doctrine.[13] One of the most famous advocates of this doctrine, Thomas Aquinas, stated concerning the change in the elements, "This is done by divine power in this sacrament; for the whole substance of the bread and wine is changed into the whole substance of the body and blood of Christ. Hence this is not a formal but a substantial conversion which is not due to any natural movement; it therefore merits a name of its own, and may be called *transubstantiation*."[14]

Advocates note two primary Scripture passages in support of this view. First, "this is My body" (Matt. 26:26) is taken to mean that the bread literally becomes the body of Christ. In addition, "this is My blood" (Matt. 26:28) is taken to mean that the drink literally becomes the blood of Christ. Second, proponents literally interpret John 6:53–56, "Jesus said to them, 'Truly, truly, I say to you, unless you eat the flesh of the Son of Man and drink His blood, you have no life in yourselves. He who eats My flesh and drinks My blood has eternal life, and I will raise him up

---

12. Wayne Grudem, *Systematic Theology* (Grand Rapids: Zondervan, 1994), 990. The terminology at which the elements are said to immediately change, "This is my body," in the Latin is *"Hoc est Corpus Meum."* One theory of the origination of the term "hocus-pocus" links it back to a corruption "by way of ridiculous imitation of the priests of the Church of Rome in their trick of Transubstantiation." For further discussion, see J. A. Simpson and E. S. C. Weiner, *The Oxford English Dictionary* (Oxford: Clarendon Press, 1989), 281.

13. J. H. Srawley stated, "The conception of a 'conversion' of the elements into the body and blood of Christ was probably derived by Ambrose . . . from Greek sources. It appears for the first time (apart from some anticipations of it in Gnostic writers) in the *Catecheses* of Cyril of Jerusalem, and was elaborated with a special theory of his own by Gregory of Nyssa." Introduction to *St. Ambrose "On the Mysteries" and the Treatise on the Sacraments by an Unknown Author*, trans. T. Thompson, ed. J. H. Srawley (New York: Macmillan, 1919), 34–35.

14. Thomas Aquinas, *The Blessed Sacrament and the Mass*, trans. F. O'Neill (Maryland: Newman Press, 1955), 20.

on the last day. For My flesh is true food, and My blood is true drink. He who eats My flesh and drinks My blood abides in Me, and I in him.'"[15] With the most literal understanding possible of these verses, transubstantiation finds its scriptural background.

The Baptist response to Matthew 26 follows along the lines of the Swiss Reformer, Huldrych Zwingli in saying that the Lord spoke figuratively and neither indicated that the bread he broke in initiating the Lord's Supper was his body nor was the drink his blood. By taking these verses symbolically, they present no problem to Baptists. More will be said on these verses at a later time.

The John 6 passage is explained by Baptists in multiple ways. First, Baptists reject the idea that this passage has anything to do with the Lord's Supper. A literal interpretation leads one to believe that you must participate in the Lord's Supper for salvation. Since salvation is by grace through faith, participation in the Lord's Supper cannot be added. The "eating" mentioned here means "believing." Second, the word for "flesh" here is *sarx* and in the discussion of the Lord's Supper, a different word is used, *soma* (body).[16] This indicates that the Lord did not intend a direct correlation of these passages. Third, at the time of this saying, the Lord's Supper had not been instituted. If Jesus spoke of the Lord's Supper, then his words would have had no meaning. Jesus spoke symbolically in this instance just as he did when he said, "This is My body."[17]

Although more scriptural proofs could be provided as to why Baptists reject transubstantiation, a comment from 1 Corinthians 11:20–21 should be sufficient. Paul states, "Therefore when you meet together, it is not to eat the Lord's Supper, for in your eating each one takes his own supper first; and one is hungry and another is drunk." Paul criticizes the church at Corinth for abusing the Lord's Supper with the result of a person being drunk. The question must arise, How would someone become drunk from drinking the wine at the Lord's Supper if the wine became the blood of Christ? Should a priest speak the magical words and the wine be changed, could someone drink all he wanted without becoming drunk? No. The reason is that no change in the elements occurs. This alone should be evidence enough to dismiss the claims of transubstantiation. Additional arguments that could be levied against this will be applied to the next error.

15. For an example of the uses of these two passages as support, see ibid., 15. Also using John 6, Ludwig Ott states, "The body and the blood of Christ together with His soul and His divinity and the whole of Christ are truly present in the Eucharist." See Ludwig Ott, *Fundamentals of Catholic Dogma* (St. Louis: B. Herder, 1954), 382.

16. See Matthew 26:26; Mark 14:22; Luke 22:19; 1 Corinthians 10:16; 11:24, 27.

17. D. A. Carson states concerning John 6:49–58, "the remainder of the discourse resorts to metaphor." For further discussion, see D. A. Carson, *The Gospel According to John*, The Pillar New Testament Commentary (Grand Rapids: Eerdmans, 1991), 294–99.

CONSUBSTANTIATION

Consubstantiation differs slightly from transubstantiation by contending that the bread and the wine contain the body and blood of the Lord but the elements themselves are not substantively changed. Martin Luther introduced this doctrine almost fifteen hundred years after Christ instituted the Supper. Luther rejected the Catholic doctrine when he wrote concerning transubstantiation, "When I learned later what church it was that had decreed this, namely the Thomistic—that is, the Aristotelian church—I grew bolder, and after floating in a sea of doubt, I at last found rest for my conscience in the above view, namely, that it is real bread and real wine, in which Christ's real flesh and real blood are present in no other way and to no less a degree than the others assert them to be under their accidents."[18] In describing this change, Luther said, "The bread is changed into his true natural body and the wine into his natural true blood."[19]

Luther stated concerning those who disagreed with his view, "Let them go, therefore, and let us adhere to the words as they read: that the body of Christ is present in the bread and that his blood is truly present in the wine. This does not mean that he is not present in other places also with his body and blood, for in believing hearts he is completely present with his body and blood."[20] From this quote, it is evident that Luther attributed the quality of ubiquity to the body and blood of Christ in conjunction with his literal understanding of "this is My body."

Baptists must also reject this view for scriptural reasons. Consubstantiation creates a Christological problem.[21] Because Luther upheld a physical presence in the Lord's Supper, he supported the ubiquity of the divine attributes. If the divine attribute of omnipresence allowed Christ's body to be present at all administrations of the Lord's Supper, then the two natures of Christ are no longer distinguishable. The natures have merged to create a *tertium quid* rather than a savior who is unconfusedly yet indivisibly fully divine and fully human.[22] Baptists infer

---

18. Martin Luther, "The Babylonian Captivity of the Church," in *Martin Luther's Basic Theological Writings*, ed. Timothy Lull (Minneapolis: Fortress, 1989), 285.

19. Martin Luther, "The Sacrament of the Body and Blood of Christ—Against the Fanatics," in Lull, *Martin Luther's Basic Theological Writings*, 252.

20. Ibid., 325. For a discussion of the debate between Luther and Zwingli over this issue, see Timothy George, *Theology of the Reformers* (Nashville: Broadman & Holman, 1988), 144–58.

21. Huldrych Zwingli, "On the Lord's Supper," in *Zwingli and Bullinger: Library of Christian Classics*, trans. G. W. Bromiley (Philadelphia: Westminster Press, 1953), 14:183.

22. The Chalcedonian formulation states, "Therefore, following the holy fathers, we all with one accord teach men to acknowledge one and the same Son, our Lord Jesus Christ, at once complete in Godhead and complete in manhood, truly God and truly man, consisting also of a reasonable soul and body; of one substance (*homoousios*) with the Father as regards His Godhead, and at the same time as regards His manhood; like us in all respects apart from sin; as regards His Godhead, begotten of the Father before the ages, but yet as regards his manhood begotten, for us men and for our salvation, of Mary the virgin, the Godbearer (*theotokos*); one and the

that without divine intervention the same physical elements cannot be in two locations at the same time. Currently Jesus Christ's body resides at the right hand of
the Father.[23] For support of this position, those holding to consubstantiation note
Matthew 28:20, "I am with you always, even to the end of the age." However, this
verse clearly applies to the spiritual presence of Christ living within believers and
not to a physical presence at the Lord's Supper or otherwise.

A second problem arises with the anticipated return of Christ. Paul states in
1 Corinthians 11:26, "For as often as you eat this bread and drink the cup, you
proclaim the Lord's death until He comes." If Christ is literally present in the
Supper, then has he not already come? In Acts 1:11 the angels say, "This Jesus,
who has been taken up from you into heaven, will come in just the same way as
you have watched Him go into heaven." If Christ is literally present in the Supper,
then has he come in like manner? Psalm 110:1 says, "The LORD says to my Lord:
'Sit at My right hand, Until I make Your enemies a footstool for Your feet.'" Again,
in Matthew 26:64, "Jesus said to him, 'You have said it yourself; nevertheless I
tell you, hereafter you will see the Son of Man sitting at the right hand of Power,
and coming on the clouds of heaven.'" If Christ is literally present in the Supper,
then how can he be at the Father's right hand, and has the second coming already
occurred?

A third problem has been well stated by a Baptist theologian of yesteryear. J. M.
Pendleton wrote, "Both doctrines presuppose the presence of the Savior's body
in different places at the same time—a notion in conflict with our fundamental
conception of material substances. Some Protestants even insist that Consubstantiation is more objectionable than Transubstantiation, so far as the interpretation
of the Savior's language is concerned; for while the latter makes him say literally,
'This is my body,' the former makes him say, 'This contains my body.'"[24] Although

---

same Christ, Son, Lord, Only begotten, recognized in two natures, without confusion, without change, without division, without separation; the distinction of natures being in no way
annulled by the union but rather the characteristics of each nature being preserved and coming
together to form one person and subsistence (*hypostasis*), not as parted or separated into two
persons but one and the same Son and Only Begotten God the Word, Lord Jesus Christ; even
as the prophets from earliest times spoke of Him, and our Lord Jesus Christ Himself taught us
and decreed of the fathers as handed down to us."

23. Mark 16:19 states, "So then, when the Lord Jesus had spoken to them, He was received up into
heaven and sat down at the right hand of God." We are also told in Acts 7:55–56 that Stephen
literally saw him: "But being full of the Holy Spirit, he gazed intently into heaven and saw the
glory of God, and Jesus standing at the right hand of God; and he said, 'Behold, I see the heavens opened up and the Son of Man standing at the right hand of God.'"

24. James Madison Pendleton, "[Thoughts on] the Lord's Supper: Number 5," *Tennessee Baptist*,
December 10, 1859. This was the second of Zwingli's two main arguments. He believed that
the ascension of Christ did away with the possibility of a literal presence of Christ's body in
the elements. Zwingli attributed omnipresence only to the divine nature of Christ and not the
human. See Zwingli, "On the Lord's Supper," 213.

Luther believes his view is a literal interpretation, no verse in the Bible ever mentions the elements "containing" the body or blood of the Lord.

Finally, an objection against both transubstantiation and consubstantiation is that if they truly contain the body and blood of our Lord, then the elements should be worshipped. Scripture nowhere indicates that the elements should be worshipped. An additional consideration is the thought of grinding the body of our Lord between our teeth when partaking of the bread results in his continual punishment or sacrifice. The New Testament never calls the Lord's Supper a sacrifice or speaks of altars, priests, or consecrations. We are told in Hebrews 7:27 that his sacrifice was offered once for all and is not a continual event. A continual chewing on the flesh of our Lord makes no sense to the logical mind relying on Scripture. Because of these objections and because proper interpretation of Scripture indicates a symbolic view of Christ's presence in the elements, Baptists reject both transubstantiation and consubstantiation.

SPIRITUAL PRESENCE

John Calvin has been credited with formulating a separate view known as the spiritual presence of Christ in the Lord's Supper. This view contends that the elements remain bread and juice, and this view presents a unique approach to the presence of Christ. One point of confusion is that Calvin does not clearly articulate his view due to the varied meaning of the term *substance*. Calvin's view guards against two faults. He states, "First, we should not, by too little regard for the signs, divorce them from their mysteries, to which they are so to speak attached. Secondly, we should not, by extolling them immoderately, seem to obscure somewhat the mysteries themselves."[25] While Calvin rejects a localized bodily presence in the Supper, he appears to support a spiritual feeding for the soul. He states concerning the body and blood, "They are therefore represented under bread and wine so that we may learn not only that they are ours but that they have been destined as food for our spiritual life . . . as bread nourishes, sustains, and keeps the life of our body, so Christ's body is the only food to invigorate and enliven our soul."[26]

This view has not found favor among Baptists for two reasons. First, Calvin did not clearly explain in what way Christ's spiritual presence during the Lord's Supper differs from his spiritual omnipresence. Cannot the gathering of believers with the Word preached and fervent prayer result in our souls being nourished? Is there some special offering of spiritual nourishment in the Lord's Supper, and if so, how is that not an infusion of grace?

---

25. Calvin, *Institutes of the Christian Religion*, 1364–65.
26. Ibid., 1362–63.

Second, Baptists do not deny that to eat and drink unworthily may result in physical detriment to the body because Paul clearly states so. However, no verse of Scripture clearly indicates that to eat and drink the Lord's Supper worthily results in special spiritual nourishment to the believer.

MEANINGFUL SYMBOLIC CELEBRATION

I have chosen to defend the position of a meaningful, symbolic celebration. I avoid the usual description of the Lord's Supper as a memorial because that describes only one facet of the Lord's Supper and leads to a misunderstanding. A memorial is for someone who is dead or celebrates a past event—Jesus is very much alive, and we celebrate his future coming. The Lord's Supper does look back to the cross in memorial, but it also looks around in fellowship and forward in anticipation of Christ's return. Thus, a complete understanding should characterize the Lord's Supper as a meaningful, symbolic celebration.

Matthew, Mark, and Luke all state that Christ took the bread and took the cup. These words provide the context, for while Jesus held the bread in his hands, he spoke the words, "This is My body." The words *is* or *am* coming from the *to be* verb many times means "symbolizes." Jesus said in John 10:9, "I am the door; if anyone enters through Me, he will be saved." No one argues that Jesus literally is a door. Jesus said in John 15:1, "I am the true vine, and My Father is the vinedresser." No one contends that Jesus actually is a vine. Jesus said in John 8:12, "I am the light of the world; he who follows Me will not walk in the darkness." All understand that Jesus uses an analogy here. Jesus said in John 10:14, "I am the good shepherd." All understand that an analogy is used here. Jesus also uses the term *is* to mean "represents" in multiple locations. Take for example the explanation of the wheat and the tares. Jesus explained in Matthew 13:38–39, "The field is [represents] the world; and as for the good seed these are [represent] the sons of the kingdom; and the tares are [represent] the sons of the evil one; and the enemy who sowed them is [represents] the devil." Thus, sound interpretation requires that when Jesus said, "This is My body," and "This is My blood" he meant those elements were symbolic or representative. If the elements themselves are symbols, then they cannot be the thing signified or they cease to be symbols. Thus, the body and blood of the Lord are not physically present at the Supper. The bread and juice symbolizing the body and blood of the Lord are present to create a meaningful celebration of our Savior.

A symbolic ordinance should not be difficult to understand. The other local church ordinance, baptism, also serves as a symbol. Baptism forms a public, symbolic action of an inward decision to place one's allegiance with Christ. In addition to being the public profession of faith, Romans 6:4 states, "Therefore we have been buried with Him through baptism into death, so that as Christ was raised from the dead through the glory of the Father, so we too might walk in newness of life." Baptism symbolizes the death, burial, and resurrection of Christ. The Lord's Supper symbolizes the body and blood of Christ, which he shed for mankind's deliverance.

Another support for the symbolic celebration view is that Christ's body is not continually sacrificed or harmed. Christ offered His body once for all. Hebrews 7:26–28 states, "For it was fitting for us to have such a high priest, holy, innocent, undefiled, separated from sinners and exalted above the heavens; who does not need daily, like those high priests, to offer up sacrifices, first for His own sins and then for the sins of the people, because this He did once for all when He offered up Himself. For the Law appoints men as high priests who are weak, but the word of the oath, which came after the Law, appoints a Son, made perfect forever." The Lord's Supper then symbolically celebrates the once-for-all sacrifice of Jesus on the cross.

THANKSGIVING

Many errors have resulted from misunderstanding Matthew 26:26, "While they were eating, Jesus took some bread, and after a blessing, He broke it and gave it to the disciples." Many have taken this verse to mean the administrator should "bless" the elements of the Lord's Supper.[27] At the time of this blessing, some believe the elements are transformed into Christ's body and blood. A complete look at the ordinance takes into account Matthew 26:27; Mark 14:23; Luke 22:19; and 1 Corinthians 11:24, which all state that Christ "gave thanks." The administrator should not confuse Romish dogma for practice in the Baptist church by asking for God to "bless" the ordinances or attempting to "bless" the ordinances himself; however, the administrator should "give thanks" to God for the provision of Christ. The prayer offered at that time should be a short prayer of thanksgiving to God and have no part in a magical transformation of the elements.

LOOKING BACK IN REMEMBRANCE

The past significance focuses on two areas: covenant and remembrance. Matthew 26:28; Mark 14:24; Luke 22:20; and 1 Corinthians 11:25 all mention the

---

27. Some may be confused by 1 Corinthians 10:16: "Is not the cup of blessing which we bless a sharing in the blood of Christ?" In the original languages the word translated bless is *eulogia* and not the usual word *makarios*. *Eulogia* combines the prefix *eu* meaning "good" with the root *logia* meaning "a word." In other verses this construction indicates adoration. First Peter 1:3 states, "Blessed be the God and Father of our Lord Jesus Christ." Thus *eulogia* is best understood as believers drinking a cup of God's "good word" and sharing in the proclaiming of a "good word" about Christ. There is no indication in these verses of blessing the elements at the Lord's Supper.

covenant. Matthew and Mark state, "This is My blood of the covenant, which is poured out." Luke and 1 Corinthians indicate that blood symbolizes the "new covenant." Thus, this covenant meal symbolizes the commitment of the believers to continue living for Jesus Christ.

Scripture indicates in Luke 22:19 and in 1 Corinthians 11:24 that participants should remember past sacrifices by saying, "Do this in remembrance of Me." The word used for remembrance is *anamnesis* and is more significant than the word for "memorial."[28] Such a strong remembrance should bring many sights to the mind's eye. For one, believers must remember the great suffering that the Lord endured for our sakes. Jesus was scourged, spat upon, "crowned" with a crown of thorns, humiliated, and hung upon a cross. As the bread is broken and the juice is poured out, believers should remember the suffering Christ endured for sinners, which should provoke thoughts of God's love. To see the height and depth and breadth of the love of God, one must look to the death of Christ at Calvary. God had but one Son, and he gave him up at Calvary. Thoughts concerning the love of God in sending his Son to die for sinners should remind participants of the justice demanded by God. God's justice demanded that he spare not his own Son to deliver mankind. It was the sinfulness of mankind that demanded the ultimate sacrifice. In examining ourselves before participation in the Lord's Supper, each believer should be confronted again with his or her sinfulness and the high price paid by our Lord, a price established by a plan from the very beginning, a price foretold in the Passover, in the serpent being lifted up in the wilderness, and in the sacrificial system. It was a price so great and given so willingly for unworthy sinners. How great is the remembrance in the Lord's Supper.

> Alas! and did my Savior bleed
> And did my Sovereign die?
> Would he devote that sacred head
> For sinners such as I?

> Was it for crimes that I had done
> He groaned upon the tree?
> Amazing pity! grace unknown!
> And love beyond degree!

---

28. Moody, *The Word of Truth*, 471. Moody notes that the use of the word for memorial, *mnemosynon*, is found in Mark 14:9. See also J. Behm, "*anamnesis*," in *Theological Dictionary of the New Testament*, ed. Gerherd Kittel (Grand Rapids: Eerdmans, 1964), 1:348–49, who says concerning 1 Corinthians 11:24, "Christians are to enact . . . the whole action of the Lord's Supper . . . not merely in such sort that they simply remember, but rather, in accordance with the active sense of [*anamnesis*].

But drops of grief can ne'er repay
The debt of love I owe:
Here, Lord, I give my self away;
'Tis all that I can do!

Refrain
At the cross, at the cross where I first saw the light,
And the burden of my heart rolled away,
It was there by faith I received my sight,
And now I am happy all the day![29]

LOOKING AROUND IN COMMUNITY

In 1 Corinthians, Paul continually focuses on the local church and community.[30] In 1 Corinthians 5:7–11, the apostle stresses that it matters *who* partakes of the Lord's Supper. The Supper is not an individual ordinance but an ordinance that must be guarded by excluding the unworthy. In 1 Corinthians 10:17, Paul states, "Since there is one bread, we who are many are one body; for we all partake of the one bread." The emphasis on the unity of the local church and the fellowship contained therein should not be overlooked in this passage as it alludes to the coming discussion in 1 Corinthians 11:29. In 1 Corinthians 11:33, Paul states, "So then, my brethren, when you come together to eat, wait for one another." Here Paul criticizes the fact that the Corinthians did not wait for one another and were disorderly in partaking of the Lord's Supper. This verse indicates that newer techniques such as allowing each one to take the Supper whenever he or she is ready are not wise. Although admirable intent lies behind allowing families to come forward together and partake of the Supper, perhaps the practice fails to understand the communal nature of the Lord's Supper.[31]

One verse potentially addressing community is 1 Corinthians 11:29. Paul states, "For he who eats and drinks, eats and drinks judgment to himself if he does not judge the body rightly." But what does "not judging the body rightly" mean? Gordon Fee puts forth the position that the "body" refers to the "church."[32] Fee states,

---

29. Isaac Watts, "At the Cross" (1707); refrain by Ralph E. Hudson (1885).
30. This principle also can be seen in the Second London Confession, which, among other things, states that the Lord's Supper is to be "a bond and pledge of their communion with him [Christ], and with each other."
31. The admirable intent referred to by this author is the attempt to reinforce the family as an important unit and to reinforce the fathers of those families as spiritual leaders. However, families should not partake of the Lord's Supper individually because the ordinance was given to the local church.
32. For further explanation, see Gordon Fee, *The First Epistle to the Corinthians* (Grand Rapids: Eerdmans, 1987), 558–69.

"This sentence now makes further sense of the short digression in 10:17, where Paul singled out the bread for interpretation and emphatically declared that their all partaking of the 'one loaf' served to demonstrate that they themselves were therefore bound together as 'one body.'"[33] He continues, "The rash of illnesses and deaths that have recently overtaken them is here being viewed as an expression of divine judgment on the whole community."[34] Thus, the abuse of the Lord's Supper and the lack of understanding concerning the community of believers demonstrated by some eating before others, some having too much while others had too little, and the division present resulted in judgment on the entire congregation. This passage demonstrates the importance of the community in the Lord's Supper.

The fact that the Lord's Supper is a church ordinance and contains meaning in community indicates that individual participation is not proper. Thus, the ordinance should not be celebrated at a wedding. The ordinance should not be celebrated at the home of shut-ins.[35] The ordinance should not be celebrated by portions of the church, such as youth groups or Sunday school classes. Such celebrations make the ordinance an individual ordinance and neglect its communal nature. It already has been demonstrated that the ordinance belongs to the local church. The local church is the gathered believers. The integrity of the ordinance must be maintained, and one must insist on the unity of the community celebrating the ordinance.

LOOKING FORWARD IN ANTICIPATION

Paul states in 1 Corinthians 11:26, "For as often as you eat this bread and drink the cup, you proclaim the Lord's death until He comes." The Lord's Supper is for a limited time. Once the Lord returns, Scripture indicates the Lord's Supper may no longer be celebrated. At that time, the marriage feast of the Lamb mentioned in Luke 14:15–24 and Revelation 19:9 will be celebrated. For the current time, believers celebrating the Lord's Supper do so in anticipation of the future coming of the Lord.

WHO SHOULD PARTICIPATE IN THE LORD'S SUPPER?

Chapter 8 in this book will present in more detail the proper participants in the Lord's Supper. However, this presentation must address briefly some issues

---

33. Ibid., 564.
34. Ibid., 565.
35. The Lord's Supper is not a private event because no "proclaiming of the Lord's death" can occur in private. Paul's statements, "when you meet together" (1 Cor. 11:20) and "so then, my brethren, when you come together to eat, wait for one another" (1 Cor. 11:33), have no meaning when the ordinance occurs in private. Such practices also make the ordinance an individual event and not a local church ordinance.

regarding those who should participate and will reflect a slightly different opinion than that supported in the following chapter. This discussion will be divided into two separate categories. First, the proper recipients will be discussed. Second, the proper administrator will be discussed. I will contend that the proper recipient must be a person who could be accepted into the membership of that Baptist church, but participation does not have to be restricted to the members on the roll of a particular local church. The administrator should be a person recognized as an example by the local church. Thus, ordination is not required to administrate the ordinance, but wisdom dictates that the pastor or other church officers should be the normal administrators of the ordinance.

Before beginning this discussion, a definition of terminology must be presented. No consistent terminology to discuss this issue has been used throughout history. Communion has been discussed in three primary categories. The first category is that of close Communion. This also has been known as closed, strict, and restricted Communion.[36] Close Communion for the current discussion will mean that only members of a particular local church are allowed to participate in Communion. Christians of similar beliefs belonging to other churches or members of other denominations are not allowed to partake in communion.[37] The second category is transient Communion.[38] This practice also has been referred to as "denominational Communion" or "closed intercommunion."[39] This chapter will use "transient Communion" to refer to that view that allows non-church members to partake in Communion on the condition of like faith and practice. Such a per-

36. Pendleton used *close* in *Three Reasons Why I Am a Baptist with a Fourth Added on Communion* (Nashville: Graves, Marks, and Co., 1857), 199. Edward Hiscox used *close* but acknowledged the terms "strict or restricted" in *The New Directory for Baptist Churches* (Philadelphia: Judson Press, 1894), 448. W. T. Conner used "close" in *Christian Doctrine* (Nashville: Broadman Press, 1937), 289. J. R. Graves used the terms "strict or restricted" Communion in *Intercommunion: Inconsistent, Unscriptural and Productive of Evil* (Memphis: Baptist Book House, 1881), 10, 14. J. L. Dagg used the term "strict," in *Manual of Church Order* (Charleston, SC: Southern Baptist Publication Society, 1858; reprint, Harrisonburg: Gano Books, 1990), 225. Among current scholarship, H. Leon McBeth used the term "closed" in *The Baptist Heritage: Four Centuries of Baptist Witness* (Nashville: Broadman Press, 1987), 81, and Slaydon Yarbrough, *Southern Baptists: A Historical, Ecclesiological, and Theological Heritage of a Confessional People* (Nashville: Fields, 2000), 109, related the terms *close* and *closed*, stating that they both mean "only members of the particular congregation are allowed to partake." A new term, *consistent Communion*, has been proposed by Nathan Finn in a recent article titled, "Baptism as a Prerequisite to the Lord's Supper," which is available at http://www.baptisttheology.org.

37. This author recognizes that not all authors have used this term to signify the closest form of Communion. For example, McBeth left open the possibility of intercommunion among Baptist churches (denominational or transient Communion). He defined closed Communion as "meaning that only those who had received believer's baptism by immersion might join in the supper" (McBeth, *The Baptist Heritage*, 81).

38. Dagg, *Manual of Church Order*, 214, used "transient communion."

39. Graves, *Intercommunion*, 11, used "denominational communion." Yarbrough, *Southern Baptists*, 110, used "closed intercommunion."

son should be one who could be accepted into that particular church's membership. The third category is open Communion.[40] This type of Communion allows any Christian to partake in Communion because it belongs to Christ and is thus open to all children of God. This practice also has been referred to as "mixed Communion."[41]

RECIPIENTS

BELIEVERS (OPEN COMMUNION)

At the very minimum, almost every Baptist church restricts the Lord's Supper to believers. Although a complete understanding of the Lord's Supper cannot be drawn from the Passover, a correlation exists at this point. Exodus 12:43–45 states, "The LORD said to Moses and Aaron, 'This is the ordinance of the Passover: no foreigner is to eat of it; but every man's slave purchased with money, after you have circumcised him, then he may eat of it. A sojourner or a hired servant shall not eat of it.'" The Passover was restricted to only those for whom it had meaning—the children of Israel.[42] Likewise, the Lord's Supper is restricted to only those for whom it has meaning—believers.

The New Testament also supports believers as the proper participants in the Lord's Supper. First Corinthians 10:21 indicates that one cannot be a servant of two masters. It states, "You cannot drink the cup of the Lord and the cup of demons; you cannot partake of the table of the Lord and the table of demons." First Corinthians 11:26 discusses the proclaiming of the Lord's death by stating, "For as often as you eat this bread and drink the cup, you proclaim the Lord's death until He comes." A person who does not believe in the Lord Jesus Christ cannot proclaim his death until he comes. Lastly, in 1 Corinthians 11:33 Paul states, "So then, my brethren, when you come together to eat . . ." Paul's "brethren" can only mean believers. Thus, believers are the only proper participants in the Lord's Supper. Therefore, the administrator of the Supper should in all instances instruct those who are not believers in Christ to abstain from participation.

In addition, Paul issues strict warnings concerning the state of the believer. First Corinthians 11:27–30 states, "Therefore whoever eats the bread or drinks the cup of the Lord in an unworthy manner, shall be guilty of the body and the blood of the Lord. But a man must examine himself, and in so doing he is to eat of the

---

40. This term has been widely used. See, for example, Dagg, *Manual of Church Order*, 214; Hiscox, *The New Directory for Baptist Churches*, 447; Yarbrough, *Southern Baptists*, 110; and McBeth, *The Baptist Heritage*, 81.

41. Thomas F. Curtis, *Communion: The Distinction Between Christian and Church Fellowship and Between Communion and Its Symbols: Embracing a Review of the Arguments of Robert Hall and Baptist W. Noel in Favor of Mixed Communion* (Philadelphia: American Baptist Publication Society, 1850).

42. This would include the circumcised proselytes.

bread and drink of the cup. For he who eats and drinks, eats and drinks judgment to himself if he does not judge the body rightly. For this reason many among you are weak and sick, and a number sleep." In this statement Paul indicates that a person who properly participates in the Lord's Supper must be able to understand two things: (1) what it means to examine oneself, and (2) what it means to eat unworthily. Surely only a believer in Christ is able to understand how to examine the motives of the heart, and only a believer who seeks to follow Christ can understand what it means to eat unworthily. In addition, those groups that allow young children to participate in the Lord's Supper must be careful to ensure that these children understand what it is to examine oneself and to eat unworthily.

This view of the ordinance has been held by prominent figures like John Bunyan, Charles Spurgeon, John Hall, and John Piper. In fact, Baptists have been attributed with beginning this practice because it does not require baptism. All other denominations, including those baptizing infants, have historically believed that baptism must precede the Lord's Supper.

BAPTIZED BELIEVERS OR LIKE FAITH AND PRACTICE (TRANSIENT COMMUNION)

The majority of Baptists throughout history have held that in addition to being a believer, baptism was a prerequisite to the Lord's Supper. More specifically these Baptists believe that those participating in the Lord's Supper should be of "like faith and practice." The requirement of baptism as a prerequisite is not limited to Baptists. Pedobaptists also require baptism before participation in the Lord's Supper.[43]

Many object that a fence should not be constructed around the Lord's Table. Lack of any sort of boundaries, however, is unrealistic. There are only two real choices—restricted or wide open. The restrictions may be of varying degrees, but the two major categories are restricted—with some fencing—or wide open. If Communion is open to all, then the table is open to anyone. No fences or restrictions, if consistently practiced, would allow barbarians, infidels, Mormons, Muslims, unrepentant sinners, and perhaps even animals to the Lord's Table. Yet no one really contends for "no restrictions." All place restrictions, such as being human, being a believer, being in good standing. The restrictions that the major-

---

43. Hiscox, *The New Directory for Baptist Churches*, 456, notes the following among many others. Justin Martyr states, "This food is called by us the Eucharist, of which it is not lawful for any one to partake, but such as believe the things taught by us to be true, and have been baptized." A well-known pedobaptist, William Wall, states, "No Church ever gave the Communion to any before they were baptized. Among all the absurdities that were ever held, none ever maintained that any person should partake of Communion before he was baptized." The pedobaptist theologian John Dick states, "An uncircumcised man was not permitted to eat the Passover; and an unbaptized man should not be permitted to partake of the Eucharist."

ity of Baptists place on the Supper are: (1) believer, (2) baptism, (3) church membership, and (4) self-examination.

The reason that baptism is required finds its foundation in the New Testament. When Christ instituted the ordinance, he did so only with men who had been baptized.[44] The Great Commission of our Lord indicates that people should be made disciples, be baptized, and then learn all things (including the Supper). When Peter preached in Acts, he mentioned salvation and baptism. Salvation and baptism occurred before anyone participated in the Lord's Supper. Throughout the New Testament, there is a consistent pattern of baptism before the Lord's Supper.

This view has enemies primarily because Baptists believe that the only proper baptism is believer's baptism by immersion. Thus, this view does not allow pedobaptists to partake of the Lord's Supper. The real issue of difference between pedobaptists and Baptists is not the Lord's Supper but the doctrine of baptism.

Because Baptists firmly believe that the New Testament teaches baptism should be by immersion of believers only, they cannot allow Pedobaptists to partake of Communion. To do so would be to affirm knowingly an errant theological view. Suppose a person believed you could lose your salvation, that baptism is essential to salvation, or that the church should not be made up of believers. Such a person would not be allowed to join a Baptist church because he does not agree with them, and unless two agree they cannot walk together. Should this person be allowed to join, it would be incumbent upon the church to begin immediate correction for improper doctrine. If the person refused to change his beliefs after being clearly shown from Scripture, then church discipline would follow and the person would not be allowed to partake of the Lord's Supper. This would be the case if a pedobaptist joined a Baptist church.

Another opposing voice can be heard from those who deny the right to allow those of "like faith and practice" to participate in the Lord's Supper. The primary advocate of this position is J. R. Graves. His work *Intercommunion: Inconsistent, Unscriptural and Productive of Evil* presents the position that Baptists should not participate in transient Communion.[45] Other Baptist theologians of that time period, such as J. M. Pendleton, Edward Hiscox, and John Dagg, believed that

---

44. John 4:1–2 states, "Therefore when the Lord knew that the Pharisees had heard that Jesus was making and baptizing more disciples than John (although Jesus Himself was not baptizing, but His disciples were . . .)." Although Scripture does not record the baptism of the disciples, they would not have been baptizing without having first been baptized themselves.

45. Graves wrote at least three books on the Lord's Supper. His most detailed work is *Intercommunion*. His other works include: *The Lord's Supper: A Church Ordinance, and So Observed by the Apostolic Churches* (Texarkana, AR-TX: Baptist Sunday School Committee, 1881); and *What Is It to Eat and Drink Unworthily?* (Texarkana, AR-TX: Baptist Sunday School Board, 1881).

transient Communion caused no harm but could not be insisted upon. For any individual to insist upon the right to participate would deny the autonomy of the local church.[46] Because each church is autonomous and has the responsibility to maintain the integrity of the ordinance, no individual can demand inclusion. However, Pendleton, Hiscox, and Dagg believed that out of courtesy people of "like faith and practice" should be included.

The primary scriptural battleground over this is Paul's trip to Troas. Acts 20:6–8 says, "We sailed from Philippi after the days of Unleavened Bread, and came to them at Troas within five days; and there we stayed seven days. On the first day of the week, when we were gathered together to break bread, Paul began talking to them, intending to leave the next day, and he prolonged his message until midnight. There were many lamps in the upper room where we were gathered together." There are multiple questions concerning this passage. First, was there a church at Troas? Second, do the verses above describe the Lord's Supper? If the answer to both of those questions is yes, then the Bible presents a case for transient Communion. Some may suggest that Paul was an apostle and thus, this does not establish policy; however, this passage in Acts is a "we" passage, indicating that Luke also participated. The second question is perhaps the easiest to answer. On the first day of the week they gathered to "break bread." Most commentators indicate that this is in fact the Lord's Supper.[47]

J. R. Graves chose to deny that Troas was a church and, by correlation, that Acts 20:7 refers to the Lord's Supper, thus eliminating this as a case of transient Communion. Those wishing to support that a church did exist at Troas note Acts 16:8–11: "and passing by Mysia, they came down to Troas. A vision appeared to Paul in the night: a man of Macedonia was standing and appealing to him, and saying, 'Come over to Macedonia and help us.' When he had seen the vision, immediately we sought to go into Macedonia, concluding that God had called us to preach the gospel to them. So putting out to sea from Troas . . ." It appears that Paul and his companions visited Troas before Acts 20. One could logically conclude that Paul preached and converts remained. Upon Paul's return he gathered with these converts to celebrate the Lord's Supper and established the only scriptural case of transient Communion.

46. See Pendleton's letter to J. J. D. Renfroe, where he disagrees with Graves over this issue. Pendleton also responds to Graves's argument that Troas is not a church by saying that if Troas is not a church because the word is never mentioned in connection to the location, then the same could be said of Berea. This letter can be found in *Selected Writings of James Madison Pendleton*, ed. Thomas White (Paris, AR: Baptist Standard Bearer, 2006), 407–10.

47. John Calvin, *Commentary on the Acts of the Apostles* (Grand Rapids: Baker, 1999), 235–36; John MacArthur, *Acts 13–28* (Chicago: Moody, 1996), 203; F. F. Bruce, *The Book of Acts* (Grand Rapids: Eerdmans, 1998), 384; and Simon Kistemaker, *Acts*, New Testament Commentary (Grand Rapids: Baker, 1990), 716.

MEMBERS OF THE CONGREGATION (CLOSE COMMUNION)

J. R. Graves and others who believe like him hold that the integrity of the Lord's Supper cannot be maintained without insisting upon the closest form of Communion—only members of that local church can participate. In order to do this, they must deny that Troas was a legitimate church. Graves does this by claiming that Paul immediately upon his arrival at Troas in Acts 16 received the Macedonian call and left without establishing a church or any converts to Christ. Thus, in Acts 20 no intercommunion or transient Communion occurred. After establishing this fact, close Communion can clearly establish itself as the most consistent practice and the most assured of maintaining the integrity of the Lord's Supper.

Close Communion can all but ensure the integrity of the Lord's Supper because only members of that local church are allowed to participate. This understanding has the easiest time adhering to Paul's warnings in 1 Corinthians concerning the oneness of the body and not eating with a person such as the man mentioned in 1 Corinthians 5. Graves points out that any other form of Communion risks allowing members of other churches currently under discipline to participate in the Lord's Supper. Such action renders meaningless the discipline of a sister church.

While I believe that close Communion is the most consistent form and empathize with that practice, the evidence in Acts 20 concerning Troas indicates that transient Communion may be allowed for those of "like faith and practice." Transient Communion could allow one church to unknowingly commune with a person who is under the discipline of another church. But then close Communion could result in a guest preacher who is qualified to fill the pulpit not being allowed to partake of Communion because he is not a member of that congregation.[48] Such courtesy between churches has historic precedence among Baptists. Baptists continually accept the ordaining of one church as sufficient for other churches. Churches should maintain that believers baptized by immersion who are church members in good standing can participate in the Lord's Supper of a Baptist church; however, individuals must not demand participation as a right. Because of autonomy, each local church must decide whether "like faith and practice" or only those on the church roll may participate in the Lord's Supper.

THE ADMINISTRATOR

The administrator should be a person recognized as an example by the local church. Ordination is not required to administrate the ordinance, but wisdom dictates that the pastor or other church officers should be the normal administrators of the ordinance.

---

48. Not that this one example should cause one to choose another view. There is no theological problem with a church deciding to refuse the Lord's Supper to a visiting preacher. If the preacher demanded participation, that would jeopardize the autonomy of the local church.

In addition to the primary administrator, generally the pastor of the church, the deacons usually serve the bread and the juice to the congregation. This practice is not mandated by Scripture but has traditionally occurred because of Acts 6. Seven men of good report were chosen out from among the congregation to serve the tables. While the meaning of Acts 6 was broader than the Lord's Supper, many Baptist churches have established the practice of the deacons serving at the Lord's Supper to reflect this passage. In addition, this continually reinforces the role of the deacons as servants of the congregation and not rulers over the congregation.

THE FREQUENCY OF THE LORD'S SUPPER

The Bible never specifically addresses how often the Lord's Supper should be observed. Acts 20:7 indicates that they broke bread on the first day of the week. Acts 2:42 states, "They were continually devoting themselves to the apostles' teaching and to fellowship, to the breaking of bread and to prayer." This verse gives no specific time but indicates the continual practice of breaking of bread. Acts 2:46 states, "Day by day continuing with one mind in the temple, and breaking bread from house to house, they were taking their meals together with gladness and sincerity of heart." This verse seems to indicate they participated in the breaking of bread daily. From the *Didache* 14:1 one can find support for weekly observance of the Lord's Supper. The Bible never clearly states how often the Lord's Supper should be observed.

Several in history have supported the weekly observance of the Lord's Supper, such as Calvin, Wesley, and Spurgeon. Many Baptists observe the Lord's Supper quarterly or monthly because a weekly observance might make it a meaningless ritual. However, many Baptist churches have relegated the ordinance to a Sunday night or tack it on at the end of a service. Either of these practices diminishes the importance of the Lord's Supper. The ordinance deserves frequent practice with the exact timing to be determined by the local church; however, each practice should be meaningful and explained as clearly as possible.

CONCLUSION

Greek legend tells that whenever mariners passed through the Strait of Messina, they dealt with two horrific obstacles. On one side of the strait, Scylla, a frightful monster with twelve feet and six heads, each with three rows of teeth, lay in wait to snatch sailors off ships that came too close to the smooth, sheer rock from which she preyed. On the other side of the strait, Charbdis, a whirlpool where the sea "forever spouted and roared and the furious waves mounting up touched the very sky," lay ready to swallow up whole ships if they came too close.[49] Only sailors like Jason of Argon, Odysseus, and Aeneas, who had help from gods, were able to make it through—and even Odysseus lost six soldiers to the various heads of the Scylla. The legendary feelings experienced by mariners who knew this daunting task lay before them is similar to that of the Baptist theologian seeking to present the theology of the Lord's Supper. On one side lay the Catholic view of infusion of grace and change of the elements, the Lutheran view of consubstantiation, and the ill-defined mystical view of John Calvin. On the other side exists a "mere symbol" or a "meaningless symbol" that undermines the importance of the Lord's Supper. The Baptist theologian must properly navigate this strait and present a view that results in a meaningful, symbolic celebration barren of needless mystical infusions. Such a meaningful celebration will encourage the believer to contemplate his sinfulness and our great and gracious God.

> And can it be that I should gain
> An interest in the Savior's blood?
> Died He for me, who caused His pain—
> For me, who Him to death pursued?
> Amazing love! how can it be,
> That Thou, my God, shouldst die for me?[50]

---

49. Edith Hamilton, *Mythology: Timeless Tales of Gods and Heroes* (New York: Penguin Books, 1982), 127.
50. Charles Wesley, "And Can It Be That I Should Gain?" (1738).

8

Fencing the Table

THE LORD'S SUPPER, ITS PARTICIPANTS, AND ITS RELATIONSHIP TO CHURCH DISCIPLINE

EMIR F. CANER

RADICALLY OPEN COMMUNION

In the spring of 2004, the General Conference of the United Methodist Church, the top policy-making body of the denomination that meets every four years, gathered in Pittsburgh, Pennsylvania, in order to revise the official church handbook (*The Book of Discipline of the United Methodist Church*) and adopt resolutions that speak to current affairs.[1] The recently implemented ecumenical theme, "Open hearts. Open minds. Open doors." took center stage once again, this time over the issue of Communion. In particular, questions were raised as to who should participate in the Eucharist and who should be considered worthy. The document, affirmed by the overwhelming majority of the more than one thousand delegates, asserted, "The church is to consciously identify and seek out those who feel unwelcome, even excluded, from its congregations, and to invite them to become part of the body of Christ and join in its celebrations of Holy Communion."[2] Just a few weeks after its adoption, United Methodist pastor Rev. Dr. Harvey C. Martz expanded upon the new statement, saying, "Today, at this table, Jesus does the same thing; he eats with Democrats, Republicans, Libertarians, Independents, former Baptists, former Catholics, gays and straights, people who are pro life and people who are pro choice. Christ welcomes everyone. This is our United Methodist belief and even in our most heated debates in our General Conference three

---

1. *The Book of Discipline of the United Methodist Church* (Nashville: Abingdon Press, 2005).
2. The General Board of Discipleship, "This Holy Mystery: A United Methodist Understanding of Holy Communion" (Nashville: United Methodist Publishing House, 2004), 34, available from GBOD Web site, at http://www.gbod.org/worship/thisholymystery/default.html (accessed September 28, 2006).

weeks ago, no one was ever turned away from Christ's table because of their opinions and beliefs and no one will be."[3]

With such progressive statements, one can easily see why the term "open communion" has lost any historical significance or meaning. The term, once generally equated as accepting all who profess faith in Jesus Christ to the Supper, now largely discards even this minimal requirement. Indeed, *The Book of Discipline of the United Methodist Church* adds a radically new flavor upon the chronological sequence of becoming a member of their denomination.[4] It states, "The United Methodist Church acknowledges that all persons are of sacred worth. All persons without regard to race, color, national origin, status, or economic condition, shall be eligible to attend its worship services, participate in its programs, receive the sacraments, upon baptism be admitted as baptized members, and upon taking vows declaring the Christian faith, become professing members in any local church in the connection."[5]

Yet, for all of the criticism that can and should be leveled at the United Methodist Church, our Southern Baptist Zion does not seem to fare much better when it comes to a theological understanding and meaningful participation in the Supper. The Lord's Supper is usually confined to a footnote of a church service with little time given to its meaning and even less time set aside for true introspection. Perhaps more than any other time in our history, Southern Baptists are ignorant of what makes their view of the Lord's Supper unique from other denominations and Christian bodies.

But the blame cannot be placed merely at the feet of members who disregard the importance of the Supper. Pastors must shoulder a significant portion of the blame, as they often have acted with criminal indifference toward the ordinance. Baptists have given a great deal of attention to those who wish to alter the meaning or mode of believer's baptism while ignoring the lackadaisical attitudes expressed at the Supper. Indeed, many are guilty of espousing in the Lord's Supper the same faulty hermeneutic as those whom they ardently criticize regarding baptism. Moreover, Baptist scholars also must share in the culpability for deeming the topic unworthy of our literary attention. The nearly empty shelves found at our bookstores are a glaring indictment of the lack of solid theological resources available to our people.

3. Harvey C. Martz, "Who Belongs at the Table?" (sermon preached at St. Andrew United Methodist Church, Centennial, CO, May 23, 2004). Available at http://st-andrew-umc.com/sermons/2004/052304.htm (accessed September 28, 2006).
4. *The Book of Discipline of the United Methodist Church* (Nashville: Abingdon Press, 2000).
5. United Methodist Office of Public Information, "Living Our Promise," at http://archives.umc.org/interior.asp?ptid=6&mid=9549 (accessed September 28, 2006).

A Historical Overview: Two Witnesses as the Typical Example of Strict Communion

Southern Baptists would do well to look to our forefathers on the issue and realize the importance of the Lord's Supper as a Baptist distinctive. J. M. Pendleton (1811–1891), professor of theology at Union University and pioneer of Landmarkism, wrote a book in 1857 titled *Three Reasons Why I Am a Baptist with a Fourth Reason Added, on Communion*. In this work Pendleton emphasizes the Baptist distinctives of believer's baptism, immersion as the essential mode of baptism, and congregational church government. He then adjoins the fourth reason for his embrace of the Baptists: "Baptists alone scripturally observe the Lord's Supper."[6] Here, Pendleton represents well the general view of Baptists at the time known as "closed Communion" or sometimes "strict Communion." This is generally defined as limiting admission to the Lord's Supper to those who have been born again and have subsequently received believer's baptism via immersion by a believers' church.[7] In this chapter Pendleton expounds upon his thesis, stating the following:

1. "The doctrine of Baptists has ever been, that the Lord's Supper is a Church ordinance, to be observed as a memorial of the death of Christ."
2. "Baptists, with comparatively few exceptions, have ever considered Baptism a prerequisite to the Lord's Table."
3. "Recognizing a New Testament church as composed of immersed believers, [Baptists] of necessity deny the church membership of Pedobaptists, and considering the Lord's Supper as exclusively a church ordinance, they cannot, without disloyalty to the King of Zion, invite Pedobaptists to the table of the Lord."[8]

Adding to his polemics against pedobaptists, Pendleton poignantly notes a glaring inconsistency among these men. He writes, "Their baptized infants, so called, are ineligible to their communion. It is manifest from the New Testament that the baptized had a right to commune at the Lord's Table, unless by acting unworthily of the Christian character. . . . As God has joined Baptism and the Lord's Supper together, they ought not to be divorced."[9]

6. J. M. Pendleton, *Three Reasons Why I Am a Baptist with a Fourth Reason Added, on Communion* (Nashville: Graves, Marks, and Co., 1857), 172.
7. See Mark Dever, ed., *Polity: Biblical Arguments on How to Conduct Church Life* (Washington DC: Center for Church Reform, 2001). As one author explained, "Since Baptists rejected alien immersions, even believers who received immersion at the hands of a pedobaptist minister were not baptized" (ibid., 25).
8. Pendleton, *Three Reasons Why I Am a Baptist*, 177, 178, 192.
9. Ibid., 198.

Perhaps what is lacking in today's Southern Baptist life is a Pendletonian appreciation for the true church, that is, unless one can argue that the Supper is somehow disconnected from the local body of believers as well as divorced from scriptural baptism. Yet, Pendleton's positions fell prey to the same contemporary emotional attacks that we hear today as many viewed his belief as unloving and narrow-minded. He responded,

> I am aware that the practice of Baptists, in regard to communion, is often pronounced illiberal, uncharitable, and indicative of bigotry. I answer, *that* is a spurious liberality which transcends the liberality of the New Testament, and *that* is a false charity which rejoices in anything but the truth. As to bigotry, it can have no place in the heart of that man whose supreme attachment is to the truth of God, and not to the dogmas of a sect. If, therefore, the New Testament justifies the course which Baptists pursue, they are neither illiberal, nor uncharitable, nor bigoted.[10]

Interestingly, as seen above, Pendleton's work is a response to the growing ecumenical affinity of some in the Southern Baptist Convention to an open communion. Yet the rampant inclusivism of the twenty-first century is far more advanced than its nineteenth-century counterpart. Then, as Pendleton himself points out, incipient ecumenism was met with strong resistance by most denominations. Furthermore, the ecumenism was inconsistent as "[Episcopalians would] allow Presbyterians and Methodists to come to their table, but [Presbyterians and Methodists would] not reciprocate the act."[11]

Alongside Pendleton, R. B. C. Howell, pastor of the First Baptist Church of Nashville and most definitely no friend of Landmarkism, wrote, in 1846, *The Terms of Communion at the Lord's Table*. Here, he espoused a position similar to Pendleton's, arguing that the prerequisites to the Table are repentance, faith, and baptism. In typical nineteenth-century prose, Howell titled a chapter, "We cannot unite with Pedobaptists in sacramental communion without an actual abandonment, or practical falsification of all our principles on both baptism and the Lord's Supper."[12] In this chapter, Howell's insistence upon separation between the Baptists and Pedobaptists in the Supper includes the following:

---

10. Ibid., 201.
11. Ibid., 204.
12. R. B. C. Howell, *The Terms of Communion at the Lord's Table* (Philadelphia: American Baptist Publication Society, 1846), 118. At that time, Howell was still pastor of the First Baptist Church in Richmond, Virginia.

1. "We are not at liberty to adopt any terms of communion not instituted and established by our Lord Jesus Christ."
2. "Were I, as a minister of Jesus Christ, to go to the Pedobaptist communion table, without hypocrisy, and in the exercise of a good conscience, I should, in that act, acknowledge, as we all agree that baptism is an indispensable preliminary to communion, that those who surround me, and who have only been sprinkled in infancy, have, in that ceremony, been truly baptized."
3. "Having bravely fought the battle, and, during eighteen hundred years, maintained the faith once delivered to the saints, shall we, so near the goal of all our hopes, ignobly put off our armor, and ingloriously perish in the affectionate embraces of fraternal liberalism?"[13]

Howell's argumentation, blending the historical and biblical, intertwines the paramount importance of a believers' church with the troublesome rise of ecumenism. Indeed, as the second president of the Southern Baptist Convention serving from 1851–1859, Howell devoted much of his life to advancing the convention against the two troublesome foes of Landmarkism and liberalism. Yet, whereas his condemnation of liberalism was doctrinal, his disapproval of Landmarkism was more denominational. Note in the following quote Howell's successionism of the Baptist church in history:

> I have frequently in the preceding chapter spoken of the church now called Baptist, as having existed in all ages since the days of the apostles. I am aware that there are many who will regard these claims as preposterous ... I assert that the Baptist church has existed, in a state of comparative purity, connected with neither Papists nor Protestants, in every period since Christ, and that in this sense God has not left himself without witness.[14]

In the subsequent pages, Howell places strong emphasis on the history of the believers' church. His argument, as seen above as well, is that Baptists should not fall into the newfound theory of ecumenism when Baptists for eighteen hundred years have followed the road less traveled.

In a portrait of irony, these two men, who represented diametrically opposite views on how the convention should be run, were unified as to whom should

---

13. Ibid., 118, 120, 128. For a brief biography of R. B. C. Howell, see Emir Caner and Ergun Caner, *A Sacred Trust: Sketches of the Southern Baptist Convention Presidents* (Nashville: Broadman & Holman, 2003), 5–8.
14. Howell, *Terms of Communion at the Lord's Table*, 248. It is obvious from this work that Howell believes we are lineal descendents of the Anabaptists.

participate in the Lord's Supper. They represented the traditional view of formative Southern Baptist life, the view of closed Communion. The most popular and
disseminated American Baptist confession, *The New Hampshire Confession of 1833*,
illustrates well the common view of the Lord's Supper. It maintains:

> [We believe] that [baptism] is prerequisite to the privileges of a
> church relation; and to the Lord's Supper, in which the members
> of the church, by the [sacred] use of bread and wine, are to com-
> memorate together the dying love of Christ; preceded always by
> solemn self-examination.[15]

Baptists were nearly unanimous, it seems, on closed Communion. Yet Pendleton did take his view of the Supper a step further than Howell. He claimed, "No
member of a Baptist Church can claim it as a right, to commune with any other
Baptist church."[16] While Howell was more concerned with unity in the convention
and thus held to interchurch communion, Pendleton believed the purity of a local
church could be compromised when communion was open to nonmembers. He
asserted, "The truth is, no church can of right be required to invite to its communion those over whom it has no power of discipline."[17] In the end, Pendleton was
not staunch in his position that Communion among like-minded Baptist churches
should not be exercised. But he did worry that a local church's autonomy could be
compromised if Baptist churches were forced to give the Supper to a member of
another Southern Baptist church. Ultimately, a local church may give the Supper
to someone out of "courtesy" but never out of coercion.

A Historical Anomaly: Spurgeon as the Quintessential Example of Open Communion

These two theologians serve as a reminder that most American Baptists held to
a strict Communion, one that was not open to those who did not follow their salvation experience with believer's baptism. In fact, the notable exceptions among Baptists resided mostly among the English Baptists,[18] men such as C. H. Spurgeon,

---

15. W. J. McGlothlin, *Baptist Confessions of Faith* (Philadelphia: American Baptist Publication Society, 1911), 306. As the author points out, the Free Will Baptists were the exception to closed
Communion, arguing that "every true believer in Christ, being a member of his body, and a
part of his visible church, has not only the right to partake of his body and his blood in the
communion, but is under obligation thus to commemorate his death" (ibid., 326). On the other
hand, confessions from Baptists in Germany (1908), France (1879), and Sweden (1848) all hold
to closed Communion.

16. Pendleton, *Three Reasons Why I Am a Baptist*, 206.

17. Ibid., 209.

18. But even in English Baptist life, closed Communion was common, especially as one sees the
confessions of faith. John Smyth's *Short Confession of Faith* explained, "The Holy Supper, accord-

Robert Hall Jr., and John Bunyan.[19] American Baptists, with the exception of some
Free Will Baptists, were ardently firm in their view of a closed Communion.[20]

Of these three men, Spurgeon provides Baptists with a unique perspective of
a man who held steadfastly to a believers' church that practiced regular church
discipline, yet opened the Supper to all believers in Christ, regardless of denominational affiliation or baptismal practice. He is noted to have encouraged believer's
baptism before the Supper, but he did not make the ordinance a prerequisite to the
Lord's Table. At the end of his sermon, "The Feast of the Lord," he pleaded,

> In conclusion, let every ungodly person here know that he has
> no part nor lot in this matter. Thy first business, sinner, is with
> Christ himself. Go thou and put thy trust in him. Oh! go this
> night. Thou mayest never have another night to go in. And then
> when thou best believed, then obey his command in baptism, and
> then also come to his table and show his death until he come. The
> Lord bless you for Christ's sake. Amen.[21]

Yet in his sermon, "A Question for Communicants," Spurgeon's view becomes
crystallized as he contends that the one who must be excluded without question is
the one who does not know the Lord and thereby cannot remember his sacrifice.
Others, though not obedient in believer's baptism or perhaps rebellious in other

---

ing to the institution of Christ, is to be administered to the baptized" (McGlothlin, *Baptist Confessions of Faith*, 62). Article 72 of *Propositions and Conclusions Concerning True Christian Religion*
declares that the Lord's Supper is an ordinance "which only baptized persons must partake"
(ibid., 79). The First London Confession (1646) affirms, "Baptism is an ordinance of the New
Testament, given by Christ, to be dispensed upon persons professing faith, or that are made
disciples; who upon profession of faith, ought to be baptized, and after to partake of the Lord's
Supper." Finally, the Second London Confession is oddly silent on the issue, even though one
of its main signers, William Kiffin, was a strong supporter of closed Communion. But this is
not to say that this confession somehow advocates open Communion.

19. Due to his contention for open (mixed) membership in the church, historians still debate
whether Bunyan should be considered a Congregationalist or a Baptist. See Bunyan's 1673 publication, *Differences in Judgement About Water-Baptism: No Bar to Communion*. For a discussion
of these three theologians, see Timothy George, "Controversy and Communion: The Limits
of Baptist Fellowship from Bunyan to Spurgeon," in *The Gospel in the World: International Baptist Studies*, Studies in Baptist History and Thought, ed. D. W. Bebbington (Waynesville, GA:
Paternoster, 2002), 1:38–58.

20. For a good introduction on the issue, see John S. Hammett, *Biblical Foundations for Baptist
Churches: A Contemporary Ecclesiology* (Grand Rapids: Kregel, 2005), 283–88. Also see Nathan
Finn, "Baptism as a Prerequisite to the Lord's Supper," White Paper 3 (September 2006), pub-
lished by The Center for Theological Research, Southwestern Baptist Theological Seminary,
Ft. Worth, TX, at http://www.baptisttheology.org/documents/BaptismasPrerequisteforSupper
.pdf.

21. Charles Haddon Spurgeon, "The Feast of the Lord," from The Spurgeon Archive, *Metropolitan
Tabernacle Pulpit* (1916), at http://www.spurgeon.org/sermons/3501.htm (accessed September
29, 2006). He preached this sermon on August 6, 1871, at the Metropolitan Tabernacle.

ways, should be able to partake in communion because of its nature and intent. He
exclaimed,

> I cannot shake off from myself the idea that this makes up a large
> part of the meaning of the Lord's supper, the communion of
> saints with each other as well as the communion of the saints
> with Christ. May we enjoy it to-night! For my part, I like to feel,
> when I come to the table, that I am going to have communion,
> not only with this church, large as it is, not merely with the mem-
> bers of one denomination (I wish there were no denominations),
> not merely with the company of one body of Christians—would
> to God, there were but one body of Christians throughout the
> world!—but freely inviting all who belong to any part of the vis-
> ible church; I delight to think that at this table to-night I shall
> have fellowship with the brethren in the United States, of all
> names, and sorts, and ages, and ranks. There cannot be two
> churches of Christ. There is but one Church, one Head, and one
> body. Though there are some very naughty children in the Lord's
> family, they must not be kept without their supper; there is some
> other way of chastening them; and as long as there is true liv-
> ing communion between one Christian and another, where God
> has given the thing signified, I dare not keep back the sign. If he
> gives them to have fellowship with Christ, who am I that shall say,
> "Thou shalt have not fellowship with me"? I dare not say it.[22]

The reader is able to glimpse into the heart of the beloved Spurgeon, who was
resolute in separating from his denomination over theological liberalism but was
unwilling to segregate the Lord's Supper from those who were fundamentally
orthodox in the faith. Anyone who was born again was welcome to participate. In
short, it was unconscionable to limit communion since the church cannot be limited to one location but, instead, represents the visible locale where God, on any
particular day, had brought his people together under the banner of the cross.

However, Spurgeon's argumentation was not welcomed by most American Baptists, many of whom regarded the astute homiletician as something less than a
true Baptist due to his views on the Supper. Gregory Wills details the numerous
examples of those who questioned Spurgeon's loyalty to Baptist life:

---

22. C. H. Spurgeon, "A Question for Communicants," from The Spurgeon Archive, *Metropolitan
Tabernacle Pulpit* (n.d.), http://www.spurgeon.org/sermons/2268.htm (accessed September 29,
2006). This sermon was delivered by the pastor on June 1, 1890.

The Columbia Baptist Association in South Carolina in 1859 called Spurgeon a "semi-Baptist" for his open communion views. The same year, and for the same reason, Joseph Walker, the editor of Georgia's Baptist Champion, judged that Baptists could not recognize Spurgeon as a "sound Baptist preacher." A writer to North Carolina's Biblical Recorder in the same manner argued that "Spurgeon is a great man but no Baptist." Joseph Otis, editor of Kentucky Baptists' Western Recorder, did not consider Spurgeon a Baptist at all in 1860. He classed "Spurgeonism" with "Beecherism" and relegated both "beyond the pale of the Baptist faith."[23]

In time, many of these same American Baptists would hail Spurgeon as the greatest Baptist of his day due to his vehement opposition to theological liberalism, which to Spurgeon was nothing less than a totally new cult. To Baptists, many of whom were embroiled in a fight for the very soul of their denominations against a liberal foe who wished to blunt their only offensive weapon, the Word of God, Spurgeon's tenacity for truth clarified any question of who he was. His view of the Lord's Supper was at the most an irrelevant matter, and to some something to be considered.[24]

A HISTORICAL OMISSION: THE LOSS OF THE LORD'S SUPPER AND DISCIPLINE

By the twentieth century, the Lord's Supper, in large part, became the forgotten ordinance among Baptists due to its diminishing role as a Baptist distinctive and the ever-increasing rise of two undefined principles under the new banner of Christendom: unity and charity. Closed Communion, once held by most Christian denominations, was dismissed as divisive and destructive. As groups such as the World Council of Churches formed, closed Communion needed to be nullified in order for the movement to gain strides interdenominationally. On the other hand, the Southern Baptist Convention, which kept its sectarian roots, held to the

23. Gregory A. Wills "The Ecclesiology of Charles H. Spurgeon: Unity, Orthodoxy, and Denominational Identity—Southern Baptist Leader," *Baptist History and Heritage* (Summer–Fall 1999), from FindArticles.com at http://www.findarticles.com/p/articles/mi_mONXG/is_3-34/ai 94161024 (accessed September 29, 2006).

24. Wills's article, "The Ecclesiology of Charles H. Spurgeon," expands on this sentiment with greater detail. He wrote, "T. T. Eaton, editor of Kentucky Baptists' Western Recorder and tireless inspector of theological credentials, saw Spurgeon's action as the proof of his orthodoxy. He was the 'greatest man living,' Eaton wrote. When others questioned whether Spurgeon was still a Baptist, Eaton responded that 'he is more of a Baptist today than ever before.' Eaton defended close Communion doggedly throughout his career but seemed to indulge the error in Spurgeon. Perhaps Spurgeon would now adopt close Communion, Eaton hoped" (ibid., 8).

tenet of closed Communion, at least in principle. All three versions of the Baptist Faith and Message testify to this fact. The 2000 revision states,

> Being a church ordinance, [baptism] is prerequisite to the privileges of church membership and to the Lord's Supper. The Lord's Supper is a symbolic act of obedience whereby members of the church, through partaking of the bread and the fruit of the vine, memorialize the death of the Redeemer and anticipate His second coming.

Whereas the principle of unity removed any strict sense of Communion, the principle of charity rejected any measure of church discipline. Cast as unfairly judgmental, discipline was thrown onto the trash heap of unacceptable doctrine. Indeed, many churches in the nineteenth century could testify that at times church discipline was practiced incorrectly. George Shore, in his work, *Church Discipline in Ten Baptist Churches in Wake County, North Carolina (1850–1915)*, provides a case study of the Holly Spring Baptist Church where, during a sixty-five year period, 227 cases of discipline were brought before the congregation. Some charges were most definitely valid, including joining a club that burns houses (obviously the KKK), desertion, slave trading, abandonment of husband and children, and universalism. But other charges such as secret sins, dancing in the home, and bringing a horse into the church, illustrated the legalism that had pervaded much of the Baptist community.

By the end of the twentieth century, church discipline had become a foreign concept to most Southern Baptists. The Lord's Supper continued, although anything but a superficial meaning was lost to most. Unlike so many formative Baptists in America, modern Baptists no longer were trained to understand the profundity of the Supper, its relationship to the church, and its connection with discipline.

UNDERSTANDING CONTEMPORARY VIEWS ON THE PARTICIPANTS OF THE LORD'S SUPPER

The question of who should participate in the Lord's Supper was once upon a time a clearer issue among Baptists, who held to one of two rivaling views: open Communion (all professed believers) and closed Communion (believers who had been scripturally baptized in the proper place). But over the last century, these two theories have evolved into many subsets. Certainly, it would be unfair to lump some open Communionists with more radical open Communionists. Likewise, closed Communionists are to varying degrees closed. Today, I see no less than five competing theories as to who should partake of the Lord's Supper. In each of these theories, one must consider three doctrines: soteriology, baptism, and ecclesiology.

First, some hold to what I define as "Laissez-faire Communion." The bread and the wine are open to all who wish to partake. Here, salvation has become a completely subjective experience that has no foundation within the pages of Holy Writ. Radical openness in Communion is consistent with a universal view of salvation. For example, Covenant Church in Houston, Texas, a Baptist church birthed from a Southern Baptist congregation, verbalizes this view very well.

> The service itself reflects the broad range of the congregation's faith backgrounds including Catholic, Jewish, and a spectrum of prior Protestant affiliations from Baptist and Church of Christ to Episcopalian and Unitarian. Worship is most often planned around a liturgical format that will include prayers of confession, intercession, dedication, and thanksgiving, and an affirmation of faith. These elements are chosen by the worship planners and include selections from worship guides, contemporary literature, and original compositions from Covenant participants. . . . Communion is included in a variety of forms approximately once each month and is open to the full participation of any who so choose.[25]

With such a radical view, it is not difficult to recognize the annihilation of any form of church discipline. Moreover, it can be stated without any hyperbole that the New Testament church has ceased to exist in such a body.

The second view, "Open Communion," I have chosen to define as allowing all believers in Jesus Christ to partake of the Supper. Thus, one's soteriology remains exclusivistic—that is, only those who are true followers of Christ as mandated by Scripture are permitted to take the bread and the cup—while one's view of the church is inclusivistic. The church is generally defined as universal and invisible, many times quoting passages such as 1 Corinthians 12:13, "For by one Spirit we were all baptized into one body—whether Jews or Greeks, whether slaves or free—and have all been made to drink into one Spirit."[26] Yet, there is no mention of believer's baptism as connected either to the church or to the Supper. The Second Baptist Church of Houston, Texas, delineates such a position, articulating,

> The Lord's Supper is an ordinance of the church. It was instituted when the Lord had the Passover meal before His crucifixion. We

---

25. "Worship," at http://www.covenanthouston.org/worship.htm (accessed September 30, 2006).
26. All Scripture quotations are from the New King James Version (NKJV).

> observe the Lord's Supper on a regular basis in remembrance of
> Jesus Christ['s] atonement for our sins. It is a proclamation of His
> death and an assurance of His second coming. We ask only those
> who have made a profession of faith in Jesus Christ to participate
> in the Lord's Supper. The elements of bread and grape juice are
> used as symbols of Christ's body that was broken and His blood
> that was shed for the remission of our sins.[27]

Note the definitional connection of one's salvation to the partaking of the elements while little else is mentioned in the brief statement.

The third view, "Cracked Communion," is characterized by its emphasis on believer's baptism, though it is not explicitly associated with a believers' church. Thus, a person is welcome to the Table if, subsequent to conversion, he or she has been baptized by immersion. Based on "like faith and practice," churches holding this view accept those to the Supper who have been baptized after believing, placing heavy emphasis on mode even more so than on meaning. Thus, these churches will accept to the Table those who were baptized individually and not by the authority of any church whatsoever.

The fourth view, "Closed Communion," is still left untouched from its historical precedent, recognizing that a person must be a believer and must accept believer's baptism by immersion under the authority of a New Testament church. The clearest expression of this view is held by local churches that adopt the Baptist Faith and Message (2000). Not only is importance placed upon true conversion and scriptural baptism, but the church is defined explicitly as well. Article VI states:

> A New Testament church of the Lord Jesus Christ is an autonomous local congregation of baptized believers, associated by covenant in the faith and fellowship of the gospel; observing the two ordinances of Christ, governed by His laws, exercising the gifts, rights, and privileges invested in them by His Word, and seeking to extend the gospel to the ends of the earth. Each congregation operates under the Lordship of Christ through democratic processes. In such a congregation each member is responsible and accountable to Christ as Lord. Its scriptural officers are pastors and deacons.

---

27. Second Baptist Church, "Our beliefs" (Houston, TX), at http://www.second.org/global/our beliefs.aspx (accessed September 30, 2006). The Scripture verses used for justification are 1 Corinthians 1:21–32; 5:11–13; and Matthew 26:29.

Article VII adds, "Being a church ordinance, [baptism] is prerequisite to the privileges of church membership and to the Lord's Supper." Hence, the three doctrines of salvation, baptism, and the church are unambiguously knitted together.

Finally, the fifth view, "Locked Communion," takes the final step in arguing that a believer should partake of the Supper only at the local church in which he or she is a member. Building upon the fact that Paul establishes the ordinance under the umbrella of the local church in Corinth (1 Cor. 11:20: "when you come together in one place"), proponents point to 1 Corinthians 5:1–13 as evidence for the connection between discipline and the Lord's Supper. In this passage, a young man's excommunication from the Corinthian fellowship (v 5: "deliver such a one to Satan") is explicitly correlated with the Supper through Old Testament imagery. He is "purged out" so that the church may be a "new lump" and represent well "Christ, our Passover." The question is then raised by the advocate of this position, If one can take communion at any church, can any church thereby disfellowship any or all from other churches? The Lord's Supper, quite simply, is a means by which brothers and sisters in Christ can share in their ardent love for one another through mutual accountability.[28]

In 1857, John Leadley Dagg (1794–1884) published his *Manual of Theology*, the first systematic theology written by a Baptist in America. In it, Dagg puts forth a convincing case for the significance of the Lord's Supper as it regards its participants and the Word of God. Beginning with the intent, he writes, "The Lord's Supper was designed to be a memorial of Christ, a representation that the communicant receives spiritual nourishment from Him, and a token of fellowship among the communicants." The rite, he argues is to be "commemorative" and "preach the doctrine that Christ died for our sins, and that we live by his death" (see John 6:53). Furthermore, it was meant "to signify the fellowship of the communicants with one another" (see 1 Cor. 10:16–17, 21).[29]

The Lord's Supper also was "designed to be celebrated by each church in public assembly." Additionally, "Faith is also a requisite to the receiving of the supper." The ordinance was "designed to be social" (see 1 Cor. 11:2, 23) and "should be celebrated by the church, in public assembly" (see 1 Cor. 11:26). Church discipline

---

28. A. H. Strong condemns open Communion since "it tends to do away with all discipline . . . since the Lord's Supper, the highest expression of church fellowship, is open to every person who regards himself as a Christian." *Systematic Theology* (Valley Forge, PA: Judson Press, 1907), 978. More worrisome to Strong is the possibility that open Communion could lead to open membership. It should be noted as well that some (like Strong) would argue for a milder form of "Locked Communion" in which they could take the ordinance in more than one church if sufficient evidence proved they were accountable to both (e.g., college students who were away for months at a time).

29. J. L. Dagg, *Manual of Theology* (Harrisonburg, VA: Gano Books, 1982), 209–11.

was to be exercised as "every such wicked person was to be accounted as an heathen man and a publican" (see 1 Cor. 5:11). Ultimately, in arguing against any form of open Communion, Dagg stated, "We have seen that the Lord's supper has been committed to the local churches for observance and perpetuation; and that local churches, if organized according to the Scriptures, contain none but baptized persons. It follows hence, that baptism is a prerequisite to communion at the Lord's table."[30]

A fair scriptural assessment of the Lord's Supper, therefore, leads to several questions that must be answered by Christians:

1. Is baptism intimately connected with the church? If so, can one enter the continuing ordinance of the Supper before entering into the initiatory ordinance of baptism?

2. Does the Scripture, in particular 1 Corinthians 5 and 11, regard the Lord's Supper as a local church ordinance, or is it considered a universal church ordinance?

3. Since the Supper requires both commitment to Christ and to fellow Christians, can someone who is not baptized actually make such a commitment? Can such extensive commitment be made beyond one's local church?

4. Can a believer affirm genuine unity with the body of Christ at the Supper without partaking in baptism?

5. If one does not need to be a member of the church to partake of the Lord's Supper, would it be appropriate for someone to partake of baptism without wanting to unify with the church?[31]

A FORGOTTEN THEOLOGIAN SPEAKS TO THE FORGOTTEN ORDINANCE

Our retrieval of meaningful corporate participation in the Lord's Supper can be accomplished only if we first examine ourselves personally and ensure our own preparedness to take of the elements. Perhaps no one can remind us of the importance of the ordinance like Balthasar Hubmaier (1480–1528), the largely unknown Anabaptist figure who helped shape the Baptist movement. While known most for his works on religious liberty and believer's baptism, Hubmaier went to great lengths to write on the Lord's Supper as well.[32] This pastor-theologian, who

---

30. Ibid., 212–14.
31. Some questions are modifications of arguments used by Hammett, *Biblical Foundations for Baptist Churches*, 284–88.
32. Balthasar Hubmaier wrote three books on the subject of the Supper: *Several Theses Concerning the Mass* (1525), *A Simple Instruction* (1526), and *A Form of Christ's Supper* (1527).

baptized more than six thousand men and women within a fourteen-month period, demanded that the proper participants of the Lord's Supper take seriously and understand thoroughly the ordinance they were about to partake. His work, *A Form of Christ's Supper*, was so respected that it was one of the first old texts to be reprinted and, in fact, is one of the few adapted for use even to this day.

In this timeless piece, Hubmaier outlines the necessary characteristics of a meaningful Lord's Supper. I have broken them down into seven key principles:

1. The Lord's Supper must be corporate and not individual. "The brethren and Sisters who wish to hold the table of the Lord according to the institution of Christ . . . shall gather at a suitable place and time, so there may be no divisions, so that one does not come early and another late and that thereby evangelical teaching is neglected."
2. The Lord's Supper incorporates both private and communal confession. "It is not inappropriate that the priest first of all should fall on his knees with the church and with heart and mouth say the following words: 'Father, we have sinned against heaven and against thee.'"
3. The Lord's Supper must be preceded with scriptural exposition of its meaning. "Now let the priest sit down with the people and open his mouth, explaining the Scriptures concerning Christ."
4. The Lord's Supper involves scriptural and personal examination. "Those who are present have the opportunity and the authority to ask, if at any point they should have some misunderstanding or some lack . . . concerning proper, necessary, and Christian items, and having to do with Christian faith and brotherly love."
5. Introspection includes examining one's faith, desire for God, thankfulness for God's love, and pledge toward other Christians. "First, that one believes. . . . Second, let a person test himself, whether he has a proper inward and fervent hunger. . . . Third, confirm himself in gratitude. . . . Fourth, publicly assuring her [the church] . . . making her a sacrament or a sworn pledge."
6. The Lord's Supper is concluded with a word of admonition.
7. The Lord's Supper is concluded with a word of encouragement. "Arise and go forth in the peace of Christ Jesus. The grace of God be with us all. Amen."[33]

In the end, the enormous importance of the Lord's Supper is not only found within Paul's first epistle to the Corinthians or within the Gospel record of Christ's Last Supper itself; it is also clearly seen within the very passage that exhorts us to

33. H. Wayne Pipkin and John H. Yoder, *Balthasar Hubmaier: Theologian of Anabaptism* (Scottdale, PA: Herald Press, 1989), 393–97, 406.

win the lost, the Great Commission of Matthew 28:19–20. Alongside of going, making disciples, and baptizing, is the often forgotten phrase, "Teaching them to observe all things that I have commanded you." For the Great Commission to be carried out biblically, the Lord's Supper must be performed properly. In fact, to water down the meaning or makeup of the Lord's Supper is to water down the meaning and makeup of the Great Commission. Proclaiming the Lord's death through this beautiful commemoration illustrates to the world the sacrifice of Christ for the world. To somehow diminish its significance would be to diminish the command to which Christ has called us. God forbid. Truth is immortal.

9

Southern Baptists and Church Discipline

DEVELOPMENT AND DECLINE

GREGORY A. WILLS

B aptists in the South practiced a thorough church discipline for about two hundred years. They did so because they believed that Christ commanded it. Between 1845 and 1900 they disciplined about 1.3 million members and expelled about 650,000.[1] But by 1950 only a fading memory of the practice remained. Southern Baptist churches had abandoned New Testament church discipline. Southern Baptist pastors and denominational leaders knew that the abandonment of discipline represented a failure to obey Christ, and for two generations they complained of the failure and urged the churches to recover church discipline.

Southern Baptists experienced three tectonic shifts that reshaped Baptist identity and rendered church discipline implausible for both conservatives and progressives. First, they lost confidence that Christ commanded a specific ecclesiology and based church practices on pragmatic concerns, on human standards of effectiveness. Second, they adopted a new view of Baptist identity that led them to redefine ecclesiology and theology according to human experience, which among other things recast God in humanitarian terms and weakened their sense of the

---

1. From the membership and exclusion data of 1,875 Baptist association records in the South, representing 76 different associations in 10 southern states, I calculated the average exclusion rate per decade (number of exclusions divided by the number of church members) and multiplied the exclusion rate by the total number of Southern Baptists, yielding an estimate of 682,812 members excluded between 1845 and 1900 inclusive. Based on data from church minute books in Georgia, churches excluded between 40 and 50 percent of those whom they brought under discipline proceedings, and hence the total number of members brought under discipline was about twice the number of those excluded. For a discussion of the extent of church discipline among Southern Baptists, see Gregory A. Wills, *Democratic Religion: Freedom, Authority, and Church Discipline in the Baptist South, 1785–1900* (New York: Oxford University Press, 1997), 22–23, 116–17.

fear of God. Third, they took guardianship of the social order, which secularized the churches and eroded their commitment to separation from the world.

These commitments so altered Baptist piety that, all things considered, church discipline seemed ill suited to advance the aims of the contemporary church. It seemed ineffective for church growth and irrelevant for ministry in modern society. Southern Baptist pastors finally chose relevance over obedience and quieted their consciences over the loss.

ORIGINS OF CHURCH DISCIPLINE AMONG BAPTISTS

The early English-speaking Baptists practiced church discipline in ways similar to those of the Puritan churches from which they separated. The Puritans valued John Calvin's teaching on the church and its discipline. Calvin and the Puritans viewed church discipline as an essential element of the true church. Discipline set the boundaries of admission to the Lord's Supper and therefore was necessary to its pure administration. Calvin was prepared to suffer death rather than distribute the communion bread and wine to the wicked and impenitent, and he was expelled from Geneva in 1536 because of this. In 1538 he made the establishment of discipline in the Genevan churches a condition of his return.[2]

Calvin's English admirers had less success. Thomas Cranmer convinced Parliament to establish Protestant doctrine and Protestant worship, but he failed to persuade them to adopt Protestant church discipline. When Puritans established churches, in England or in exile, they established them on a platform that included church discipline.[3]

Anabaptists may have influenced early English-speaking Baptists in the practice of discipline, but little evidence supports the idea. The early English-speaking Baptists came out of Puritan churches, and they construed discipline in the same way that the Puritan Independents did. Baptists did not use the social ostracism of the ban, which Anabaptists made an essential element of excommunication. And the Separate Baptists, who so largely contributed to the Southern Baptist movement, withdrew from New England Congregational churches whose principles of church discipline they endorsed.

But Baptists felt no allegiance to Puritanism, whether in seventeenth-century England or eighteenth-century New England. They required scriptural justifica-

---

2. See Robert Kingdon, "The Geneva Consistory in the Time of Calvin," in *Calvinism in Europe, 1540–1620* (Cambridge: Cambridge University Press, 1994), 21–34.
3. See James C. Spalding, "*Reformatio Legum Ecclesiasticarum* of 1552 and the Furthering of Discipline in England," *Church History* 39 (1970): 162–71; Gerald Bray, "The 1552 Reform of English Church Discipline," *Churchman* 116 (2002): 201–19; and J. William Black, "From Martin Bucer to Richard Baxter: 'Discipline' and Reformation in Sixteenth and Seventeenth-Century England," *Church History* 70 (2001): 644–73.

tion for their church practices. They therefore rejected the infant baptism and the sprinkling of the Puritan churches. But they judged that the discipline of the Puritans was correct in the main, and they practiced discipline in similar ways. The most striking differences between the Baptist and the Puritan practice were that Baptists maintained the practice much longer and insisted on a stricter separation from the world.[4]

THE SHAPE OF BAPTIST CHURCH DISCIPLINE

Baptists sought to practice church discipline in accordance with the New Testament. The New Testament doctrine of regenerate church membership logically presupposed church discipline, but Baptists did not build their practice on it. They based their practice of discipline on the explicit command of Jesus Christ in Matthew 18 and on the normative character of apostolic practice, as revealed especially in 1 Corinthians 5 and 2 Corinthians 2.

Baptists set themselves to obey the commands of Christ regardless of costs or consequences. When colonial authorities ordered John Waller not to preach, he preached nevertheless, for Christ commanded it.[5] When a Georgia planter threatened to whip his wife and to kill John Leland if he dared to baptize her, he ventured his neck and she her back, for Christ commanded it.[6] When a disgruntled congregant sought to hire thugs to beat W. B. Johnson for preaching election, he was undeterred, for Christ commissioned him to preach the Scriptures.[7] When a church member burned the meetinghouse and threatened "powder and lead" to prevent church discipline, the congregation proceeded to excommunicate, for Christ required it.[8] They had no more freedom to neglect church discipline than they had to neglect baptism, communion, or preaching repentance and faith in the name of Christ. They believed that Christ commanded a specific church order and pledged to carry it out no matter how impractical or ineffective it appeared. And they believed that God commanded them to be separate from the world, regardless of the scorn of cultured society. They would obey God, whom they feared more than man.

---

4. For discussion of the church discipline practices of the New England Congregationalists, see Emil Oberholzer, *Delinquent Saints: Disciplinary Action in the Early Congregational Churches of Massachusetts* (New York: Columbia University Press, 1956).

5. Robert Semple, *A History of the Rise and Progress of the Baptists in Virginia* (Richmond: John Lynch, 1810), 15–16.

6. John Leland, "Events in the Life of John Leland," in *The Writings of the Late Elder John Leland*, ed. L. F. Greene (New York: G. W. Wood, 1845), 20, 27.

7. William B. Johnson, "Reminiscences," South Caroliniana Library, University of South Carolina, Columbia, 16–17.

8. Bethel Baptist Association (Georgia), *Minutes* (1841), 14–16.

They also believed that God would bless their faithful administration of discipline, that he wrought spiritual benefits through the faithful exercise of church discipline. Discipline kept the church pure. It removed stumbling blocks to faithfulness. This visible reminder of the heinous character of sin strengthened believers in their zeal for righteousness. It upheld the honor of Christ by excluding those who professed his name in unrighteousness. It presented offenders proper inducements to repent and return to an orderly Christian walk. It was a gospel remedy for sin and temptation, an essential part of the means that God provided for sanctifying believers. And they believed that God would generally visit spiritual power and revival on churches that obeyed Christ in discipline.

Baptists believed that Jesus required the churches to exercise church discipline in the case of practically every outward sin. The churches did not condone inward sin; they reproved it. But Christ designed the church's discipline to notice outward sins. The church could not see inward sins in order to weigh them. Outward sins were visible and amenable to discipline.

Baptists disciplined members who committed such gross immoralities as murder, abortion, arson, assault, theft, fraud, blasphemy, falsehood, drunkenness, abuse, fornication, and adultery. They disciplined others who were guilty of hostility, anger, slander, or threats. They disciplined still others who sinned against their church duties by habitual absence, refusal to submit to the church, indulging in worldly amusements, or participation in open Communion. They also disciplined those who incited factions or division in the church, and they disciplined those who spread erroneous doctrine or embraced heresy.

Baptists held that the New Testament established two rules of procedure for discipline. For offenses of a "personal" nature and for less serious offenses generally, church members ought to follow the "gospel steps" delineated in Matthew 18. For "public" offenses and for grave offenses generally, church members generally brought the matter directly to the church, as Paul commanded the Corinthian church to do in 1 Corinthians 5.

In the nineteenth century Baptists attended to discipline matters at their monthly church conference or business meeting, usually on a Saturday. In some cases, individuals accused themselves of sin, made confessions, and sought forgiveness. But in most cases, one of the deacons introduced the matter for the attention of the church. The moderator then asked the accused member for a response. If the accused was absent, the church "cited" him or her to appear before the church at the next meeting to give an answer.

In virtually all cases, the church appointed a committee to investigate. They wanted to have confidence that they had all relevant evidence of guilt or innocence before them. They also wanted relevant information regarding the circumstances.

Just as important, they wanted to know the state of the heart and mind of the accused.

After talking to the relevant witnesses and "laboring with" the accused, the committee submitted its report to the church. The report included the committee's opinion on guilt or innocence and the relevant factual basis for their finding, including mitigating and aggravating circumstances. The report finally recommended a course of action for the church. If the church was satisfied that the committee had executed its duty well, they received the report and dismissed the committee. If not, they instructed the committee to complete its task.

Three outcomes only could ensue. First, the church could find the accused innocent and dismiss the charges. Second, the church could rebuke the offender but forgive him and retain him as a member of the church. Third, the church could exclude, or excommunicate, the offender.

Exclusion always ensued if there was no repentance. But repentance did not always save. For grave sins that brought particular dishonor to the Savior or that involved habitual deceit or fraud, churches usually excluded even if the accused repented. About 50 percent of those whom the church brought before its discipline experienced exclusion.

The churches sought the restoration of those excluded. When they asked for readmission, the churches granted the request if in their judgment the offenders had in fact repented. Churches gauged this by weighing the character and gravity of the offense against the evidence of sincerity. They tested the repentance based on what the individual did and said. They expected that the individual had been constant in attending the church's services and had indeed abandoned unchristian conduct. For sins that were especially grave or involved deceit, churches generally expected a longer period of time to prove repentance, up to about one year. They made no rules on this but developed a common sense of what was suited to each situation.

Persons seeking restoration also had to express the right mind and heart in their request for restoration. The church expected them to admit their guilt, to avow their repentance, to justify the church's action, and to pledge to walk according to righteousness, all in a proper spirit of sorrow and humility. The church would then restore. If the individual sought to justify himself or accuse others in the least, the church took it as evidence of a proud heart inconsistent with true repentance and would not restore. In the nineteenth century, 30 to 40 percent of those excluded sought and gained restoration.

Members seem to have been cautious in bringing charges against fellow members. In those cases in which the clerk noted the response, the vast majority confessed their guilt. And the churches seem to have been remarkably fair. In about half of all cases in which the accused denied guilt, the church acquitted, an acquittal rate far higher than in criminal courts. If a member brought an accusation against another without sufficient cause, the church generally charged the accuser with slander or hostility.

The discipline was far more effective than is apparent from the statistics. In a general way it helped sustain the regenerate character of the church and reminded members of their covenanted duties and the meaning of membership. It sustained the church's purity not only by expelling the impure but also by its clear and present warning to the members to guard against sin. But it also resulted in repentance in many instances before the matter could rise to the attention of the whole church, as members followed the steps of Matthew 18. It also reminded members of their corporate responsibility for the purity and faithfulness of the church. Their commitment to New Testament congregationalism meant that every member was responsible and that the congregation jointly exercised authority over the fellowship.

In Praise of the Old Discipline

In the 1880s the use of church discipline began a steady decline in Southern Baptist churches. By the 1930s, churches excluded members at rates 80 to 90 percent lower than they had done before 1880. But the decline was even steeper than the statistics showed. By the 1930s most exclusions did not involve discipline proceedings at all. The churches were cleaning their rolls of their inactive members and reporting these erasures as exclusions. Discipline proceedings became rare.

But many Southern Baptists resisted this result. Pastors and members rallied again and again to stop discipline's slide. They praised the old discipline and thought not to bury it. It nevertheless slipped into the grave.

Southern Baptists began to sense they were losing their grip on church discipline in the 1870s. William H. Whitsitt, professor at the Southern Baptist Theological Seminary in Greenville, South Carolina, for example, complained in 1874 that "it is now very difficult to exclude a person for drunkenness or any other ordinary crime."[9] In 1878, J. C. Hiden, pastor of Greenville, South Carolina, First Baptist Church, wrote a series of articles in the *Baptist Courier* lamenting the recent trend of lax discipline.[10]

For several decades Baptists published their warnings to return to the old discipline in their state newspapers and association reports. The Texas *Baptist Standard*,

---

9.   William H. Whitsitt, *Journal*, William Heth Whitsitt Collection, James P. Boyce Centennial Library, Southern Baptist Theological Seminary, Louisville, Kentucky, 266.

10.   J. C. Hiden, "Church Discipline, No. I," *Baptist Courier*, March 14, 1878, 2. Hiden wrote at least three additional articles in the series.

for example, published George Truett's plea for traditional church discipline in 1911.[11] In 1922, South Carolina's *Baptist Courier* published Furman president William McGlothlin's concern that the "abandonment of discipline" had harmed not only the churches but also the entire community.[12]

Although exhortations to restore the old discipline became less frequent as the twentieth century progressed, Southern Baptist leaders occasionally urged its restoration as late as the 1950s and 1960s. In the 1958 *Southern Baptist Encyclopedia*, the article on discipline described it as "indispensable" to Baptist churches.[13] The Tennessee *Baptist and Reflector* pressed the matter as late as 1962, when Southern Seminary professor Glenn Hinson commended the recovery of church discipline in a full-page article.[14]

Developments in church life made discipline more difficult. Urbanization in the South entailed the loss of face-to-face culture, promoted a culture of civility, and expanded the privileging of the individual over the group. As city churches grew large, the press of urgent financial matters and the development of a program-oriented church life tended to push discipline to the sidelines where it withered from neglect. Changes in church and society made church discipline more challenging, but these seem insufficient causes in view of the strong belief of Baptist leaders and pastors that the Bible required it. Southern Baptists did not intend to abandon their discipline. No one urged its neglect. All seemed to agree that it should be restored. But they failed to see that they had embraced new commitments incompatible with church discipline. First, they now based church practices on their apparent effectiveness more than on an apostolic pattern. Second, they redefined Baptist identity in ways that privileged subjective values and individual freedom and thus undermined the church's authority to judge belief and behavior. Third, they modified the church's mission to include curing social ills, which diminished their sense of separation from the world and secularized the churches. Southern Baptist leaders embraced these new commitments in the period from about 1880 to about 1930. They were tectonic shifts with expansive consequences. Together they undid discipline.[15]

11.   George Truett, "Church Discipline," *Baptist Standard*, September 23, 1923, 1–2.
12.   William McGlothlin, "Reflections on Reading an Old Church Book: Number Two," *Baptist Courier*, November 16, 1922, 5.
13.   Theron Price, "Discipline," in *Southern Baptist Encyclopedia* (Nashville: Broadman Press, 1958), 1:366.
14.   E. Glenn Hinson, "Early Christian Discipline and Ours," *Baptist and Reflector*, December 6, 1962, 12–13.
15.   There were other factors at work, but these three represented structural shifts within which the practice of discipline appeared contrary to reason. For a discussion of other factors, see Wills, *Democratic Religion*, 116–38.

THE NEW CHURCH: THE RAGE FOR EFFICIENCY

In the first of these shifts, Southern Baptists embraced a new understanding of the church. They paid their respects to the old ecclesiology, but they lost confidence in it. Efficiency was the watchword of the new church. The proponents of efficiency assured their fellow Southern Baptists that only efficient churches would prosper under the new conditions of modern society. And the proponents multiplied rapidly. It did not take long for the new ecclesiology to relegate the old to irrelevance. As a result, church discipline had to play a new role. Efficiency experts did not recommend neglecting discipline; they rather made efficiency its purpose. But somehow the discipline did not produce the anticipated results, and the churches felt that somehow they were not skilled enough to operate the machinery in the way the experts demanded.[16]

In the traditional ecclesiology, Baptists held that the best way to ensure the efficiency was by obedience. Churches that maintained New Testament doctrine, ordinances, and discipline would receive God's blessing. Churches that failed in these areas, God would chastise or blight.

They were confident that the chief agency in all spiritual work was the Holy Spirit. Only the Spirit could make preaching effective for the conviction and conversion of sinners. Only the Spirit could make prayer powerful. Only the Spirit could make church discipline effective for the restoration of straying saints and the vivification of the church. The Spirit would bless churches that were truly spiritual, that pursued obedience in all things, great and small. Worldliness and wickedness in the church, on the contrary, grieved the Spirit.

James P. Boyce, pastor of Columbia First Baptist Church and later president of the Southern Baptist Theological Seminary, argued additionally that unless the church exercised church discipline, it could not fulfill the Great Commission. Only church discipline would keep worldliness from the church and promote holiness even in small things. Only by learning such self-denial would the church exert that earnest and constant effort necessary to evangelize the world. But before that, Boyce said, was the fact that the Holy Spirit would assist only pure and holy churches. Without the Spirit's assistance, the church can have no success.[17]

Before the 1870s, when conversions were few or spirituality waned, leaders attributed it to either soft preaching or soft discipline. The Sunbury Baptist Association expressed it well in 1868: "[The] only way to secure the strength and effi-

16. Southern Baptists here followed the powerful cultural trends of the Progressive Era—among them reliance on experts, professionalization, and the social sciences—toward rational ordering of social institutions and efficiency.
17. James P. Boyce, "Church Discipline—Its Importance," *Baptist Courier*, February 18, 1852, 2.

ciency of the churches is to keep them pure."[18] By the 1880s, however, it became common to blame denominational problems on lack of system, order, and plan. The church's greatest defect was lack of organization.[19] Efficiency, not purity, was the answer to the church's fundamental problems.

Church leaders promoted efficiency with striking regularity during the period in which church discipline withered. They made efficiency the practical test of faithfulness to the Great Commission. Efficiency consisted not in purity or obedience, but in system, organization, and rationality in all areas of church activity. Indeed, pastors saw their role increasingly as organizing the activity of the members. Formerly, pastors received high praise for ably leading their churches to maintain pure morals and doctrine through faithful preaching and church discipline. By the 1880s, pastors increasingly won praise instead for reducing their churches to efficient systems of finance, missions giving, training, and labor.[20]

By 1900 the old ecclesiology was waning fast. Southern Baptist Theological Seminary professor E. C. Dargan's 1905 *Ecclesiology: A Study of the Churches* was its swan song. Dargan promoted a church polity based on the authority of the apostolic pattern. But progressive church leaders held that the church in the modern age needed a polity based not on ancient authority but on science, rationality, and system. They looked to social scientists and efficiency experts such as Frederick Winslow Taylor, who in this era developed management into a science for producing efficient organizations.[21]

Shailer Mathews, dean of the University of Chicago Divinity School, represented well the new approach. He urged the churches to adopt scientific management, which meant efficient organization of the church's labor. The essential nature of the church came under revision. "Theoretically the church should be regarded as a body of workmen ready to perform definite tasks as these are outlined for them by its committee of management. . . . This is precisely what the philosophy of efficiency demands." The pastor, Mathews said, should look to perform a social function more than to proclaim a message. Seminaries therefore should "send them out trained in efficiency rather than merely informed as to orthodoxy."

---

18. Sunbury Baptist Association (Georgia), *Minutes*, 1868, 6.
19. Flint River Baptist Association (Georgia), *Minutes*, 1900, 13.
20. See Wills, *Democratic Religion*, 131–34.
21. E. C. Dargan, *Ecclesiology: A Study of the Churches*, 2nd ed. (Louisville: C. T. Dearing, 1905). The first edition was published in 1897. Frederick Winslow Taylor, *Principles of Scientific Management* (New York: Harper and Brothers, 1911). This transition from traditional to scientific ecclesiology appears most suggestively in the change of titles for Dargan's chair. Dargan was professor of homiletics and ecclesiology, but Charles S. Gardiner, who replaced him in 1907, was professor of homiletics and Christian sociology.

Efficiency, rather than scriptural purity and orthodoxy, became the standard of measure.[22]

In the Southern Baptist Convention, Gaines Dobbins, professor of church efficiency at Southern Seminary, promoted the new ecclesiology most successfully. He explained in his 1923 classic, *The Efficient Church*, that the principles of efficiency were central because the church was in large measure a "business enterprise" and was subject to the "laws which govern business affairs."[23] The New Testament itself taught efficiency, he wrote, because it required Christians to "test men and institutions" by their fruit, "precisely the test of the modern efficiency expert." Dobbins explained that Jesus' "ministry, his training of the Twelve, his plan of organization for his churches, his program of world-conquest, all exhibit the perfection of efficiency." Although apparently unnoticed before, the book of Acts was in fact a "manual of church efficiency." And Paul, he wrote, was the "world's greatest efficiency expert in religion."[24]

But the ecclesiology of efficiency did not intend to repudiate church discipline. It intended discipline to play a key role: to help maintain efficiency. Efficient churches must establish "high and worthy standards" to advance the order, morale, and management of the church. Discipline was necessary to challenge members to rise to these standards and maintain them.[25] In the old church, discipline was for the good of the accused, the honor of Christ, and the purity of the church. In the new church, discipline sustained efficient management.

Church discipline in the new church operated primarily by cutting off inefficient members. Members who did not sustain the church's programs of worship, Sunday school, training, and evangelism were burdens on the church. They did not take their place in the church's organized labor. The efficient pastor sought to reclaim them from their waywardness or, more often, indolence and indifference. He sought to persuade them to "enlist" in service. But those who resisted enlistment and remained aloof were inefficient and had to be cut off. In fact, by the early twentieth century, Southern Baptist church discipline consisted mostly of such exclusions, a jettisoning of the "dead weight" of inactive members.[26]

22. Shailer Mathews, *Scientific Management in the Churches* (Chicago: University of Chicago Press, 1912), 36–37, 45. This book originated in lectures that Mathews presented to the 1911 Sagamore Beach Sociological Conference.

23. Gaines Dobbins, *The Efficient Church: A Study of Polity and Methods in Light of New Testament Principles and Modern Conditions and Needs* (Nashville: Sunday School Board of the Southern Baptist Convention, 1923), 93, 11.

24. Dobbins, *Efficient Church*, 25–26. Dobbins later moderated some of these claims.

25. Ibid., 20. Efficiency expert Harrington Emerson included "discipline" as one of his twelve principles of efficient management. See Harrington Emerson, *Twelve Principles of Efficiency*, 4th ed. (New York: Engineering Magazine, 1916), 135–64.

26. See Wills, *Democratic Religion*, 129.

As Southern Baptists moved into the middle of the twentieth century, the rage to measure the church primarily in terms of efficiency subsided, but the new ecclesiology based on pragmatism and effectiveness had taken hold. The most durable legacy of the rage for efficiency was the overthrow of the apostolic model of the church. Discipline might be apostolic, but it could not pass the efficiency test and fell into disuse. Southern Baptists no longer believed that God revealed the shape and methods of the church and commanded its methods, modes, and forms. Christ commanded churches to exercise church discipline, but it seemed to undermine the church's social relevance, its missionary and benevolent giving, and its enlistment of efficient laypersons in the church's program of work. Without conviction that Christ had ordained the shape and methods of the church, churches could not sustain discipline.

THE NEW BAPTIST: THE REVOLUTION OF INDIVIDUAL FREEDOM

The second shift in Baptist life entailed a thorough recasting of theology and ecclesiology based on a new view of Baptist identity. A new idealist philosophy provided a basis for this reorientation. Developments in science, scholarship, and society made the redefinition plausible and finally persuasive to most Southern Baptist leaders. This revolution made the old church discipline altogether implausible.

The new approach redefined theology and practice by appeal to the authority of the alleged "essence" or "genius" of the Baptist movement. This essence went by many names: the voluntary principle, the spiritual principle, personhood or personality, or individualism. But undergirding all was the principle of freedom: the free individual deciding voluntarily to relate to the personal God and other free individuals. The redefinition of Baptist identity took root and flourished in the period from about 1880 to about 1920. It proved as powerful and durable as the commitment to efficiency. It transformed Southern Baptist theology and ecclesiology in profound ways. It even seemed to absorb the doctrine of efficiency and to subordinate it to its own principles.[27]

The old theology came under pressure from Darwinism. Educated Americans increasingly accepted the theory of evolution and sought ways to retain both evolution and the Christian faith and its Bible. But evolution of any sort posed problems for a traditional interpretation of the Creation account in Genesis, and many

---

27. The concern to determine the essence of Christianity was a particular preoccupation of the Protestant liberal era. See, e.g., Adolf von Harnack, *What Is Christianity?*, trans. Thomas Bailey Saunders (New York: G. P. Putman's Sons, 1901); and William Adams Brown, *The Essence of Christianity: A Study in the History of Definition* (New York: Charles Scribner's Sons, 1902). For discussion of the idea of essence in modern theology, see Gary Dorrien, *The Word as True Myth: Interpreting Modern Theology* (Louisville: Westminster John Knox Press, 1997), 22–25.

persons could no longer accept its accuracy. This meant that if they wished to keep the Bible in its central place in Christianity, they had to accept a theory of inspiration that could make the Bible authoritative without the burden of being historically true.[28]

The new critical approach to the Bible also put pressure on the old theology. Its first principle was to interpret the Bible like any other book. Rules of interpretation, they said, must have universal application or they are not rational. The only rational rule for interpreting the Bible, therefore, was to interpret it according to the same methods used to interpret merely human books. The result was that apparent contradictions turned into real contradictions and accounts of miracles often turned out to be mere legend or myth. Christians who adopted these conclusions similarly needed a theory of inspiration that retained an authoritative Bible that was not necessarily true in its historical statements.[29]

Idealist philosophy suggested the most attractive solution. In one popular form it taught that history is the temporary expression of the eternal spirit. God does not change, but the particular expressions of God's activity in history do. Or in a more basic form, all physical objects are transitory and imperfect expressions of an eternal ideal. The objects pass into and out of existence, but the eternal ideal does not change. "Modern Liberalism," Harvard University's W. W. Fenn wrote in 1913, "is usually inspired by some form of monistic idealism." Idealism was fundamental to liberalism's understanding of the Christian faith, and in its light "many, perhaps most, theological doctrines are surprisingly transformed."[30]

In the new view of inspiration, the Bible's permanent element was thus inward. Its expressions and forms were part of the changing outer husk of history. God's activity in history was a transitory expression or revelation of his purposes for the progress of human society. The Bible was the record of such revelations. These revelations could be examined to discover God's redemptive purposes by discovering their inward value. Even if cloaked in the form of legend or myth, they revealed spiritual truths and principles, liberals said. The Bible could then be inspired and authoritative but did not need to be true in its historical statements. It taught eternal spiritual principles but did so through imperfect and often inaccurate historical statements, that is, through myth.

---

28. This view of inspiration had important proponents, especially in Europe, before Darwin published his *Origin of the Species* in 1859, but in America particularly the spread of Darwinian science played a key role in the spread of the new view of inspiration. See Gary Dorrien, *The Making of American Liberal Theology: Imagining Progressive Religion, 1805–1900* (Louisville: Westminster John Knox Press, 2001), 109–10, 286–88, 298–302.
29. Ibid., 334–58.
30. W. W. Fenn, "Modern Liberalism," *American Journal of Theology* 17 (1913): 512.

The basic method was to examine all the particular historical statements of the Bible in order to discover the unchanging eternal principles that lay beneath them. The eternal resided in the spiritual kernels that were hidden under the husks of historical language. The task was to remove the temporal and changeable husk of history to reveal the unchanging spiritual essence. Liberals applied the method not only to Scripture but also to the history of the church. The church's theology and forms were merely temporary expressions of the spiritual experience of Christians. These changed, but the God whom they experienced did not. This meant that Christianity itself was not about doctrine but about life.

Many educated Southern Baptist leaders embraced this new understanding of Christianity. They began to view theology and ecclesiology as changing expressions of spiritual experience. These changed to meet the needs of changing social conditions. "Theologies change every day," North Carolina editor J. W. Bailey wrote. "Boyce has one, Strong another, Clarke another."[31] "Baptists," he wrote, "stand for a Principle of Life" rather than "formulated dogmas."[32] The reconstruction in theology promised renewed health for the churches. One benefit was that "dogmatic clamor" was passing away, said Virginia Baptist leader W. R. L. Smith.[33] Outward theology was impermanent, but the experience of vital relation to God abided always.

Traditional conservatives in the Southern Baptist Convention found such statements troubling, but they were not sure that they understood them. They felt that Christianity was both a doctrine and a life and that the life could not be sustained without the doctrine given once for all by Christ and his apostles. They could not stretch to grasp the idealism that was foundational to progressive reconstruction in theology, and they saw no reason to question traditional realism. Such conservatives retained a majority in the Southern Baptist Convention, but the progressives possessed the citadels of learning and exercised broad influence.

Progressive leaders redefined doctrine. The principle of individual freedom led many to oppose traditional Baptist commitments to such doctrines as penal substitution in the atonement and the eternal election of individuals.[34] It led other Baptists to bootstrap the old doctrines to the new theology by an appeal to the ideal of individual freedom. E. Y. Mullins, for example, rather miraculously established the doctrine of hell on this principle. Heaven was the rational and spiritual

---

31. J. W. Bailey, "The Appeal to the Scriptures," *Biblical Recorder*, December 2, 1903, 8.

32. J. W. Bailey, "The Danger of Denominationalism," *Biblical Recorder*, November 5, 1902, 8.

33. W. R. L. Smith, "The Baptist Law of Conduct," *Biblical Recorder*, November 25, 1903, 2.

34. E.g., W. R. L. Smith, "Wherein Lies the Efficacy of Jesus' Work in the Reconciliation?" in *Eighteenth Annual Session of the Baptist Congress* (New York: Baptist Congress Publishing, 1900), 85–94. Broadly, see Paul Harvey, *Redeeming the South: Religious Cultures and Racial Identities among Southern Baptists, 1865–1925* (Chapel Hill: University of North Carolina Press, 1997), 152–54.

outcome of choosing fellowship with God by faith, and hell was the rational and spiritual outcome of rejecting that fellowship. Hell was essentially the absence of that fellowship, and it operated in the soul by the laws of the moral and spiritual universe.[35] Human freedom rather than divine holiness made hell necessary; thus, "God could only annul hell by annulling freedom." Persons entered hell by "free choice," he said. By their unbelief and sin they "choose it for their final abode."[36] When Jesus said to the wicked, "Depart from me, ye cursed, into everlasting fire, prepared for the devil and his angels" (Matt. 25:41 KJV), Mullins explained, Jesus meant that "men damn themselves to suffering" and that "in a real sense a man makes his own hell."[37] Freedom became the touchstone of truth.

The progressives redefined the doctrine of human nature to accord with the ideal of individual freedom. "The essence of man," New Orleans Baptist Theological Seminary professor Frank Stagg held, is "his God-given freedom for self-determination."[38] God ordained freedom as the highest good and made it the central endowment of human nature.

Progressive leaders also applied the idealist method to Baptist identity. They looked across the generations of "Baptists" and looked for the unchanging essence that lay beneath the various theological opinions and church practices. What they discovered was that the fundamental element of Baptist identity was individual freedom. This was the Baptist contribution to the world. Each denomination, progressive Baptists said, "make their particular contribution to the saving of the world."[39] The Presbyterians, one popular pastor said, contributed the family principle; Methodists, the tribal; Episcopalians, the national; and Roman Catholics, the cosmopolitan. But "Baptists are individualists."[40]

The principle of individual freedom thus became the new basis of Baptist doctrine and church practice. The authority of the Bible stood upon voluntary acceptance and individual freedom of interpretation. Justification by faith was the doctrinal expression and believer's baptism the ritual expression of individual personal relationship with God. Baptist church practices similarly derived from commitment to democracy and the sovereign individual. And because the Baptist principle was in perfect harmony with God's movement of social progress toward

---

35. E. Y. Mullins, *The Christian Religion in Its Doctrinal Expression* (Philadelphia: Judson Press, 1917), 488–89.
36. E. Y. Mullins, "The Meaning of Religion," *Religious Herald*, July 24, 1919, 4.
37. Mullins, *Christian Religion*, 489.
38. Frank Stagg, letter to Clifton Mathews, March 16, 1955, Box 2, Folder 4, Frank Stagg Collection, Samford University, Birmingham, Alabama.
39. William L. Poteat, "Religion in Education," in *The Baptist Message* (Nashville: Sunday School Board of the Southern Baptist Convention, 1911), 65. See similarly, A. T. Robertson, "The Distinctive Baptist Principle," *Biblical Recorder*, September 16, 1903, 2.
40. W. W. Landrum, "Baptist Self-Respect—A Drawing Force," in *The Baptist Message* (see note 39), 76.

the kingdom of God, Baptists were in the best position to influence the masses and were therefore gaining hegemony among the denominations. "Our success," George McDaniel wrote, "is conditioned upon our loyalty to these principles."[41]

The view that the essence of the Baptist movement was individual freedom could not well accommodate traditional church discipline. Even so, the proponents of this new theology did not quite repudiate discipline. They redefined it as an element of the actualization of personality, of the intersection of individual freedom and interpersonal relationship. They strained to recast exclusion as the personal choice of individual members. "Strictly speaking," as Frank Stagg explained exclusion in 1947, "the church does not *exclude* him; it simply recognizes that he is not one of them."[42]

This strained credulity. It did not make sense to make freedom the central Christian value and then go about excluding people from church against their will. The church had to respect individual freedom. As Southern Seminary professor Harold Tribble explained, the church did not coerce: "There is no justification for any sort of government within the church that suppresses the freedom of any individual member. . . . There is no justification for any practice that imposes upon individuals conformity to ecclesiastical polity that does not arise spontaneously from the experience of fellowship with Christ."[43] Voluntarism formed the essence of individual and church life. Discipline seemed rather involuntary. The new view of Baptist identity reduced discipline therefore to persuading individuals, without a hint of coercion, voluntarily to withdraw.

The idealist redefinition of Baptist identity, ecclesiology, and theology had profound ramifications. The idealist method inevitably measured theology and ecclesiology by the standards of human experience and values. Perhaps the most revolutionary result was the reconceptualizing of God according to humanitarian values. Many Southern Baptist leaders accepted the idea of the humanitarian God.[44] In this view, God gave commands and ordered history according to the humanitarian standard of the common good rather than according to the scriptural standard of divine purpose and holiness. This tended to marginalize such traditional doctrines as the justice and wrath of God. It could not come to terms with

41. George W. McDaniel, *The People Called Baptists* (Nashville: Sunday School Board of the Southern Baptist Convention, 1919), 61. See also pp. 39–60.

42. Frank Stagg, *New Testament Theology* (Nashville: Broadman Press, 1962), 275.

43. Harold Tribble, "typescript on the church," Harold Tribble Papers, Reynolds Library, Wake Forest University, Winston-Salem, North Carolina.

44. James Turner's discussion of this reconceptualization of God as a source of theological reconstruction and "doctrinal doubts" is helpful and suggestive of similar dynamics among Southern Baptist leaders. See James Turner, *Without God, Without Creed: The Origins of Unbelief in America* (Baltimore: Johns Hopkins University Press, 1985), 142–43.

the God who visited the iniquity of the fathers upon the sons and who put to death Ananias and Sapphira.[45] It tended to view the fear of God not as the beginning of wisdom, not as virtue, but as superstition and cowardice. The humanitarian God seemed averse to church discipline. The new Baptist identity, and the new theology and ecclesiology it produced, proved incompatible with the old discipline.

A New Stewardship: Saving the Nation from Its Earthly Perils

A third shift that undermined church discipline was an expansion of the mission of the church to include stewardship of the social order. After the Civil War a generation of Southern Baptist leaders arose who taught that the mission of the church included more than evangelization and discipleship. It included also the creation of Christian civilization in the South, the nation, and the world. Southern Baptist leaders began to feel that they had stewardship for both the church and the social order. But the more solicitous they became to purify society, the less concerned they were to purify the church.[46]

America's progressive civic leaders generally held that the church played a central role in the social order. They argued that the safety of American freedom depended on civic morality, and civic morality depended on strong churches. So they called the churches to do their part for establishing a good and orderly society and protecting it from ruin. The churches complied.

Henry Grady, editor of the *Atlanta Constitution*, for example, viewed the southern churches as pillars of the social order. The South's matchless civilization rested in significant measure on the "straight and simple faith" of the people, who were markedly religious "along the old lines of Christian belief."[47] The combination of orthodox faith and commitment to American democracy had saved the South from social peril. The rest of the nation, Grady insinuated, was in jeopardy of ruin due to the spread of anarchy and socialism in politics, and of heresy and speculation in religion. The South, Grady suggested, may be "the last hope" for saving orthodox religion and American republicanism, the two pillars of freedom.[48]

---

45. See W. O. Carver, *Acts of the Apostles* (Nashville: Sunday School Board of the Southern Baptist Convention, 1916), 55–56; Frank Stagg, *The Book of Acts: The Early Struggle for an Unhindered Gospel* (Nashville: Broadman Press, 1955), 83–84.
46. Parts of this section are adapted from Gregory A. Wills, "The First One Hundred Years of Baptist Home Mission in America: Civilization, Denominationalism, and Americanization" (a paper presented at the Fourth International Conference on Baptist Studies, Acadia College, Nova Scotia, Canada, July 2006, to be published in the volume of conference papers).
47. Henry Grady, *The New South* (New York: Robert Bonner's Sons, 1889), 154.
48. Ibid., 185–86.

Southern Baptist leaders generally accepted this challenge to help save civilization. Their churches would contribute to the uplift of southern education, economy, culture, and order. By such social service the churches won the respect and gratitude of all "right-minded" persons and expanded their influence over the region. And Baptists rejoiced in the respect and influence they had gained. The result, Rufus Weaver argued, was that Southern Baptists had the "opportunity of weaving these [Baptist] principles into the civilization of the New South, and making the new social order in warp and woof baptistic."[49] They would not suffer irrelevance. They would stand in the breach as a great bulwark to save civilization from ruin.

While true religion aided the social order, the mission to rescue society from its earthly perils also generated support for denominational efforts. Many Baptist leaders seemed to sense that the commission to evangelize and make disciples was an insufficient basis for their denominational success. In order to win wider support among Southern Baptists, denominational leaders needed a grander vision, a more compelling justification. They found it in a commission to civilize society.

The most striking expressions of this vision came in pleas for support of the Home Mission Board of the Southern Baptist Convention. In the South, home mission promoters argued, the Christian faith was sounder and purer than in the North. The new theology of modernist rationalism had enervated northern churches. Their forces were no longer adequate to meet the perils to American civilization. The destiny of America and the world now depended on the success of southern home mission efforts.

Richard Edmonds, editor of the *Manufacturer's Record*, promoted the home mission cause for the Home Mission Board. The forces of materialism, superstition, and socialism threatened "the civilization of the world." But, he suggested, God had raised up the South to meet these threats. "The salvation of America largely depends upon the South," he wrote. If southerners would support the efforts of the Home Mission Board, then the board's evangelistic and educational efforts would save the South, America, and the world from vice, ignorance, lawlessness, and barbarism. Southern religion was the hope of the world, and Southern Baptists were the hope of southern religion. "Upon the Baptists of the South," Edmonds concluded, "may rest the salvation of America and of the world from chaos and from sinking back into the darkness of the middle ages."[50] Save the South and you save the world.

---

49. Rufus M. Weaver, "The Baptist Opportunity in the World of Modern Thought," in *The Baptist Message*, 106.

50. Richard H. Edmonds, *The South, America and the World* (Atlanta: Home Mission Board of the Southern Baptist Convention, [c. 1920]), 1–3.

Victor Masters, publicity director of the Home Mission Board 1909–1921, pressed the same argument in the first two decades of the twentieth century. In his many books and pamphlets promoting home mission, he enumerated the familiar perils: immigration, Roman Catholicism, socialism, materialism, Mormonism, and urbanization. He added also the perils of German rationalism, evolution, and the new modernist theology. These evils endangered American civilization and Christianity. The immigrants must be Americanized, and home mission alone could accomplish it. "Never was there in any nation a need for Home Mission effort comparable to that which now confronts American evangelical Christian bodies."[51]

William L. Poteat, president of Wake Forest College and Southern Baptists' best-known liberal, told the messengers of the 1910 Southern Baptist Convention meeting that Baptists were in the best position to save civilization and that they would do it primarily through supporting Baptist colleges. The educational institutions of America were becoming thoroughly secularized, Poteat warned. Secularized education could not produce virtue, and without virtue, democratic institutions would fail. The result would be "national disorder, disintegration, and decay." But religion, the religion of Baptists, not only taught persons their duty but also gave them heart to do it. In this way religion was the "organizing force" of American democracy. The nation's hope for safety was "not policemen, but God." Baptist principles would save civilization.[52]

Southern Baptist leaders in this way made religion serve the social order. They construed piety as a means of economic growth, social stability, and cultural advance. They subordinated concern for man's eternal fate to anxiety about the nation's political welfare. They seemed to fear social disorder more than God. The church became more relevant to society, but it was a poor trade. Spirituality diminished and worldliness increased.

Church discipline could survive only if the pastors led their churches to a scriptural standard of separation from the world. But they feared social disorder, the ostracism of the cultured and literate, and the inconveniences of rebuke and correction, and they shaped the churches accordingly. Yoking the church to the welfare of society erased much of the distance between the church and the world. Separation from the world seemed ineffective for church growth and seemed to relegate the church to irrelevance. Southern Baptists no longer felt themselves separated from the world. Church discipline could not survive this transformation.

---

51. Victor I. Masters, *Making America Christian* (Atlanta: Home Mission Board of the Southern Baptist Convention, 1921), 52.
52. William L. Poteat, "Religion in Education," in *The Baptist Message* (see note 39), 67, 61.

Most ordinary Southern Baptists and pastors kept aloof from the progressive ideals that undergirded these three tectonic shifts. But they too tended to embrace the new definition of the church and were influenced by the new understanding of Baptist identity. They too failed to lead their churches to practice New Testament discipline. The ideas advanced by progressive Southern Baptist leaders influenced the conservative denomination more profoundly than is generally realized.

These three transformations in Baptist life withered the traditional church discipline. It was unintentional. But in combination they condemned the old discipline to implausibility and impracticality. In theory, Southern Baptist pastors still believed in the necessity of church discipline. But commitment to the efficient church overcame the Christ-ordained order. Commitment to the new view of Baptist identity remade God as a humanitarian, rendered the fear of God irrational, and reconstituted ecclesiology according to the standard of individual freedom. Commitment to saving society overwhelmed commitment to separation from the world.

10

The Reestablishment of Proper Church Discipline

One of the most glaring omissions in modern Baptist church life is the absence of the regular practice of biblical church discipline. The demise of this practice may well rest in the fact that, by and large, contemporary Baptists have not been taught or do not understand the concept of a New Testament church. The majority of Baptist churches today do not perceive themselves as believers joined together by the bond of the Spirit and associated by covenant in a shared confession of faith in the Lord Jesus Christ and a common fellowship of the gospel. Contemporary Baptists seem instead to understand themselves as autonomous individuals casually associated together in loose-knit groupings called churches. The concept of spiritual accountability to God and to one another is tragically lacking or ignored.

The neglect of church discipline as a regular and meaningful part of church life is a departure from our Baptist roots. Historically Baptists have believed that church discipline is not merely a matter of obedience; church health and vitality depend upon it. Baptists believed that our beliefs, mission, witness, proclamation, spirituality, governance, fellowship, and morality are all tied to the faithful practice of discipline.

American Baptists in the nineteenth century gave careful attention to the procedure and practice of church discipline. Baptist historian Gregory Wills notes, "To an antebellum Baptist, a church without discipline would hardly have counted as a church."[1] Baptist churches would devote entire days to deal with disciplinary matters. Congregations would gather to heal breaches of fellowship, admonish

---

1. Gregory A. Wills, *Democratic Religion: Freedom, Authority, and Church Discipline in the Baptist South 1785–1900* (New York: Oxford University Press, 1997), 12.

wayward members, rebuke the obstinate, and, if required, excommunicate the unrepentant. By engaging in these activities, Baptists believed that they were following the biblical pattern established by Christ and the apostles for the health and effectiveness of the church.[2]

The spiritual revitalization of Baptist churches requires that we assume the mantle and once again practice this important church ministry. The health of our churches will continue to suffer from a spiritual malaise and slide into moral decay and cultural accommodation until we are faithful to practice what Christ has instructed us to do. New Testament churches practice church discipline. No church can genuinely claim to be a New Testament church or a Baptist church if it is unfaithful to what the Bible teaches on the practice of church discipline.

Biblical Teaching on the Doctrine of Church Discipline

The practice of church discipline is directly commanded by the Lord. In his instructions regarding the future church, Jesus gave his disciples the procedure for discipline. Matthew 18:15–20 is typically considered to be the most important and definitive text for church discipline. The promise of divine authority is found in verse 18 in Jesus' statement, "I assure you: Whatever you bind on earth is already bound in heaven, and whatever you loose on earth is already loosed in heaven."[3] The terminology of "binding and loosing" also is used by Jesus in Matthew 16:19. In response to Peter's great confession, Jesus promised, "I will give you the keys of the kingdom of heaven, and whatever you bind on earth is already bound in heaven, and whatever you loose on earth is already loosed in heaven." Binding and loosing were concepts used by the Jewish rabbis in the first century to refer to the power of judging matters on the basis of the revelation of God. The Jewish authorities would determine how the Scriptures applied in a specific situation, and they would then render a judgment either by binding (to restrict) or by loosing (to liberate). Christ has given the church the necessary authority to restrict a sinful person under a disciplinary process or to liberate a repentant believer from the process. The church exercises discipline with the authority of heaven, for the Lord is with them, providing assurance and guidance in the process.

The basis for church discipline directly rests upon the holiness of God. God demands that his children be holy. Throughout the Bible, the people of God are characterized by his holiness. This moral purity is not their own achievement but the work of God in their midst. The New Testament describes the church as the

---

2. R. Albert Mohler Jr., "Church Discipline: The Missing Mark," in *Polity: Biblical Arguments on How to Conduct Church Life*, ed. Mark E. Dever (Washington, DC: Center for Church Reform, 2001), 44.

3. All Scripture quotations are from the Holman Christian Standard Bible (HCSB).

people of God who are to be known to the world by their purity of life and integrity of message. Peter reminded the church of this ideal in his quotation of select Old Testament texts in 1 Peter 2:9–10: "But you are a chosen race, a royal priesthood, a holy nation, a people for His possession, so that you may proclaim the praises of the One who called you out of darkness into His marvelous light. Once you were not a people, but now you are God's people; you had not received mercy, but now you have received mercy." The apostle then admonished his readers, "Dear friends, I urge you as aliens and temporary residents to abstain from fleshly desires that war against you. Conduct yourselves honorably among the Gentiles, so that in a case where they speak against you as those who do evil, they may, by observing your good works, glorify God in a day of visitation" (vv. 11–12). Baptist theologian Albert Mohler provides commentary on the implications of this passage for the concept of church discipline.

> As the new people of God, the church is to see itself as an alien community in the midst of spiritual darkness—strangers to the world who must abstain from the lusts and enticements of the world. The church is to be conspicuous in its purity and holiness and steadfast in its confession of the faith once for all delivered to the saints. Rather than capitulating to the moral (or immoral) environment, Christians are to be conspicuous by their good behavior. As Peter summarized, "Just as he who called you is holy, so be holy in all you do" (1 Peter 1:15).[4]

Individual believers and particular churches are therefore to be characterized by the holiness of God (Heb. 12:7–11). The church is now the sanctuary for the presence of the Holy God, his temple where his holy presence resides. God requires that his church reflect his holy character (1 Peter 1:16). Failure to discipline indicates unwillingness on the part of the church to ensure that his character is rightly and clearly reflected. God has chosen to make his name and glory known through the church. Only a pure, holy church can radiate the glory of God to the world. Church discipline is one means of preserving the holiness of the church.

The church is to practice discipline because God himself disciplines those he loves. Every child of God has at one time or another experienced the chastening work of God. "For the Lord disciplines the one He loves, and punishes every son whom He receives" (Heb. 12:6). As an expression of familial relationship, God disciplines those who belong to him. As an expression and reflection of this aspect of his character, God requires his church to discipline its members.

---

4. Mohler, "Church Discipline," 48.

The writings of Paul reveal that the early church put into practice the instructions of the Lord. First Corinthians 5:1 recounts the incident of a man who was "living with his father's wife," a reference to an incestuous relationship. Paul rebukes the Corinthian church for their failure to deal with the matter. In fact, Paul rebukes the church for its pride and toleration of such aberrant, sinful behavior (v. 2). He instructs the Corinthians believers to "turn that one over to Satan for the destruction of the flesh" (v. 5), a call for the church to excommunicate the man. This process appears to have had the desired effect, because 2 Corinthians 2:4–8 indicates that the apostle had to remind the congregation to forgive and comfort the repentant man and to restore him back into the fellowship.

Other passages in the New Testament also reveal instances where the early church obeyed the command of Christ and practiced church discipline. Galatians 6:1 provides instructions for restoration and cautions against pride. The church at Thessalonica was to warn and eventually withdraw from those who were lazy and those who rejected apostolic teaching (2 Thess. 3:6–15). Elders/overseers who sin are to be rebuked publicly as a warning to others (1 Tim. 5:19–20). Titus was to issue warnings to divisive people to cease from their controversial and heretical speculations. After appropriate warnings, Titus was to "reject," or withdraw from them (Titus 3:9–11).

CHURCH DISCIPLINE IN BAPTIST THOUGHT

The identification of proper church discipline as a mark of a New Testament church dates as far back as the Belgic Confession of 1561.

> The marks by which the true Church is known are these: If the pure doctrine of the gospel is preached therein; if she maintains the pure administration of the sacraments as instituted by Christ; if church discipline is exercised in punishing of sin; in short, if all things are managed according to the Word of God, all things contrary thereto rejected, and Jesus Christ acknowledged as the only Head of the Church. Hereby the true Church may certainly be known, from which no man has a right to separate himself.[5]

Church discipline and its implications for church membership were prominent emphases in the early writings and practices of the Anabaptists. The origin of those early followers of Ulrich Zwingli who would later be called Anabaptists is often believed to have arisen from their pursuit of a faithful church separate from the state and free from the error of infant baptism. These beliefs certainly were

5. Philip Schaff, *The Creeds of Christendom*, rev. David S. Schaff (New York: Harper and Row, 1931), 3:419–20.

primary convictions that undergirded this movement. However, it is equally valid to note that development of the Anabaptist movement also was precipitated in part by their concern for dealing with sinful offenders within their fellowship according to the pattern of Matthew 18. The term "rule of Christ" (referring to Matthew 18) was already a fixed phrase in their vocabulary by 1524.[6]

Several factors led the early Anabaptists to reject infant baptism. The inability of the child to exercise his or her faith and to repent of sin clearly was problematic. In addition, the Anabaptists rejected the practice of infant baptism because of the clear lack of biblical teaching on the matter. They also repudiated infant baptism because they believed that the one who requested baptism should be able and willing to submit to the mutual obligation of giving and receiving "admonition" from the congregation. An infant cannot do this. For example, before his discussion on whether water has a saving effect or whether unbaptized children are lost, Conrad Grebel wrote in September 1524 that "even an adult is not to be baptized without Christ's rule of 'binding and loosing.'"[7] The issue, therefore, is not simply the age of the one desiring baptism but also the ability of the individual to make a commitment to enter into the covenant community with a clear understanding of congregational accountability.

Balthasar Hubmaier argued that the willingness to be "admonished" by the church should be a primary consideration to determine whether or not someone is an appropriate candidate for baptism. In his catechism, Hubmaier writes:

Q. What is the baptismal pledge?

A. It is a commitment which one makes to God publicly and orally before the church, in which he renounces Satan, and his thoughts and works. He pledges as well that he will henceforth set all his faith, hope and trust alone in God, and direct his life according to the divine Word, in the power of Jesus Christ our Lord, and in case he should not do that, he promises hereby to the church that he desires virtuously to receive fraternal admonition from her members and from her, as is said above.

Q. What power do those in the church have over one another?

A. The authority of fraternal admonition.

Q. What is fraternal admonition?

A. The one who sees his brother sinning goes to him in love and admonishes him fraternally and quietly that he should abandon such sin. If he does so

---

6. The Anabaptists appear to have reached this position prior to any final conclusions about the form of the church, the practice of the baptism of believers, or the church's autonomy from the state.

7. Conrad Grebel, "Letters to Thomas Muntzer," in *Spiritual and Anabaptist Writers*, ed. George H. Williams and Angel M. Mergal (Philadelphia: Westminster Press, 1957), 80.

he has won his soul. If he does not, then he takes two or three witnesses with him and admonishes him before them again. If he follows him, it is concluded, if not, he says it to the church. The same calls him forward and admonishes him for the third time. If he now abandons his sin, he has saved his soul.

Q. Whence does the church have this authority?

A. From the command of Christ, who said to his disciples, "all that you bind on earth shall be bound also in heaven and all that you loose on earth shall also be loosed in heaven."

Q. But what right has one brother to use this authority on another?

A. From the baptismal pledge in which one subjects oneself to the Church and all her members according to the word of Christ.[8]

One of the oldest Anabaptist articles of faith, the Schleitheim Articles (1527), discusses the "ban" (excommunication) as a principal point for their union to which all members must agree and submit.[9] In his treatise "The Church of God" (1560), Dietrich Philips identified as one of the seven "ordinances" or marks of the true church "evangelical separation, without which the church of God cannot stand or be maintained."[10] Peter Rideman addressed the issue of exclusion when he stated, "Therefore, do we watch over one another, telling each other his faults, warning and rebuking with all diligence. But where one will not accept the rebuke, but disregardeth it, the matter is brought before the Church, and if he hear not the Church, then he is excluded and put out."[11] Menno Simons also wrote prolifically on church discipline.[12]

Church discipline and its implications for church membership were also prominent emphases in the writings and practices of the early Baptists. John Smyth declared that Christ has granted the church the power to excommunicate and that final appeal for disciplinary matters rests with the church.[13] In his English Declaration at Amsterdam, Thomas Helwys noted,

8. Denis Janz, ed., *The Reformation Catechisms* (New York: Edwin Mellen Press, 1982), 135–36.

9. William L. Lumpkin, *Baptist Confessions of Faith* (Valley Forge, PA: Judson Press, [c. 1959]), 25.

10. Dietrich Philips, "The Church of God," in *Spiritual and Anabaptist Writers*, 246–48.

11. Peter Rideman, *Account of Our Religion, Doctrine, and Faith* (Rifton, NY: Plough Publishing House, 1970), 131–32.

12. Menno Simons, "A Kind Admonition on Church Discipline" (1541), in *The Complete Writings of Menno Simons*, trans. Leonard Verduin, ed. John C. Wenger (Scottdale, PA: Herald Press, 1956), 407–18; idem, "A Clear Account of Excommunication" (1550), in *Complete Writings of Menno Simons*, 455–85; and idem, "Instruction on Excommunication" (1588), in *Complete Writings of Menno Simons*, 959–98.

13. Lumpkin, *Baptist Confessions of Faith*, 101.

> That Brethren impenitent in one sin after the admonition of the Church, are to bee excluded the cōmunion off the Sainets. Mat. 18.17. 1 Cor. 5.4, 13. & therefore not the cōmitting off sin doth cut off anie from the Church, but refusing to heare the Church to reformacion.[14]

The First London Confession of the Particular Baptists (1644) states that every member is subject to congregational discipline and that "the Church ought with great care and tenderness, with due advice to proceed against her members."[15] The Charleston Church Discipline (1774) defines three types or degrees of church censure: (1) the rebuke, admonition, or brotherly reproof; (2) suspension "from office, from the Lord's table"; and (3) excommunication, or exclusion "from union and communion with the church, and from all rights and privileges thereof."[16] Church discipline was a prominent theme in the writings of J. R. Graves and was a key factor in his argument for local church practice regarding the Lord's Supper.[17] The Abstract of Principles of The Southern Baptist Theological Seminary (1858) identifies the three essential marks of a New Testament church as order, discipline, and worship:

> The Lord Jesus is the head of the Church, which is composed of all His true disciples, and in Him is invested supremely all power for its government. According to His commandment, Christians are to associate themselves into particular societies or churches; and to each of these churches He hath given needful authority for administering that order, discipline and worship which He hath appointed. The regular officers of a Church are Bishops or Elders, and Deacons.[18]

This sampling of the evidence demonstrates that church discipline was regarded by our Baptist ancestors as a biblical practice. Our history also reveals that church discipline was widely practiced by the majority of Baptist churches prior to the twentieth century. One of the convictions of our denominational forebears was

---

14. Ibid., 121.
15. Ibid., 168.
16. "A Summary of Church-Discipline Shewing the Qualifications and Duties, of the Officers and Members, of a Gospel Church, by the Baptist-Association, in Charleston, South Carolina, 1774, V," in *Baptist Church Discipline*, ed. James Leo Garrett Jr. (Nashville: Broadman Press, 1962), 42–45.
17. J. R. Graves, *The Lord's Supper: A Church Ordinance* (Texarkana, AR-TX: Baptist Sunday School Committee, 1928), 14, 28–30, 36–39.
18. "The Abstract of Principles of The Southern Baptist Theological Seminary," at http://www .sbts.edu/About_Us/Beliefs/Abstract of_Principles.aspx (accessed March 2, 2007).

their pledge to separate themselves from the world and to submit themselves to Christ and to each other. Church discipline was considered one means of achieving this distinction.

The Occasion for Discipline

The New Testament does not explicitly state the criterion for determining which offenses are worthy of discipline. Although the Bible does join church discipline with the purity of the church, the biblical pattern reveals that the disciplinary process was practiced with discretion and care. The apostle Paul has much to say about the sins of the people in the church at Corinth, among which are divisiveness, sexual immorality, and disorderly conduct. However, Paul instructs only the discipline of the man involved in the incestuous relationship. We find this same discretionary care for church discipline exercised throughout the New Testament. No attempt is ever made to make the church sinlessly perfect by disciplining every sinful deviation or infraction.[19]

The common theme that seems to tie together the instances of church discipline in the New Testament are those sins that have a harmful, public effect upon the congregation in some way. Several categories of offense in the New Testament that require discipline include difficulties between members of a church (Matt. 18:15–17; 1 Cor. 5:5–6), disorderly conduct (2 Thess. 3:6–15), divisiveness (Rom. 16:17–18; Titus 3:9–10), and blatant immorality (1 Cor. 5:1–13). Along with the sins of sexual immorality, Paul also lists greed, idolatry, drunkenness, abusive speech, and swindling as worthy of discipline (1 Cor. 5:11). False teaching also is identified as an offense that merits church discipline (1 Tim. 1:20; 2 Tim. 2:17–18; Rev. 2:14–16). These false teachings are not lesser or minor issues of biblical interpretation but rather involve the fundamental doctrines of the faith.[20]

All the sins that were explicitly disciplined in the New Testament appear to be known publicly or were outwardly evident and probably had been occurring over a period of time. The public nature and knowledge of the sins brought reproach upon the church, impugned the integrity of its message and mission, and dishonored the cause of Christ. Further, the church's failure to address such matters would have signaled the approval of the congregation and could have encouraged others to follow the sinful practices that were publicly tolerated in the fellowship.[21]

Without being too reductionistic, we can cluster all of these various sins that are the occasion for church discipline into three main categories: fidelity to orthodox doctrine, purity and holiness of life, and unity of the fellowship. Each of these

19.   Robert Saucy, *The Church in God's Program* (Chicago: Moody, 1972), 120–21.
20.   Ibid., 121.
21.   Wayne Grudem, *Systematic Theology* (Grand Rapids: Zondervan, 1994), 896–97.

three areas is essentially and vitally important for the health and integrity of the faith and practice of the church.

THE PURPOSE OF CHURCH DISCIPLINE

Church discipline is the process by which a local church works to restore a professing Christian who has fallen into sin. The errant person may be the leader of an entire denomination or a low-profile member of a small rural church. All members are subject to the disciplinary action of the church.

The primary purpose of church discipline is restoration (of the offender to right behavior and attitude) and reconciliation (with other believers and with God). Church discipline is an act of love to bring repentance and restoration in the life of the errant brother or sister. With discipline comes hope for renewal (1 Cor. 5:6–8). Sin hinders fellowship among believers and with God. Reconciliation and restoration can occur only when the church confronts and deals with the offender. A church that disciplines is acting in love to reclaim a straying brother or sister, restore that person to right fellowship, and to rescue him or her from destructive patterns of life that equally threaten the ministry and message of the church. Even the act of excommunication is taken with the hope that the errant individual will repent and be restored to the fold of God. If the church will remember the ultimate purpose for church discipline, then it will be easier for the Christians involved to act genuinely with love and concern as they participate in the disciplinary process.

Church discipline also keeps sin from spreading to the rest of the fellowship. Churches that regularly and faithfully practice biblical church discipline are following a biblical prescription that will keep sin from spreading and contaminating the rest of the fellowship. The author of Hebrews alludes to the corporate, contaminating effect of sin when he states, "See to it that no one falls short of the grace of God and that no root of bitterness springs up, causing trouble and by it, defiling many" (Heb. 12:15). The apostle Paul makes mention of this dynamic when he warns the Corinthian church, "Don't you know that a little yeast permeates the whole batch of dough? Clean out the old yeast so that you may be a new batch" (1 Cor. 5:6–7). The sinful effects of the undisciplined may well spread to others who are aware of the problem and know that the church did nothing about it. Such neglect on the part of the church could cause some within the fellowship to think that sin is not as bad as they thought, thereby tempting them to commit similar kinds of sin. Church discipline helps the church avoid the contamination of sin. In fact, the public discipline of wayward elders before a congregation serves warning to the church to deter the members from similar sins (1 Tim. 5:20).

Church discipline also preserves the communal purity and holiness of the congregation. The Lord Jesus Christ wants to present to himself a church "in splendor, without spot or wrinkle or any such thing, but holy and blameless" (Eph. 5:27). Christ is the head of the church, and its character reflects upon its testimony of him. Even angels and demons look at the church and see the manifold wisdom of God (Eph. 3:10). Paul exhorts Christians to "walk worthy of the calling you have received" (Eph. 4:1). The moral purity and spiritual holiness of the church are to reflect the character of God to the world. When a church member continues to sin outwardly in a way that is evident to the world, Christ is dishonored and the integrity of the church's work and witness is impugned. The apostle Peter encourages believers to "make every effort to be found in peace without spot or blemish before Him" (2 Peter 3:14). Christians are to live in obedience to the Word of God and to be exemplary in their conduct.

THE DECLINE OF THE PRACTICE OF CHURCH DISCIPLINE

Several factors in Baptist life have contributed to the decline of the practice of church discipline in our Baptist churches. The cultural shift of the twentieth century precipitated the rise of a stringent individual autonomy. Christians have bought into the "every-man-is-an-island" mentality so prevalent in our age. In addition, the relativism so pervasive in Western secular society has managed to seep slowly but surely into our churches. As a result, the church is awash in a brash individualism that effectively denudes its ability to make moral judgments. The common mantras of this attitude are "mind your own business" and "who are we to judge?" Because of the reticence of Christians to make moral judgments based on the Word of God, some of the sins that automatically led to ecclesiastical censure or possible excommunication in the past are now regarded by the church as justifiable or acceptable. The movement of the church away from communal accountability toward autonomous individualism is one factor that destroys the authority or will of a church to exercise discipline.

Another reason for the decline of church discipline may be traced to a general lack of respect for authority within the church. The anti-institutional mood of the past four decades has effectively eroded ecclesiastic authority. Our Baptist ancestors held a high view of the authority of the church and regarded church discipline as a grave matter. In contrast, church authority today (especially in our free church tradition) is met with skepticism and contempt. The attitude of disrespect for church and ministerial authority common outside the church has made significant inroads into the church. The result is that many Christians imbibe the secular disdain for authority in general and authority within the church in particular.

Differing denominational policies also contribute to the demise of church discipline. Some denominations in essence have no discipline. Other denominations are lax or lack the wherewithal to follow whatever rules or guidelines they may have. In addition, local congregations do not honor the disciplinary actions of sister churches. Anyone who is disciplined or censured consequently can leave one denomination or local church and join another without any difficulty. This denominational laissez-faire attitude significantly reduces the effectiveness of discipline.

Confusion concerning Christian accountability within the local church further erodes the church's ability to discipline its members. To belong to the Lord is to belong to his church and to submit to the discipline of his people (Matt. 18:15–18; Gal. 6:1–2). Few Christians today, however, desire or agree to be accountable to other believers. Spiritual accountability is all but nonexistent in many Baptist congregations.

Behind the cultural, philosophical, and theological factors that contribute to the deterioration of church discipline lie two "fears" that likewise precipitate its decline. The first of these fears is the pragmatic loss of revenue. The potential of an "empty offering plate" is a major reason why some churches simply will not practice discipline. Leaders in these Baptist churches fear that if discipline were in fact practiced, a massive exodus would ensue, leaving the church unable to meet its financial obligations. Further, the potential for a loss of tithes and contributions becomes particularly acute when the church must confront and possibly excommunicate its largest contributor. Of course, this attitude is immediately recognized as a compromise of the truth and conviction of God. The local church cannot be "held hostage." Baptist churches must trust the Lord to take care of their needs and obediently practice what Christ has commanded.

The second fear with regard to the exercise of discipline is the rising fear of litigation. Those who practice discipline might find themselves being subjected to lawsuits by the recipients of the church's disciplinary activity. More and more churches fear a legal backlash if they make any attempt to discipline their members. Churches should be sensitive, loving, and careful whenever it is necessary to discipline a member, but the church must be faithful to the biblical mandate to discipline despite the threat of potential legal action. In response to a situation in which a church was sued by a former member, Chuck Colson noted the following: "It will be sad news if the court should emasculate the church by holding that it can't enforce biblical standards on its members; but it will be even worse news if it turns out that by ignoring our biblical responsibilities we have done it to ourselves."[22]

---

22.   Chuck Colson, "The Church Should Mind Its Own Business," *Jubilee* (April 1984): 3.

Each of these reasons poses formidable and real challenges to our Baptist churches in the reclamation and practice of church discipline. For that matter, however, every generation of Baptists has had to contend with its own unique cultural and pragmatic pressures that could potentially jeopardize its practice of church discipline. Prior to the twentieth century, most Baptist churches were able to face and overcome these challenges. The twentieth century, however, has witnessed the almost complete capitulation of most Southern Baptist churches to the numerous philosophical and societal pressures. As we move into the twenty-first century, we must confront and overcome any and all challenges that threaten to undermine our fidelity to biblical church discipline.

A COVENANT COMMUNITY

The Baptist Faith and Message (2000) states that a New Testament church is a group of believers "associated by covenant in the faith and fellowship of the gospel." Part of our Baptist ecclesiology is that a true church is a group of followers of Christ joined together in voluntary covenant with God. The early Baptists believed that a church should be a group of converted individuals gathered from the world at large and united for the purpose of serving together under the lordship of Christ.

Seventeenth-century Baptists customarily formed new congregations by "covenanting" with God and one another to walk together in all the ways of Christ. The persons who were to be constituted as members of a church would write their covenant, and they would sign their names to the document at a public meeting. This act of covenanting made explicit in writing the vows and commitments made in baptism. The formal act of signing the covenant was considered the means of constituting the church. New members would be expected to affirm in writing their consent to the dictates of the covenant. Entire congregations would periodically have occasions when, as a church body, they would renew their covenant vows. Some Baptist churches would combine their covenant renewals with their observance of the Lord's Supper.[23]

Benjamin Keach, a leading seventeenth-century Baptist, used the concept of covenant in his definition of a Baptist church. Although the actual word is not used, the language used by Keach is descriptive of the idea of covenant. For Keach, a church is "a congregation of godly Christians, who at a stated assembly (being first baptized upon profession of faith) do by mutual agreement and consent give themselves up to the Lord, and one to another, according to the will of God."[24]

---

23. Norman H. Maring and Winthrop S. Hudson, *A Baptist Manual of Polity and Practice* (Valley Forge, PA: Judson Press, 1963), 72.
24. Ibid.

Covenant language varied from church to church and was often shaped by cultural and contextual factors. Certain basic concepts, however, were quite common. The essential idea could be expressed in a statement such as, "We do hereby give ourselves up to the Lord and to one another, agreeing to walk together in all of the ways he makes known to us." Declarations of binding duties and obligatory behaviors would often, though not always, follow the introductory statements. Covenants were perceived as the most suitable way to remind church members of their spiritual commitments and corporate responsibilities.[25]

A church covenant underscores that individual believers through the act of regeneration are moved by the Spirit to unite together as the church. The Baptist concept of a covenant community asserts that the church is the result of the free activity of God in the lives of individual believers. Our "association by covenant in the faith and fellowship" stands in sharp contrast to the notion that the church is an organization created by coercive governmental authority or institutional/territorial, ecclesiastical manipulation.

Covenant implies that church life must be experienced in local congregations. The covenant community is by nature local, the result of a particular, visible group of believers united in confession. For Baptists, the covenant that joins believers together in the church of Jesus Christ is sealed in believer's baptism.[26]

The notion of covenant therefore points to the truth that a church is a group of people united together in their joint confession of Jesus Christ as Lord. The church consists of those called out by the preaching of the gospel to live in union with God and other believers. Because all members of a congregation confess allegiance to Christ, they are a people joined together in corporate confession of and submission to God through Christ. This idea is expressed in the Baptist Faith and Message (2000) statement, "In such a congregation each member is responsible and accountable to Christ as Lord."[27] Their mutual confession of Jesus as Christ also means that the believers are united to one another in fellowship and service; they are committed as disciples of Christ to one another. Christians within a covenant community mutually agree to walk together as the people of God. Each individual believer should have a sense of belonging to God and to one another.[28]

---

25. Ibid., 72–73.
26. Stanley J. Grenz, *Theology for the Community of God* (Nashville: Broadman & Holman, 1994), 611–12. Although much about Grenz's theological method and constructions in this work are problematic, his observations about the importance and role of covenant for a local church are instructive.
27. The Baptist Faith and Message at http://www.sbc.net/bfm/bfm2000.asp (accessed March 2, 2007).
28. Robert T. Handy, "The Philadelphia Tradition," in *Baptist Concepts of the Church*, ed. Winthrop S. Hudson (Philadelphia: Judson Press, 1959), 36.

PRACTICAL CONSIDERATIONS FOR THE REESTABLISHMENT OF CHURCH DISCIPLINE

The reclamation of the doctrine of church discipline is absolutely essential for the present and future viability of our Baptist churches. I readily concede that the implementation of church discipline within a congregation that is currently not practicing it will be a slow and tedious process. The old adage, "You cannot turn a ship on a dime," equally applies to effecting change in the culture of a church. "You cannot transform a church overnight." This observation, however, is qualified by the fact that God could bring immediate change to a local congregation. God can change anything immediately and completely. The immediate transformation of the culture of a church on this or any other matter certainly lies within the powerful prerogative of God. But barring this kind of powerful intervention from God, transformation of beliefs and practices will require a commitment to an intentional process from the pastor and leadership of a local church.

The adoption or revision of a church covenant is one place to begin the process of the reestablishment of biblical church discipline. Whether a church is a new work or a well-established congregation, each Baptist church should have a covenant. Church covenants are usually written, and each person must agree to the covenant as a condition for membership in a local congregation. Covenants are based upon and must reflect biblical principles. Although they may state the various beliefs of the congregation, the covenant of a Baptist church should affirm the following: the lordship of Jesus Christ over the church and its members; the divine inspiration, inerrancy, and authority of the Bible; the membership of the church consisting only of regenerate persons who have professed their faith in believer's baptism by immersion; and the mutual consent of each member to congregational accountability as expressed in a willingness to submit themselves to the disciplinary ministry of the church. The regular, voluntary affirmation of the terms of the covenant by all the members of the congregation addresses the issue of a regenerate church membership, reminds each church member of the integrity of church membership, and requires a recommitment to the disciplinary ministry of the local church. By the act of actually signing the covenant, each member declares his or her voluntary consent to an affirmation of the terms of the covenant, of which church discipline is a part.

As part of this process, I would also recommend a careful reexamination and, when necessary, a revision of the legal documents of the church. Because of our highly litigious society, some churches and Christian leaders have concluded that biblical church discipline can no longer be practiced without severe legal consequences. Although the courts on occasion have ruled against certain churches regarding their disciplinary practices, these rare instances should not lead us to conclude that Baptist churches can no longer practice church discipline. The issues of redress in these situations focused upon the inappropriate manner in which a church exercised church discipline and not the fact that the church practiced discipline. A critical examination of the bylaws of a church in its statements about church discipline will not only ensure that a congregation acts appropriately and legally when it exercises church discipline, but also will remind the members that church discipline is an essential part of its biblical and ministerial identity. The theology and methodology regarding discipline should be stated clearly in the constitution and other legal documents of the church.

The rediscovery and implementation of church discipline must be an intentional part of the preaching and teaching ministry of a local church. The pastor and church leadership must regularly instruct and prepare the church for this ministry. As such, the senior pastor should periodically preach and teach on church discipline. The doctrine of church discipline, as well as congregational accountability and integrity, should be taught in new member classes and in the Bible study ministries. This step is preliminary to the proper exercise of discipline and should be a regular part of the ongoing ministry of the church.

The church must understand the purposes of God for corrective discipline. The ultimate goal of this ministry is always restoration and reconciliation. These ideals must be kept before those involved in this ministry. Failure to do so can result in harmful diversions. For example, one temptation in this process is to focus on the procedural mechanics of the process. Ignoring the issues in hopes they will go away or seeking to find a "middle ground" of compromise as opposed to calling for repentance and reconciliation are not biblical solutions. Clever parliamentary or administrative tactics may prevail in an argument or dispute, but such maneuverings will not achieve the biblical ideal of restoration. Another temptation in this process is to interpret all matters that merit discipline therapeutically. In this regard, I recognize that certain instances requiring discipline may also require some form of biblical counseling. The inclusion of counseling may be regarded as part of the restorative and reconciling process, but counseling itself should not be equated with church discipline. Likewise, some disciplinary instances may require some form of mediation as part of the process. As in the case of counseling, however, mediation is not identical with church discipline. The goal is not simply to settle a dispute or resolve a misunderstanding. The goal is rather for the wayward church member to repent and be reconciled to God and to the church.

The proper exercise of church discipline also requires understanding what offenses are "discipline worthy" as well as who is a proper subject of discipline.

Certain diagnostic questions can help a church establish whether an offense calls for discipline. Does the offense fall within those sins that Scripture teaches merit discipline? Is the sin a violation of orthodox doctrine? Does the offense taint the purity and holiness of the life of the congregation? Will this sin disrupt the unity of the fellowship? If the sin requires discipline, is the wrongdoer a member of the church? Is the sin public or private? Private sins call for one-on-one encounters. Public sins may require that the discipline process begin in a more formal, public manner.

THE PROCEDURE FOR DISCIPLINE

The first step in the discipline process is the recognition that an offense has occurred. "If your brother sins against you, go and rebuke him in private. If he listens to you, you have won your brother" (Matt. 18:15). This face-to-face contact is an essential part of the disciplinary process. The offended individual is first to seek reconciliation privately with the offender. If the offender recognizes his sin and repents, the offended person has been restored. The need for privacy is important, because this limits the extent of the injury created by the sin and prevents a public confrontation that would further exacerbate the problem.

The initial private confrontation may not, however, end in repentance and restoration. If this step fails to elicit reconciliation, then other members of the church are to be included in the process. "But if he won't listen, take one or two more with you, so that by the testimony of two or three witnesses every fact may be established" (Matt. 18:16). In this verse, Jesus quoted Deuteronomy 19:15, a text that requires the testimony of multiple witnesses to establish the facts. Jesus draws on the Old Testament prohibition that a person may not be convicted of a crime on the basis of a single witness (Num. 35:30; Deut. 17:6; 19:15). At least two witnesses are necessary to ensure that a charge is brought with integrity, truthfulness, and in an unprejudiced manner. The inclusion of others in the disciplinary process does not have the purpose of establishing the original charge (the truth of which is taken for granted). The presence of others is to bring moral pressure upon the offender and to observe his attitude if it should become necessary to testify before the church. The witnesses are to assist in the attempted restoration of the errant church member, but if the attempt fails, they will serve as witnesses, not of the original transgression, but of the failure to repent. Bringing a sin to a brother or sister's attention in the presence of witnesses is not to threaten or intimidate but to reinforce the severity of the sin and to strengthen the appeal for repentance.

Steps one and two need to be repeated as long as the offender demonstrates genuine openness to listen and consider the gravity of his or her sin. Love demands that more than one meeting may be necessary, with sufficient time and prayer between each step.

If the offender will not listen and repent in the presence of others, then the process transitions into the third phase. Jesus instructs his disciples to "tell the church" (Matt. 18:17). The leadership of the church should be included and provide direction for guiding the church to address the matter as a corporate body, following Paul's instructions that the "spiritual" are to restore those overtaken in a fault (Gal. 6:1). Offenses that merit disciplinary action are always serious. The inclusion of the entire church body, however, intensifies the severity of the situation and further strengthens the appeal for repentance. The church must discern the facts of the situation and render a judgment based upon the teachings of the Word of God. The deportment of the church in this stage must always be Christ-like, with the goal being the restoration of the sinning brother or sister. The public inclusion of the congregation in the process indicates that the church body is ultimately responsible for the discipline of its membership.

The role of the church leadership is crucial in this phase. The leaders should contact the offender to communicate that the matter has moved to a more public format. At this juncture, the leadership, along with the appropriate lay leadership, should commit themselves to diligent and intense prayer and Bible study. The leaders would be wise to dedicate a day to prayer and fasting to seek the direction and discernment of God on the particular disciplinary issue. The pastor and other church leaders likewise should devise an appropriate plan to transition the entire membership into the process over a period of time. The objective in this third stage is to purposefully and appropriately broaden the circle of congregational involvement. As the congregation is involved, the pastor and other leaders should spiritually equip and prepare the fellowship for their inclusion in the disciplinary process.

Jesus provides further instructions for the church should this third step fail to bring reconciliation and restoration: "But if he doesn't pay attention even to the church, let him be like an unbeliever and a tax collector to you" (Matt. 18:17). This fourth step is a formal decision rendered by the congregation. A formal meeting of the church should be convened to address the particular disciplinary matter. The offender should be given notification that a meeting of the church will be conducted to determine his or her status as a member in good standing. Discussion of the particular sin of the errant individual should not be done in an open worship service. Safeguarding the integrity and privacy of the fellowship is crucial. Order and decency should prevail. Only church members should be allowed in the disciplinary meeting. Clear biblical instructions should be given regarding the manner of treatment by the church toward the unrepentant individual, and only the necessary facts about the offense should be communicated.

Should the individual refuse to repent of the offense (the individual may or may not be present at the meeting), the church is to treat the unrepentant individual as an unbeliever. The congregation is to "withdraw fellowship," or "excommunicate," the errant individual. The separation is to be real and public. Church members should be instructed to keep the matter silent and view the offender as a non-Christian who needs prayer and a gospel witness. The church should communicate its decision to the offender in a manner similar to the following:

> We find your present conduct unacceptable and contrary to God and this congregation. Our love for you therefore demands that we take this action, which, though painful, we hope by God's grace will result in your repentance and restoration to God and to this fellowship.

This is not an occasion for rejoicing or celebration. The congregation should mourn and weep the loss of a brother or a sister.

When a brother or sister will not submit to the discipline of the church, then he or she is no longer considered a part of the church. Membership responsibilities and privileges are removed from the unrepentant person. The excommunicant is to be treated as an unbeliever, an unregenerate person outside the community of Christ. Like any non-Christian, he or she would be welcome at a worship service (if the person's presence would not disturb those he or she may have hurt or cause other disruptions in the unity of the Spirit). Hearing the gospel proclaimed is a privilege that every unbeliever should have. Communion, fellowship, and meetings for support or ministry, however, are not permitted for the unrepentant offender. Since the offender gives no evidence of being a believer, the person is to be treated as such until he or she repents. When the opportunity arises, the church should give witness to the individual, but Christian fellowship cannot take place unless and until repentance and restoration occur first.

The church should watch and hope for the offender to repent and seek restoration and reconciliation with God and the congregation. The membership should wait prayerfully and expectantly for signs of repentance and be prepared to restore and embrace the wayward individual should he or she repent of the offense (2 Cor. 2:7–11). Visible evidence of forgiveness and full restoration must be genuinely and sincerely expressed by and for all involved in the process. A formal, public meeting of reconciliation should occur as part of the restorative process.

What should be done if questions or doubts exist regarding the authenticity of the offender's repentance? We must be careful at this point, for no one can judge the heart of another; we can only judge behavior. The church, however, is not obliged to accept every claim of repentance without verification. When the discipline process has gone beyond private admonition and has resulted in the formal removal, the repentant offender may be questioned to gain assurance that the repentance is sincere. The leadership and congregation should exhibit loving discernment in this matter. In cases where the entire assembly was involved in the process, members who may have knowledge that has direct bearing on this matter should be afforded opportunity to share appropriately that information.

Sins that are public in nature and that impact the entire congregation are the offenses that merit the disciplinary action of the church. As already noted, these include: (1) divisions and factions that destroy Christian unity and fellowship, (2) moral and ethical deviations that violate purity and holiness of life, and (3) false doctrines that reject the essential tenets of the Christian faith. Although offenses in any of these categories can trigger the discipline process, the act of excommunication is exercised upon those who fail to repent of their sin. The excommunicated are therefore doubly judged: (1) they are judged for their entrenchment in their actual sin, and (2) they are judged for their unwillingness to repent of their sin.

Although individuals and groups are involved in its various phases, church discipline is the prerogative and responsibility of the corporate body. The final act of excommunication is a corporate act of the congregation. Since the church as a body disciplines, the congregation is also to act corporately in the restoration of the repentant. The church must forgive and comfort the repentant brother or sister, as well as confirm their love toward him or her (2 Cor. 2:6–8).

CONCLUSION

In his essay, "The Church: Baptists and Their Churches in the Eighteenth and Nineteenth Centuries," Gregory A. Wills recounts the story of a significant Southern Baptist leader who was subjected to church discipline.

> On October 16, 1814, William B. Johnson, one of the most respected antebellum Baptist leaders, separated from the First Baptist Church of Savannah, Georgia. He declared himself no longer their pastor, not even a member of the church, and marched out. The congregation expressed their respect and goodwill by inviting him to fill the pulpit temporarily, if he refrained from stirring the controversy between him and the church. Johnson agreed but could not resist the temptation to rebuke the church the following Sunday—he declared them a "corrupt body." For the next five years the regular Baptist churches rejected fellowship

with him. . . . In 1819 William B. Johnson regained fellowship
with regular Baptists when he repented of his condemnation of
the Savannah church and promised to refrain from attempts to
impose his views.[29]

This episode from Baptist life illustrates several principles we have examined in
our brief survey of church discipline. No Christian, no matter how prominent or
esteemed, is above the discipline of the church. Also, restoration and reclamation
can be achieved, and a person can be restored to meaningful ministry.

One of the convictions of the early Baptists was their pledge to separate themselves from the world and to submit themselves to Christ and to each other. We
would do well to follow in their footsteps. Church discipline is one means of
achieving this distinction. Church discipline is an act of obedience to the teachings of Christ (Matt. 18:15–20) and is a means of preserving and facilitating fidelity
to right doctrine, purity of life (holiness), and unity of fellowship.[30] Church discipline is the prerogative of a local church.

Our Baptist ancestors considered church discipline a mark of a true church,
and they practiced it accordingly. This high regard assigned to church discipline
is represented in the following statement from John Leadley Dagg: "It has been
remarked, that when discipline leaves a church, Christ goes with it."[31] If such is the
case, then many of our Baptist churches are in serious trouble.

As Baptists, we should seek to maintain a clear distinction between those who
belong to Christ and those who belong to the world. We must instruct those
desiring to join our churches that their membership includes accountability to the
authority of the congregation. In addition, membership in our churches should
require a voluntary submission of the beliefs and conduct of the individual to the
judgment of the church. The gospel message will lose its integrity and power if our
churches do not remain distinct from the world. Church discipline is one means
of preserving the integrity and impact of the message and ministry of our Baptist
churches.[32]

The doctrine of church discipline certainly is not the exclusive "theological
property" of Baptists. Our contention that church discipline is a mark of a New
Testament church, however, has enjoyed strong, historical support in Baptist life,
especially prior to the twentieth century. In addition, the coupling of church

---

29. Gregory A. Wills, "The Church: Baptists and Their Churches in the Eighteenth and Nine-
     teenth Centuries," in Dever, *Polity*, 19–20.
30. Mohler, "Church Discipline," 53–56.
31. John Leadley Dagg, *A Treatise on Church Order* (reprint, Harrison, VA: Gano Books, 1982),
     274.
32. Wills, "The Church," 28.

discipline with the doctrines of a regenerate church membership and congregational polity gives our understanding and practice of church discipline a distinctively Baptist perspective. As we move forward into the twenty-first century, let us return to our historical and theological roots in the reclamation and implementation of church discipline, one of the true marks of a New Testament church.

The Priesthood of Believers

REDISCOVERING THE BIBLICAL DOCTRINE
OF ROYAL PRIESTHOOD

MALCOLM B. YARNELL III

The priesthood of believers" has been given various names in church history. Those stressing the communal nature of the doctrine have employed such terms as "the priesthood of the faithful," "the universal priesthood," "the general priesthood," "the spiritual priesthood," "the common priesthood," "the priesthood of the baptized," "the priesthood of the laity," and "the priesthood of all believers." Those expressing an individualistic understanding have utilized the terms, "the priesthood of the believer," "the priesthood of every believer," or "the believer priest." In the Old Testament, the Hebrew term was *mamlakuth cohenim*, which was translated in the Greek Septuagint as *basileion hierateuma* (Exod. 19:6). Peter followed the Septuagintal rendering (1 Peter 2:9), which may result in the first term being treated as an adjective, while John used dual substantives (Rev. 1:6; 5:10). The Holy Spirit has not felt confined to a strict reliance upon one term, for the Bible also substitutes the adjective "holy" for "royal" (1 Peter 2:5) and transforms the leading adjective (or noun) into a verb (Rev. 20:6). The preferred English terminology for the strict Biblicist may be the alternating usage of "royal priesthood," "priests and kings," and "kingdom priesthood."

The purpose of this chapter is to exegete the biblical doctrine of the royal priesthood, reflecting upon its meaning as a Baptist ecclesiological distinctive. There are numerous books and articles, ancient and modern, that have sought to elucidate the biblical basis, historical manifestations, and theological meaning of the doctrine. This essay will not seek to engage the complex bibliography of that tradition or even survey the major works. Rather, the focus will be upon a recovery of the biblical doctrine for local Baptist churches. Following a review of the biblical witness to the doctrine of the church as composed of priests and kings, a historical paradigm will be outlined, and then five theological conclusions will be offered.

THE BIBLICAL WITNESS

FIVE TYPES OF ROYAL PRIESTS

Within biblical history, there are at least five types that combine the offices of both priest and king. Leaving aside the question of the rule and priesthood of prelapsarian Adam and the continuing royal and priestly activities of the patriarchs, perhaps the earliest manifestation of a priest-king occurs with the mysterious and Christologically significant figure of Melchizedek.

First making his appearance in Genesis, Melchizedek ("king of righteousness") is described both as the "king of Salem" ("king of peace") and as "the priest of God Most High" (Gen. 14:18–20).[1] Following Abram's defeat of Chederlaomer, Melchizedek blessed both Abram and God for the former's victory. Abram then gave Melchizedek a tithe of everything he had gained. In the premiere messianic psalm, the Lord promises the Lord that the latter will be an eternal priest according to the order of Melchizedek (Ps. 110:4). Drawing upon this tradition, the author of the epistle to the Hebrews concluded that the priesthood of Christ surpassed the Aaronic priesthood since, within the loins of Abraham, Levi paid tithes to Melchizedek (Heb. 7:9–10).[2]

The Aaronic or Levitical priesthood, the second type of priest-king, combined both religious and administrative roles. Zadok, high priest under King David (2 Sam. 8:17), and his sons have been examined in detail concerning their apparent combination of the roles of priest and administrator. In the intertestamental period, the Maccabeans were the first Israelites to truly attempt a combination of the roles of high priest and ruler of Israel, but with limited success.[3] After the demise of Jewish self-rule, the Qumran community began to spiritualize the concept of priesthood at the same time that it held onto the temple priesthood.[4]

The third type of priest-king, the pagan version, was a common near Eastern phenomenon during and after the biblical period. Many cultures viewed their kings as possessing not only supreme civil power but also supreme religious authority. Their victories on the battlefield were due to their sway with the gods. In Rome, the Eastern practice was imitated, and priesthood was first brought under the

---

1. Scripture quotations are from the New King James Version (NKJV) unless noted otherwise.
2. Joseph A. Fitzmeyer, "Melchizedek in the MT, LXX, and the NT," *Biblica: Commentarii Periodici Pontificii Instituti Biblici* 81, no. 1 (2000): 63–69.
3. Deborah W. Rooke, *Zadok's Heirs: The Role and Development of the High Priesthood in Ancient Israel* (Oxford: Oxford University Press, 2000).
4. Ernest Best, "I Peter II 4–10—A Reconsideration," *Novum Testamentum* 11, no. 4 (1969): 285.

emperor's purview during the reign of Julius Caesar. The highest priesthood over all the official cults, *pontifex maximus*, was permanently added to the emperor's list of offices under Augustus, but not without controversy.[5]

The fourth type of priest-king is the Lord Jesus Christ. The description of Melchizedek as type and Christ as antitype in Hebrews 7 is not confined to priesthood but incorporates kingship. Jesus is the "sacral king" or "royal priest" *par excellence*.[6] However, it is proper to speak of Christ as possessing not merely two offices but three. The Latin theological term, *triplex munus Christi*, indicates the biblical witness to Jesus as prophet, as well as priest and king.[7] The final type of priest-king, the royal priesthood of the people, returns us to our central subject.

THE OLD TESTAMENT WITNESS TO THE ROYAL PRIESTHOOD

The first text that addresses our subject may be found in Exodus 19:6. John Hall Elliott calls this "the Exodus formula," indicating his conclusion that all subsequent biblical references were shaped by this text. Indeed, Elliott's substantiation[8] prompted Ernest Best, a not insubstantial biblical scholar, to "reconsider" his earlier claim that Exodus 19:6 is theologically insignificant to later biblical formulations.[9] In the Exodus formula, God promised to make the Israelites into a *mamlakuth cohenim*, "kingdom of priests" or "kingdom [and] priesthood" or "priestlike kings" or "royal priesthood."[10] The context is significant, for the promise was made at the initial deliverance of the covenant to Moses at Mount Sinai. If Israel would obey God's voice and keep his covenant, they would be "a special treasure" to him "above all people" (19:5). The nature of this special gift is described as "a kingdom of priests and a holy nation," a unique people. On the basis of this promise, the elders of Israel agreed to enter the covenant. Moses afterward returned to receive the covenant of the law in its awesome fullness (19:7–15).

Included within the covenant for the national priesthood was the special priesthood of the Levites, described in the book of Leviticus with its temple, regulations, and sacrifices.[11] Considering the detail with which the temple, along with the

---

5. Lily Ross Taylor, *The Divinity of the Roman Emperor* (Middletown, CT: American Philological Association, 1931), 59–60. Cf. Mary Beard, "Priesthood in the Roman Republic," in *Pagan Priests*, ed. Mary Beard and John North (London: Duckworth, 1990), 17–48.

6. Deborah W. Rooke, "Jesus as Royal Priest: Reflections on the Interpretation of the Melchizedek Tradition in Heb 7," *Biblica* 81, no. 1 (2000): 81–94.

7. Millard J. Erickson, *Christian Theology*, 2nd ed. (Grand Rapids: Baker, 1998), 780–87.

8. John H. Elliott, *The Elect and the Holy: An Exegetical Examination of 1 Peter 2:4–10 and the Phrase Basileion Ierateuma, Supplements to NT XII* (Leiden: E. J. Brill, 1966), 50–128.

9. Ernest Best, "Spiritual Sacrifice: General Priesthood in the New Testament," *Interpretation* 14 (1963): 273–99; and idem, "I Peter II 4–10—A Reconsideration."

10. John I. Durham, *Exodus*, Word Biblical Commentary (Waco, TX: Word, 1987), 263.

11. It often has been noted that the Old Testament universal priesthood did not invalidate the Old Testament particular priesthood. E.g., C. E. Pockree, *The Priesthood of All Believers* (London: St. Charles Booklet Library, 1969).

Aaronic priesthood and its sacrifices are described, it is intriguing that the cultic duties of the *mamlakuth cohenim* are never explicitly addressed in the Old Testament. However, it may be surmised that the liturgical-ethical responsibilities of the priestly people are described periodically in sacrificial terms: "Offer the sacrifices of righteousness, and put your trust in the LORD" (Ps. 4:5); "Offer to God a sacrifice of thanksgiving" (Ps. 50:14 NASB; cf. Lev. 7:11ff.; Pss. 27:6; 50:23; 107:22; 116:17); "The sacrifices of God are a broken spirit" (Ps. 51:17); "Take away all iniquity and receive us graciously, that we may present the fruit of our lips" (Hos. 14:2 NASB). Indeed, such activities are preferable to the cultic rituals: "I will praise the name of God with song and magnify Him with thanksgiving. And it will please the LORD better than an ox or a young bull with horns and hoofs" (Ps. 69:30–31 NASB; cf. Isa. 1:11–17; Hos. 6:6; 9:4; Mic. 6:6–8).[12]

The historical books of the Old Testament relate the sad story of Israel's continual disobedience to God's voice and violation of the covenant. This was followed by the destruction of the northern kingdom by the Assyrians and the subsequent tortured demise of the southern kingdom. Especially troubling was the presumption of the Jerusalem elite during Jeremiah's day that God would preserve the nation in spite of their disobedience. They were disabused of that notion, and the prophets proclaimed a new covenant was required. Jeremiah and Ezekiel promised Jerusalem would one day be restored and that the divine transformation of the people's minds and hearts would ensure an eternal covenant of peace. Indications of national restoration along the lines of the original Sinaitic agreement can be detected in these prophecies. "I will be their God, and they shall be My people" (Jer. 31:31–34; cf. Jer. 32:37–41; Ezek. 37:24–28).

Isaiah reiterated the promise of an eschatological restoration of the nation in a number of places, including that the Israelites would be "named the priests of the LORD" (Isa. 61:6). The promise of an eschatological priesthood was again given to the entire nation, not just to the Levites. But the universality of this promise was taken one step further at the conclusion of the book. In the end of time, all peoples will be gathered. With reference to the Gentiles, Yahweh declares, "I will also take some of them for priests and Levites" (Isa. 66:21). The new priesthood will encompass not only the godly remnant of the people of the Mosaic covenant but also many chosen from among the nations.

THE PETRINE WITNESS TO THE ROYAL PRIESTHOOD

The first letter of Peter was written to the Christians of Asia Minor, who were experiencing severe persecution. Although they resided in the earthly city and

---

12. A. Feuillet, "Les 'sacrifices spirituels' du sacerdoce royal des baptizes (1 P 2,5) et leur preparation dans l'Ancien Testament," *Nouvelle Revue Théologique* 96 (1974): 704–28.

should relate responsibly to it, their citizenship was really in the city of God.[13] Peter encouraged this community by reminding them that they were the elect of God. Collating the witness of 1 Peter, Elliott delineates the Trinitarian origin, mediation, and goal of their election: "They have been elected ('chosen,' RSV) (a) 'according to the foreknowledge of God the father' (cf. 1:17), (b) 'through the sanctifying activity of the Spirit' (cf. 1:10–12, 14–16; 4:14), and (c) 'for obedience and the sprinkling of the blood of Jesus Christ' (cf. 1:14, 19, 22)."[14] The chief image for the church in 1 Peter is *oikos tou theou*, "the household of God." Indeed, this image is joined by other metaphors in 1 Peter 2:9 to promote group consciousness, solidarity, and cohesion.[15]

The Petrine passage in which the two references to the royal priesthood are located is 1 Peter 2:4–10:

> Coming to Him as to a living stone, rejected indeed by men, but chosen by God and precious, you also, as living stones, are being built up a spiritual house, a holy priesthood, to offer up spiritual sacrifices acceptable to God through Jesus Christ. Therefore it is also contained in the Scripture, "Behold, I lay in Zion a chief cornerstone, elect, precious, and he who believes on Him will by no means be put to shame." Therefore, to you who believe, He is precious; but to those who are disobedient, "The stone which the builders rejected has become the chief cornerstone," and "A stone of stumbling and a rock of offense." They stumble, being disobedient to the word, to which they also were appointed. But you are a chosen generation, a royal priesthood, a holy nation, His own special people, that you may proclaim the praises of Him who called you out of darkness into His marvelous light; who once were not a people but are now the people of God, who had not obtained mercy but now have obtained mercy.

This passage contains a complex litany of metaphors for Christ and his church, a litany that intentionally invokes fuller theological reflection. In verses 4 and 5, there are seven metaphorical constructions. "Each metaphor qualifies and is

---

13. The three levels of Roman citizenship were *politai*, full citizens; *paroikoi*, resident aliens; and *zenoi*, strangers. Christians found themselves existing between full rights and no rights. See John H. Elliott, *A Home for the Homeless: A Sociological Exegesis of I Peter, Its Situation and Strategy* (Philadelphia: Fortress, 1981), 25. The reference to Augustine's historiography is intentional. Cf. Augustine of Hippo, *Civitas Dei*.

14. John H. Elliott, "Salutation and Exhortation to Christian Behavior on the Basis of God's Blessings (1:1–2:10)," *Review and Expositor* 79 (1982): 416.

15. Elliott, *Home for the Homeless*, 132–33; and idem, "Salutation and Exhortation," 419.

qualified by the other metaphors, all of them together pointing to realities lying behind them all."[16] In verses 6 through 8, which quote several Old Testament texts (Isa. 28:16; Ps. 118:22; Isa. 8:14–15), these metaphors coalesce around the central metaphor of Christ as the living and life-giving stone. Those who build their lives upon this stone will be blessed; those who reject him will be cursed. The church built upon this living stone is vividly pictured by the assimilation of five communal metaphors, "house" in verse 5 and "priesthood," "nation," "race," and "people" in verses 9–10, modified by five adjectives, "spiritual," "chosen," "holy," "royal," and "God's own."[17]

These metaphors find their provenance in the Old Testament and are extensively paralleled in the New Testament, which Best quaintly refers to as "the primitive tradition." The bulk of Old Testament references derive from Isaiah, the Psalms, Hosea, and Exodus; the New Testament books with the densest Old Testament usage are 1 Peter, Hebrews, and Revelation.[18] In an intriguing way, these same seven books figure prominently in the discussion of the royal priesthood and its spiritual sacrifices.

There are three major images that hold this complex of metaphors in 1 Peter 2 together as an ideological unit.[19] The primary image considers the living stone of Christ as the basis and source of life for the living stones who believe in him. The second major image considers these living stones as being continually built (*oikodomeisthe*) into *oikos pneumatikos*, "the house of the Spirit,"[20] another biblical name for the temple. The third major image considers this spiritual temple composed of stones as also a holy and royal priesthood that offers spiritual sacrifices. These three major images point to two substantive realities, Christ and his church, and two activities, the reconciliatory rule of Christ and the church's offering of spiritual sacrifices.

Peter's intentional mixing of metaphors may confuse the strict literalist, but for those willing to employ a chastened figurative and typological hermeneutic, the imagery is theologically productive. It has long been recognized that this passage, as well as most references to Christian priesthood and sacrifice in the New Testament, should not be taken in a literalist sense.[21] Rather, the literary modification, especially of *oikos*, "house," and *thusias*, "sacrifices," by *pneumatikos/pneumatikas*,

---

16. Paul S. Minear, "The House of Living Stones: A Study of 1 Peter 2:4–12," *Ecumenical Review* 34, no. 3 (1982): 242.

17. Ibid., 245.

18. For the Old Testament background, see Best, "I Peter II 4–10—A Reconsideration," 270–78. For the New Testament parallels, see ibid., 280–82.

19. Minear outlines two major images in "The House of Living Stones," 243–46.

20. Elliott, "Salutation and Exhortation," 422.

21. Frederic Gardiner, "The Use of the Words Priest, Sacrifice, and Prophet in the New Testament," *The Old and New Testament Student* 9, no. 5 (1889): 289–91.

"spiritual," demands a Spirit-led exegesis (2:5). Paul Minear states it this way: "As Paul recognized, words taught by the Spirit must be discerned by the same Spirit (1 Cor. 2:6–16)."[22] A conservative theologian would claim that the Holy Spirit who inspired the words of Scripture must illuminate those same words. Rationalist hermeneutics, such as the modern historical-critical method, fail to truly comprehend what the Spirit reveals.

How should the royal priesthood of 1 Peter be understood? The passage provides clues to both the nature and the function of the royal priesthood. First, ontologically, the royal priesthood is one among many metaphors for the church of Jesus Christ. In verse 9, Peter applies to the church the metaphors of "chosen generation" and "His own special people" from Isaiah 43:20–21 and "royal priesthood" and "holy nation" from Exodus 19:6. In verse 10, he adds communal imagery from Hosea, indicating that those who were not a people have now become the people of God (cf. Hos. 1:6, 9; 2:21–23). The ecclesial metaphors of verses 9 and 10 expand upon the introductory image of a "spiritual house" in verse 5. The inclusion of "royal priesthood" within this list of ecclesial metaphors, along with the communal nature of the metaphor itself, argues strongly for a congregational understanding of the doctrine.

Elliott translates *basileion* nominally rather than adjectivally. In other words, *basileion hierateuma* is best taken as the combination of two nouns, "palace [and] priesthood," or "royal residence [and] body of priests," rather than as a modified noun, "royal priesthood." In this way, Elliott draws closer to the idea that the nouns represent a single communal entity.[23] The structure of the words *basileion* and *hierateuma* also indicates a corporate or collective entity rather than an individual. Greek nouns ending in *-euma* normally designate a community, as do words ending in *-eion*. Whether these words should be taken in a corporate sense (a body) or in a collective sense (individuals gathered) remains an unsettled point among New Testament scholars.[24] What is beyond doubt is that this is a communal image of the church.

As to the second problem, the function of the royal priesthood, 1 Peter 2 provides details encouraging not only an immediately contextual interpretation but also a canonical interpretation. Following E. G. Selwyn, both Elliott and Minear treat verses 4–5 as introductory to verses 6–8 and 9–10.[25] Employing three cultic terms, verse 5 introduces the idea that this *hierateuma hagion*, "holy priesthood," is

---

22. Minear, "House of Living Stones," 239.
23. Elliott, *Elect and the Holy*, 73, 166, 223.
24. Ibid., 66; and Best, "I Peter II 4–10—A Reconsideration," 286–87, 290–91.
25. Edward Gordon Selwyn, *The First Epistle of St. Peter: The Greek Text with Introduction, Notes and Essays* (London: Macmillan, 1949), 268–81, 295; Elliott, *The Elect and the Holy*, 147–59; idem, "Salutation and Exhortation," 421; and Minear, "The House of Living Stones," 240.

intended *anenegkai*, "to offer up," *pneumatikas thusias*, "spiritual sacrifices." Verse 9 may be taken as indicating a second function of the royal priesthood, the proclamation of the saving gospel. The church has been elected in Christ "that you may proclaim the praises of Him who called you out of darkness into His marvelous light." The proclamation of this gospel may be taken as a second function of the royal priesthood or as one type of spiritual sacrifice. If taken as a type of spiritual sacrifice, proclamation focused on "Him who called you" should doubtless be given prominence.

SPIRITUAL SACRIFICES IN THE NEW TESTAMENT

Peter's claim that the royal priesthood offers spiritual sacrifices begs the question as to what exactly spiritual sacrifices are. Since Peter does not immediately indicate what he means by the activity, scholars have turned to the canon for explication. Typically, New Testament theologians consider the spiritual sacrifices as encompassing both proclamation and personal ethics, "These sacrifices are evidently the praise of God by words and by the living of lives that honor him in the world and so increase his glory."[26]

The textual indications for a spiritual sacrifice include the presence of certain cultic nouns and their cognates: such as *thusia*, "sacrifice," *prosphora*, "offering," *letourgia*, "service" by priests, or *latreia*, religious "service" by anyone. Also important are the verbs of offering: *paristanein*, "to present an offering," and *anapherein*, "to offer up." Also indicative of a spiritual sacrifice is the adjective *amomos*, "blameless," for one may not offer an unworthy sacrifice to God.[27] That these sacrificial actions must be taken metaphorically is indicated by the inclusion of the term *pneumatikos*, "spiritual," or by contextual application to Christians, who no longer require the cultic priesthood. "Spiritual," however, does not mean "unreal"; rather, it points to the deeper reality of the divine.

Alan Richardson discerned five forms of spiritual sacrifice in the New Testament, to which might be added two others. The compilation of these spiritual sacrifices pictures Christians as living lives of habitual service to God.

1. Christians offering their entire lives, bodies as well as souls, as holy sacrifices to God (Rom. 12:1; Eph. 5:2; Rom. 6:13).
2. Christians engaging in good deeds (Heb. 10:24; 13:16).
3. Christians sharing monetary or material gifts (Heb. 13:16; Phil. 4:18).

26. I. Howard Marshall, *New Testament Theology: Many Witnesses, One Gospel* (Downers Grove, IL: InterVarsity Press, 2004), 654. Cf. Thomas D. Lea, *The New Testament: Its Background and Message* (Nashville: Broadman & Holman, 1996), 543; Elliott, *The Elect and the Holy*, 184; and Selwyn, *The First Epistle of St. Peter*, 161.

27. Alan Richardson, *An Introduction to the Theology of the New Testament* (New York: SCM Press, 1958), 297–99.

4. Christians worshipping through praise, prayer, and confession (Heb. 13:15; Rev. 5:8; 8:3–4).

5. Christians ministering through the proclamation of the gospel (Rom. 15:16; 1 Cor. 16:15).[28]

6. The faith of others (Phil. 2:17; Col. 1:28), which of course is gained through proclamation, and yet the sacrifice is the response of faith rather than the proclamation.

7. Martyrdom on behalf of Christ and his church (2 Tim. 4:6).

THE JOHANNINE WITNESS TO CHRISTIAN PRIESTS AND KINGS

Whereas Peter focuses on the communal ontology and sacrificial function of the royal priesthood, John focuses on the Christological origin and ruling function of the doctrine. There are three passages in John's apocalypse concerning Christian priests and kings: Revelation 1:4–8; 5:6–10; and 20:4–6. The context of each passage reveals the origin and image of Christian priests and kings in the one who is the second person of the triune Godhead and who fulfills a threefold office as Prophet, Priest, and King. Considered together, the passages indicate the past, present, and future aspects of the church's royal priesthood.

The first passage, Revelation 1:4–8, contains John's salutation to the seven churches of Asia. This salutation quickly becomes a doxology, and within this doxology is a promise to the persecuted churches. Grace and peace are promised to the churches from a threefold source. That threefold source is the Father, described here as "Him who is and who was and who is to come"; the Holy Spirit, unusually pictured in Revelation as "the seven Spirits who are before His throne"; and "from Jesus Christ." The source of the churches' hope is the triune God—Father, Spirit, and Son.

John then expounds upon the Son's threefold work. First, Jesus Christ is "the faithful witness," indicating his role as the Prophet who reveals God most fully because he is God incarnate for us. Second, Jesus Christ is "the firstborn from the dead," indicating his role as the High Priest who overcomes death through the sacrifice of himself. Many commentators focus on the meaning of "firstborn" as a reference to Christ's sovereignty.[29] Although doubtless true, John emphasizes Christ's death, not his birth, by subsequently expanding upon the soteriological importance of that death: He "loves us and released us from our sins by His blood"

---

28. Ibid., 299–301. Richardson's categories have been retained, and supplemental citations have been provided. In at least one case (Rev. 14:4–5), a citation has been deleted, for the sacrifice is not apparently that offered by Christians.

29. George Eldon Ladd, *A Commentary on the Revelation of John* (Grand Rapids: Eerdmans, 1972), 25; and Robert H. Mounce, *The Book of Revelation*, New International Commentary on the New Testament, rev. ed. (Grand Rapids: Eerdmans, 1977), 48–49.

(NASB). The sacerdotal imagery is clear: as a priest, Christ offered his blood as a sacrifice to atone for our sins. The third work of Jesus Christ is his rule as King. His title is "the ruler of the kings of the earth" (NASB). Just as he excels all prophets by revealing God fully, and just as he excels all priests by atoning for all sin, so he excels all kings.

It is only after defining the person of Jesus Christ as God incarnate and the work of Jesus Christ as *triplex munus Christi* that John considers the royal priesthood of the church. "The order is important. First comes the reference to his redeeming work and only then that to the kingdom [of the people of God]."[30] "By means of his death Jesus constituted his followers a kingdom."[31] The origin of the Christian priesthood is found in this one, who is the second person of the Trinity, and who functions as Prophet, Priest, and King. This one has *epoiēsen hēmas*, "made us." The aorist active indicative form of the verb indicates a past activity; the priestly work of Christ indicates the incarnation. As the one who atoned for us as a Priest by the sacrifice of his blood, he made us priests. In other words, the priesthood does not come to Christians in the divine work of creation but in the divine work of redemption. The Christian priesthood is not a natural right inherent in created man; the Christian priesthood is a special gift created in redeemed man.

Consider the content and role of this divine gift: the churches have been made *basileion hiereis*, literally "a kingdom, priests." Some commentators take this to indicate a corporate kingdom, yet the individual priest.[32] Yet in the context of this passage, the book of Revelation, and the canon, this is an imposition. The passage is addressed to the churches; the book of Revelation consistently pluralizes the Christian priesthood; and as we have seen, the remainder of the canon treats the priesthood of the people of God communally. The role of this special creation of a kingdom of priests from redeemed humanity is implied in the words, *to theo kai patri autou*, "to his God and Father." Christ created Christians as priests in order to serve his Father. The emphasis here is not on the personal privilege of the priests, but on their profound responsibility before God. A priesthood must be blameless, and as the Jerusalem priesthood discovered, God severely judges those priests (and princes and prophets) who forsake their official responsibility (Ezek. 22:26–28). John hedges the church's priesthood by the priority of the divine, immediately reminding us of the eternal nature of God's *hē doxa kai to kratos*, "glory and power" (Rev. 1:6b). Indeed, God is *pantocrator*, literally "the power over all" (v. 8).

30.　Leon Morris, *The Book of Revelation: An Introduction and Commentary*, Tyndale New Testament Commentaries, rev. ed. (Grand Rapids: Eerdmans, 1987), 49.

31.　Mounce, *Book of Revelation*, 49.

32.　Morris, *Book of Revelation*, 50; Mounce, *Book of Revelation*, 50, 136.

The second relevant passage in John's apocalypse, 5:6–10, reveals the heavenly throne, which is preparing for the unfolding of the end of all things. Again, the Trinity is central, this time with perichoretic imagery. The Father sits on the throne of heaven (5:1), the Son stands in the midst of that throne (5:6b), and the Holy Spirit proceeds from the Son (5:6c). The Father holds a scroll that reveals the outworking of history, and nobody is found worthy to open and read it—except, that is, for the Son. John's titles for the Son are dramatic. In his vision, John sees "that the Lion is also the Lamb."[33] On the one hand, Christ is "the Lion of the tribe of Judah, the Root of David." These are Old Testament images (Gen. 49:9–10; Isa. 11:1–9; cf. 4 Ezra 11:37; 12:31) evocative of the kingly rule of David fulfilled in "the promised triumphant messianic King."[34] The New Testament repeatedly affirms the kingly rule of Christ as being fully manifested in the Judgment (cf. Acts 2:34–35; 1 Cor. 15:25–26; Heb. 1:3; Rev. 1:18; 12:7–11; 19). On the other hand, Christ is also a "Lamb." This Lamb is standing, defying all temporal logic, "as though it had been slain" (Rev. 5:6). The Lamb, of course, was identified with sacrifice, at least since the Passover, when Israel was delivered from Egypt (Exod. 12:13). The Suffering Servant of Isaiah, too, had been described as a "lamb that is led to slaughter" (Isa. 53:7 NASB). This lamb, who gave his soul as "an offering for sin," and "made intercession for the transgressors," would also "prolong His days" (Isa. 53:10, 12). In his gospel, John had picked up on the dual message of Christ as both King and priestly victim (John 1:29, 49). This same combination of ruling king and sacrificial lamb in the official work of Christ is also relayed by Peter (1 Peter 1:19; 3:22).

Before the throne of the Lion-Lamb, with his Father and the Spirit, are four living creatures and the twenty-four elders. The prayers of the saints are offered up before God at the throne, and the saints sing a new song. The song extols Christ for his atoning work, which has redeemed them to God. In an apparent fulfillment of Isaiah 66:21, these saints come from "every tribe and tongue and people and nation" (Rev. 5:9). They praise the Lion-Lamb for having made them—again, the aorist active indicative form of *poieō*, "to make"—*basileian kai hiereis*, "kingdom and priests." Rather than emphasizing the priestly role of the royal priesthood, the kingdom is now emphasized as the verbal form is also used. The saints who have been made a kingdom "rule upon the earth" or "will rule upon the earth."

The textual evidence for the verb is evenly divided between *basileuousin*, the present tense, and *basileusousin*, the future tense.[35] Most translators opt for the

---

33. John P. Newport, *The Lion and the Lamb: A Commentary on the Book of Revelation for Today* (Nashville: Broadman Press, 1986), 123.

34. Ladd, *Commentary on the Revelation*, 83.

35. The fourth-century Sinaiticus contains the future tense, while the fifth-century Alexandrinus text contains the present tense. See Kurt Aland et al., ed., *The Greek New Testament*, 3rd ed.

future tense, preferring either a futuristic present or importing the future millennial reign from Revelation 20.[36] However, the present tense may be preferable since this heavenly scene precedes the events leading to the millennial reign. Moreover, these priests are said to serve God in heaven, and many are already located there around the throne. Also, it would seem odd to ascribe a title if there is no present activity associated with that title. Finally, if the present tense is accepted, then it brings a temporal symmetry to the Johannine witness to the royal priesthood. In 1:6, Christians have been made priests; in 5:10, Christians are currently serving as a priestly kingdom before the throne of God; and, in 20:6, their kingship will come into material fullness. The royal priesthood has past, present, and future aspects to it.

If the kingdom has a present aspect of ruling upon the earth, in what way is this true? Paul provides an answer in 1 Corinthians 6:2, where he calls the Corinthian congregation to pass judgment on its members now, in light of the fact that they will one day "judge the world." In a significant work titled *Jesus and the Kingdom of God*, G. R. Beasley-Murray carefully divides the sayings and parables of Jesus concerning the kingdom between those that concern the present and those that concern the future.[37] The churches now exist in a time when the kingdom has come, but not yet in its material fullness (Matt. 13; 19:28; Mark 13:24–27, 32). The kingdom has yet to fully come, but the church, which has Christ as its King, finds its member-kings should now participate in the eternal kingdom through congregational governance.

The third Johannine reference to the Christian royal priesthood occurs in the only New Testament witness to the millennial reign of Christ, Revelation 20:4–6. This passage is commonly believed to reflect the Old Testament prophecy of the Son of Man.[38] In Daniel 7 the "saints of the most high" will share in the fifth monarchy, which is the everlasting kingdom of the one who is "like the Son of Man" (v. 13). All peoples shall uniquely serve and obey the Son of Man (v. 14), but the saints also "possess" the kingdom and exercise "dominion" over the kingdoms (vv. 22, 27). Likewise, in the Millennium, there will be thrones from which the saints and martyrs will rule (Rev. 20:4). The saints, who participate in "the first resurrection," receive three blessings: "the second death" has no power over them; "they

---

(Stuttgart: United Bible Societies, 1983), 849n. 5. The majority of the UBS committee preferred *basileusousin* as "more suited to the meaning of the context." Bruce M. Metzger, *A Textual Commentary on the Greek New Testament: A Companion Volume to the United Bible Societies' Greek New Testament*, 3rd ed. (Stuttgart: United Bible Societies, 1975), 736.

36. Ladd, *A Commentary on the Revelation*, 92; Mounce, *The Book of Revelation*, 136, 136n. 36.

37. George R. Beasley-Murray, *Jesus and the Kingdom of God* (Grand Rapids: Eerdmans, 1986), chaps. 9–12.

38. Mounce, *Book of Revelation*, 364.

shall be priests of God and of Christ"; and, they "shall reign with Him a thousand years" (v. 6). It should be noted that the saints retain a future role as priests, but the emphasis is upon the kingly role of the saints. There is no textual uncertainty about the tense of the verb *basileusousin* here: the physical rule of the saints is definitely in the future tense. Finally, this rule is to occur *met' autou*, "with Him." In the context of the apocalyptic return of *basileus basileōn kai kurios kuriōn*, "the King of kings and Lord of lords" (19:16), there should be little doubt that Christian kingship, though real, is nevertheless a client kingship. The saints shall be kings under the King of kings.

A PARADIGM FOR CHRISTIAN HISTORY

How have these texts been understood throughout Christian history? James Leo Garrett has said, "The doctrine of the priesthood of all Christians has been misunderstood, misapplied, and neglected as much as, if not more than, it has been opposed or denied during Christian history."[39] In order to analyze the historical (mis)interpretations of the biblical doctrine, a fivefold paradigm is offered. Although it is dangerous for a pure historian—a necessary fictional concept to uphold for the sake of honest research—to offer a historical paradigm without the benefit of a detailed rehearsal of the facts, the theologian is not bound as strictly by those requirements. Thus, the following historical paradigm is offered as an aid to the reader in comprehending the major trends in history for those seeking to implement the biblical doctrine of the royal priesthood. There have been five major manifestations of the doctrine among the churches in history. These manifestations may be titled Catholic sacramental priesthood, Caesarean sacred kingship, Reformation universal priesthood, congregational royal priesthood, and modern libertarian priesthood.[40]

---

39. James Leo Garrett Jr., "The Biblical Doctrine of the Priesthood of the People of God," in *New Testament Studies: Essays in Honor of Ray Summers in His Sixty-Fifth Year*, ed. Huber L. Drumwright and Curtis Vaughan (Waco, TX: Baylor University Press, 1975), 137.

40. This author's interest in the doctrine of royal priesthood came as a budding historical theologian under the tutelage of James Leo Garrett Jr. Following Professor Garrett, he grew dissatisfied with both inadequate historiographies and modern misrepresentations of the biblical doctrine. Among historians, Cyril Eastwood was the most ambitious narrator, yet his scholarship is severely wanting by reason of its selectivity at the macro level and reliance on secondary sources at the micro level. For instance, at the macro level, Eastwood does not consider either Eastern Orthodoxy or the Baptists, and he presents his attenuated historiography through the lens of modern ecumenism. See Cyril Eastwood, *The Priesthood of All Believers: An Examination of the Doctrine from the Reformation to the Present Day* (London: Epworth, 1960); and idem, *The Royal Priesthood of the Faithful: An Investigation of the Doctrine from Biblical Times to the Reformation* (London: Epworth, 1963). In a series of well-researched articles, Professor Garrett began the careful work of reconstructing the historical meaning of the doctrine. Others have since continued that reconstruction, including this author, who wrote a master's thesis on the Continental Reformation understandings of the doctrine, and a doctoral dissertation on the English

THE CATHOLIC SACRAMENTAL PRIESTHOOD

The first doctrine of royal priesthood developed largely during the first three centuries and was deepened during the medieval period. Several authors have noted a constriction of the biblical doctrine of Christian priesthood through the division of the church between the clergy and the laity, with the former often taking on the name of *hiereus* (Greek) or *sacerdos* (Latin). This was a new priesthood for the church, in that Scripture never refers to the ministers of a church as priests. Alongside the development of the new priesthood was a concomitant development of sacramental theology. Baptism became a soteriological requirement administered by the new priests to infants and converts for the removal of original sin. Confession administered by the new priests became necessary for the removal of postbaptismal sin. But with the Lord's Supper, the sacerdotal imagery was strongest. The Lord's Supper became a sacrificial Mass offered by the new priests on behalf of the people. The priesthood dispensed salvation through the sacraments, which only they could administer.

With the division of the church into clergy and laity, there was also an extending of the hierarchy of the clergy into three major orders, a number of minor orders, and an extensive clerical bureaucracy. The diaconate waxed then waned in importance, and the episcopate was elevated above the presbyterate or regular priesthood. To be in unity with Christ and his church, one must be in unity with the bishop. Cyprian of Carthage is a lynchpin theologian in the early development of this hierarchical sacerdotal ministry dispensing sacramental grace.[41] In the West, complex bureaucracies developed around the larger episcopal and archiepiscopal sees, and especially at the center of Western Christianity, the Roman curia. In the Middle Ages, the pope received to himself the see of Peter, the imperial title of *pontifex maximus*, and the vicarage of Peter, Christ, and God. He also became an Italian noble, competing with the kings and emperors of Europe. In the East, the clerical bureaucracy developed around the patriarchs, especially the major patriarchs of Alexandria and Constantinople, "the new Rome," and eventually around the new patriarchates of Eastern Orthodoxy, including "the third Rome," Moscow.

With each advance in the special priesthood of the clergy, the universal priesthood of the people was constricted. The granting of priesthood to the people

---

Reformation understandings of the doctrine. The following fivefold paradigm issues from that research and ongoing interest.

41. James Leo Garrett Jr., "The Pre-Cyprianic Doctrine of the Priesthood of All Christians," in *Continuity and Discontinuity in Church History*, ed. F. F. Church and Timothy George (Leiden: Brill, 1979), 45–61; Collin Bulley, *The Priesthood of Some Believers: Developments from the General to the Special Priesthood in the Christian Literature of the First Three Centuries* (Waynesboro, GA: Paternoster, 2000).

occurred in the passive reception of baptism and found periodic expression in the passive reception of the Mass. At the Mass, it was believed that the prayers and offerings of the people were gathered up by the priest to be presented to God along with the propitiatory sacrifice of the recently confected host. In the West, by the time of the sixteenth century, the universal priesthood had effectively been emptied of any practical import. The people received grace through the sacraments; the sacraments were administered by the priests; and the priests were ordained by the bishops, who were approved by the Roman curia. The laity were informed that their priesthood was publicly receptive or active only privately. With the constriction of grace to the sacerdotal sacraments and the general restriction of scriptural knowledge to the priesthood, the laity could be and often were accused of soteriological ignorance.[42]

THE CAESAREAN SACRED KINGSHIP

In a set of overlooked articles that appeared in the journal *Church History* in the early 1950s, Harvard historian George Huntston Williams reconstructed the beginnings of the Eastern Orthodox understanding of the emperor's sacred kingship. His thesis, substantially supported, was that Constantine's synthesis of church and state initially was uncritically accepted. Constantine incorporated the church under the pagan imperial title of *pontifex maximus* and was considered by the church historian and semi-Arian, Eusebius of Caesarea, to be *ton ektos episkopos*, "bishop of externals."[43] However, the Arian controversy caused orthodox churchmen to reconsider their initial embrace of Constantine's shepherding of the church. Arian heretics, however, were much more willing to elevate the emperor as they made him a greater type of Christ than other Christians.

The Arian Christ was not as unique as the Nicene Christ, and Arian emperors more easily bolstered their political claims by borrowing divine characteristics from this weaker Arian Christ. The Nicene proclamation of Christ as consubstantial with God thus encouraged the church's independence from the state, while the Arian subordination of Christ as less than fully God allowed them to elevate the emperor into a demigod comparable to Christ and thus subordinate the church to the emperor. Heresy in Christology thus encouraged imperial domination of the

---

42. Malcolm Yarnell, "Royal Priesthood in the English Reformation" (D.Phil. diss., Oxford University, 2000), chaps. 1–2.

43. Gratian was the first Christian emperor to surrender the title; the popes later began to use the title. See Alan Cameron, "Gratian's Repudiation of the Pontifical Robe," *The Journal of Roman Studies* 58 (1968): 96–102. The emperor's repudiation of the title was part of the Christian battle with paganism, rather than a grant to the pope. See Herbert Bloch, "A New Document of the Last Pagan Revival in the West, 393–394 A.D.," *Harvard Theological Review* 38, no. 4 (1945): 203–4, 213–15.

church.[44] The prolonged centralization of religious and civil power in the hands of the emperor also encouraged the dissolution of the empire into separate nations.[45] In iconography and in numismatics, the claim of the Byzantine emperor to be an image of the divine *pantocrator* is still evident. This is an area requiring further historico-theological research.

THE REFORMATION UNIVERSAL PRIESTHOOD

Protesting against Rome's spiritual pretensions in 1520, Martin Luther helped bring about a partial yet major dismantling of the Catholic sacramental priesthood. In his *Appeal to the German Nobility*, Luther tore down the three walls of the papacy: the ontological distinction between the sacerdotal priesthood and the quiescent laity, the Roman claim to officially interpret Scripture, and the Roman convocation of a council. In his *Babylonian Captivity of the Church*, Luther reduced the seven sacraments to those sacraments instituted by Christ that contain a promise, especially the Lord's Supper and Baptism, effectively destroying the sacerdotal hold over sacramental grace. In *The Freedom of a Christian*, he expounded upon the doctrine of justification by grace through faith alone. And in all three works, he developed his understanding of the doctrine of the universal priesthood of all Christians. The true Christian priesthood was possessed by all Christians, and the Roman curia could not keep the people from exercising discipline over corrupt clergy.

In his early Reformation understanding, Luther believed the people could dispense the sacraments without a priest. But after the Peasants' Revolt, perceiving the revolutionary political implications of his religious egalitarianism, he began to moderate his doctrine of the universal priesthood by appealing to the authority of the magistrate and the magisterially approved minister. Similar moderations of the Reformation doctrine of the universal priesthood may be detected in the Reformed and Anglican wings of the Protestant Reformation. Among the Anabaptists, however, the doctrine of universal priesthood was applied more rigorously to the congregation.[46]

---

44. George Huntston Williams, "Christology and Church-State Relations in the Fourth Century," *Church History* 20, no. 3 (1951): 3–33; idem, "Christology and Church-State Relations in the Fourth Century (continued)," *Church History* 20, no. 4 (1951): 3–26. Cf. Basil Studer, *Trinity and Incarnation: The Faith of the Early Church*, trans. Matthias Westerhoff, ed. Andrew Louth (Collegeville, MN: Liturgical Press, 1993), 127–37.

45. Adolf von Harnack, *The History of Dogma*, trans. from the 3rd German ed. by E. B. Spiers and James Millar (reprint, Eugene, OR: Wipf and Stock, 1997), 4:241–52.

46. Malcolm Yarnell, "The Reformation Development of the Priesthood of All Believers" (Th.M. thesis, Duke University, 1996); idem, "Royal Priesthood in the English Reformation," chaps. 3–7.

THE CONGREGATIONAL ROYAL PRIESTHOOD

The Continental Anabaptists developed a congregational understanding of the doctrine of royal priesthood that is quite similar to developments in England. I have outlined the development of the English Separatist and Baptist understanding of the congregational royal priesthood elsewhere and point you to those essays.[47] In sum, the English Separatists and the early English Baptists came to the conclusion, especially on the basis of their reading of Matthew 18:15–20, that the royal priesthood should be manifested in congregational governance and worship. Christ directly rules over the covenanted congregation that is separated from the world and to God. The presence of Christ in the congregation allows the congregation to mimic the *triplex munus Christi*. Because Christ is King and has made his people a kingdom, they may rule themselves. Because Christ is Priest and has made his people a priesthood, they may worship, pray, and celebrate the ordinances. Because Christ is Prophet and has made his people a prophethood, they may freely proclaim his Word. No longer may one look to the Roman sacerdotal priesthood or to the magisterially approved Reformation ministry for authority; rather, one must look to the ruling King within the covenanted congregation.

THE MODERN LIBERTARIAN PRIESTHOOD

After Protestants and Baptists came to America, some coupled their fear of the Roman Catholic priesthood (and by extension any "priesthood") with theological liberalism and Enlightenment individualism. The result was the identification of the priesthood of believers with the American theory of individual rights. In the early twentieth century, "the priesthood of the believer" was granted an innate right of access to God apart from any priest, an idea to which E. Y. Mullins contributed his novel term, "soul competency."[48] This doctrine of priesthood, sometimes shortened to "the believer priest," meant that every Christian could exercise the right of private judgment as an expression of freedom in Christ. The believer priest with his soul competency was elevated above the pastor and often pitted against the church. In the middle of the twentieth century, some theologians began raising objections to this understanding. While discussing moral pride, Reinhold Niebuhr lamented, "The fact is the Protestant doctrine of the priesthood of all

47. Malcolm Yarnell, "Changing Baptist Concepts of Royal Priesthood: John Smyth and Edgar Young Mullins," in *The Rise of the Laity in Evangelical Protestantism*, ed. Deryck Lovegrove (London: Routledge, 2002), 236–43; idem, "Congregational Priesthood and the Invention or *Inventio* of Authority," *Journal for Baptist Theology and Ministry* 3 (2005): 110–35. Cf. Reggie McNeal, "The Priesthood of All Believers," in *Has Our Theology Changed? Southern Baptist Thought Since 1845*, ed. Paul A. Basden (Nashville: Broadman & Holman, 1994), 204–29.
48. Yarnell, "Changing Baptist Concepts of Royal Priesthood," 243–49.

believers may result in an individual self-deification against which Catholic doctrine has more adequate checks."[49]

During the conservative resurgence of the Southern Baptist Convention (SBC) in the late twentieth century, the moderate faculties of Southern Baptist seminaries, universities, and colleges resurrected the doctrine as a means of denying confessional integrity. Following Mullins, and indeed taking him further, they made this doctrine the premier Baptist distinctive, the mother of all Baptist distinctives. The doctrine, as preached by moderate Southern Baptists, seemed to encourage doctrinal chaos in the denomination and in the churches. In 1988, the SBC adopted a "Resolution on the Priesthood of the Believer," which decried the vacuous meaning of the term and its subjection "to both misunderstanding and abuse," especially "the undermining of pastoral authority in the local church." The 1988 resolution affirmed an undefined biblical doctrine under the same name.[50] Shortly afterward, a 1993 "Report on Freemasonry" presented by the Interfaith Witness Department of the Home Mission Board treated the doctrine of "the priesthood of the believer" as supportive of Christian freedom.[51] Although theologians in the SBC were aware of the difficulties with the modern doctrine, they failed to reach a consensus concerning a positive definition of an obviously central Baptist distinctive.

In 2000, however, the convention adopted a revised version of its confession. In the 1963 version of the Baptist Faith and Message, the preface had affirmed "the priesthood of the believer." The 2000 committee at first omitted any reference to the doctrine, but after a short but intense uproar, the committee inserted the following sentence into the new preface: "We honor the principles of soul competency and the priesthood of believers, affirming together both our liberty in Christ and our accountability to each other under the Word of God." In a brilliant move, the committee thus reaffirmed Southern Baptist commitment to the doctrine, while moving the convention closer to a biblical understanding by reverting to a communal meaning, both by rendering the term in the plural and by coupling accountability with liberty.

Moderate Southern Baptists, however, continue to stress both individualism and libertinism in their terminology and practice. For instance, immediately after the new confession was adopted, a moderate North Carolina church declared its

---

49. Reinhold Niebuhr, *The Nature and Destiny of Man: A Christian Interpretation* (New York: Scribner, 1964), 1:202.
50. "Resolution on the Priesthood of the Believer" (June 1988), Southern Baptist Convention, at http://www.sbc.net/resolutions/amResolution.asp?ID=872 (accessed September 27, 2006).
51. "Report on Freemasonry," in *Annual of the Southern Baptist Convention* (Nashville: Executive Committee of the Southern Baptist Convention, 1993).

right to affirm a homosexual union by appealing to "local church autonomy." The church's pastor declared, "We also respect the individual rights of believers as their own priests before God, and we respect the right of individuals to participate as they feel led."[52] Simultaneously, a moderate Texas church reaffirmed the desire of the Baptist General Convention of Texas (BGCT) to maintain the 1963 confession, appealing to seven "historic Baptist principles," including "the priesthood of every believer and the autonomy of the individual soul before God."[53] William M. Pinson Jr., a moderate Baptist leader affiliated with the BGCT and Baylor University's George W. Truett Theological Seminary, continues to maintain the modern libertarian doctrine of "the priesthood of the believer," while also now recognizing the communal term.[54]

THEOLOGICAL CONCLUSIONS

WHAT THE BIBLICAL DOCTRINE DOES NOT INCLUDE

In the church's history, a number of conceptions have been connected with the biblical doctrine of the royal priesthood. Certain of these conceptions have reflected the political and religious trends of the times more than biblical teaching. This critique may be applied to both Catholic and Protestant accretions and to some Baptist innovations.

First, it should be readily evident that the confinement of the effective rule of the church to either the emperor, following the Caesarean sacred kingship, or the pope, as an extension of the Catholic sacramental priesthood, lacks biblical warrant. The Christian royal priesthood is a communal conception within Scripture. The egalitarian nature of this communal concept militates against the confinement of ecclesiastical authority to any single person or group of persons within the churches. It is true that just as the Bible affirms the royal priesthood in relation to the church, so it also speaks of ministerial leadership in relation to the church (cf. Acts 20:17–38; Eph. 4:7–16; 1 Tim. 3:1–13; Heb. 13:17). But Scripture does not indicate the exact relationship between the royal priesthood and the ministry. Using this silence, some early churches incorporated an unfortunate division between clergy and laity and then constructed a hierarchy on top of that distinction. As R. C. Moberly declared, "That the priest was holy, while the layman was

---

52. Todd Starnes, "Conservative, Moderate Baptists Speak Out on Wake Forest Homosexual Union," *Baptist Press*, September 12, 2000. Available at http://www.bpnews.net/bpnews.asp ?id=6489 (accessed June 22, 2007).

53. "Two Churches Reaffirm Ties to BGCT," *Baptist Standard* (October 2, 2000).

54. William M. Pinson Jr., "Baptists: What Makes a Baptist a Baptist?" at http://www.baptist-dis tinctives.org/textonly2.html (accessed September 27, 2006); idem, "Baptists: The Priesthood of the Believer or of *Believers*?" http://www.baptistdistinctives.org/textonly7.html (accessed September 27, 2006).

not; that the priest performed God's service in the layman's stead; that the priest propitiated God on the layman's behalf; that, when the layman's time came, the priest could come in and make right his relation with God—here was indeed a distorted development of ministerial theory."[55]

Second, as a result of the development of the Catholic sacramental priesthood, the royal priesthood was directly tied to the doctrines of baptism and the Lord's Supper. Although one's entrance into the royal priesthood logically correlates with entrance into the church through baptism, there is no direct biblical connection in this regard. Indeed, there is no biblical evidence for the medieval assumption that baptism is ordination into the royal priesthood. And, although one's participation in the ecclesial celebration of the Lord's Supper should be an occasion for engaging in spiritual sacrifices, there is also no biblical connection in this regard.[56] As a result, the effective confinement of the laity's public practice of its royal priesthood to the eucharistic Mass according to the medieval Catholic sacramental priesthood is especially problematic.

A third instance of a common conception lacking a biblical connection is the idea that the Christian royal priesthood entails the inherent right of unmediated access to the throne of God. The idea that direct access to God is a function of the Christian royal priesthood first appeared during the Reformation but came into its own with the modern libertarian priesthood. Advocates of this position turn to Hebrews 4:16 for their claim that our priesthood results in the right of direct access to God. However, this is difficult to support. "In Hebrews, although the language of access to the sanctuary (10:19ff.) implies a privilege belonging specially to priests, the Christians are never explicitly addressed in these terms."[57] Rather, Christians are encouraged to see their lives as a continuing pilgrimage in Christ. Unmediated access to God is simply unavailable in this life.[58] "In fact, believers of the New Covenant are not without a mediator."[59] The profound reason why Christian priesthood and access to God are unconnected in Scripture is that we need the continual intercession of a priest. We need a priest, and his name is Jesus Christ! This brings us to our first positive conclusion.

---

55. R. C. Moberly, *Ministerial Priesthood: Chapters (Preliminary to a Study of the Ordinal) on the Rationale of Ministry and the Meaning of Christian Priesthood* (London: John Murray, 1897), 93.

56. Elliott, *Elect and the Holy*, 224.

57. John Dunnill, *Covenant and Sacrifice in the Letter to the Hebrews*, New Testament Studies 75 (Cambridge: Cambridge University Press, 1992), 234.

58. Ibid., 256–59. In an early article, Best defined access to God as a "function" of the general priesthood, but he based this claim on an "implicit" witness in Hebrews to the general priesthood. His tortuous exegesis was singularly unconvincing, and after the appearance of Elliott's sober dissertation, Best neglected the idea. Best, "Spiritual Sacrifice," 280–86; and idem, "I Peter II 4–10—A Reconsideration."

59. "De fait, les croyants de la nouvelle Alliance ne sont pas sans médiateur." C. Spicq, *L'Épitre Aux Hébreux* (Paris: Librairie LeCoffre, 1977), 91.

THE PRIMACY AND UNIQUENESS OF CHRIST'S PRIESTHOOD

It is notable that in the context of each of the New Testament references to the royal priesthood of the church, there is an emphasis upon the royal priesthood of Jesus Christ. The priesthood of believers is subsidiary to the primary doctrine of the eternal priesthood of Jesus Christ. The second person of the Trinity, the Son of God, became man in order to function as both Priest and sacrifice. "Therefore, holy brethren, partakers of the heavenly calling, consider the Apostle and High Priest of our confession, Christ Jesus" (Heb. 3:1). His priesthood surpasses that of Aaron, for his priesthood is like that of the enigmatic Melchizedek (chap. 7). His priesthood, unlike theirs, is eternal (5:5–11). His priesthood, unlike theirs, is "holy, harmless, undefiled, separate from sinners, and has become higher than the heavens" (7:26). His covenant surpasses that of Moses, for his covenant is without fault (8:7–13). His sacrifice surpasses the old sacrifices, for he did not offer it for himself. And he need not repeat it, for it is a one-time sacrifice with eternal consequences (7:27–28). Unlike the old animal sacrifices, which were mere shadows that could not take away sin, he sacrificed his own body, which can redeem all sinners (10:1–4). His tabernacle surpasses the old tabernacle, for his tabernacle is not even part of creation, but is of eternity (9:11). The priesthood of Jesus Christ is primary because it is the only effective priesthood; his sacrifice is primary and unique because it is propitiatory, satisfying the wrath of a Holy God. It is only by reason of his sacrifice and through his priesthood that the church may boldly approach the throne of grace:[60]

> Seeing then that we have a great High Priest who has passed through the heavens, Jesus the Son of God, let us hold fast our confession. For we do not have a High Priest who cannot sympathize with our weaknesses, but was in all points tempted as we are, yet without sin. Let us therefore come boldly to the throne of grace, that we may obtain mercy and find grace to help in time of need. (Heb. 4:14–16)

The Christian priesthood is not a participation in the unique priesthood of Christ, for that entails the offering of propitiatory sacrifice, a sacrifice effective for the removal of sin. John's revelation is quite clear that Christ "made" us into a priesthood (Rev. 1:6; 5:10). We do not share in his priesthood; he makes us a priesthood. There is an unbridgeable, qualitative distinction to be maintained between Christ's priesthood and Christian priesthood. Christian priesthood is ontologically inferior to Christ's priesthood. Christ's priesthood is by nature

---

60. Ibid., 93.

eternal; Christian priesthood is by nature created. Christ's sacrifice is by necessity propitiatory and eternal; Christian sacrifices are spiritual, not propitiatory, and are temporal. Christ's tabernacle is eternal and in the very presence of God; our tabernacles require grace to experience God's presence. Christ gives the covenant out of his grace; we enter the covenant as a result of his grace.

THE CONGREGATIONAL NATURE OF CHRISTIAN PRIESTHOOD

This brings us to a second positive conclusion. With every mention of the royal priesthood, in the New Testament as in the Old, the doctrine is rendered in the plural. Moreover, the context is always the congregation of the people of God. This congregation may be Israel, the church, or those in glory, but it is the gathered people of God who receive the promise of the royal priesthood and are made the royal priesthood. Finally, there is never any hint that qualitative distinctions are to be maintained within the membership of the royal priesthood. No priest in Scripture is ever given a greater priesthood within the royal priesthood. One must leave Scripture in order to transform this doctrine into an egalitarian individualism or a hierarchical individualism.

The congregational nature of Christian priesthood should not limit Christians from practicing their priesthood in every aspect of their lives, including that which is private. For instance, some of the spiritual sacrifices seem to imply individual activity as well as corporate activity.[61] And yet, "such sacrifices are certainly not to be reduced to mere spiritual thoughts or pietistic words." The most obvious context for the gathering of spiritual sacrifices in worship to God occurs during congregational worship (cf. 1 Cor. 5:7–8; Col. 3:16–17).[62] The congregational nature of Christian priesthood eliminates the idea that individuals may appeal to their personal priesthood in order to oppose the congregation or its leadership. This limitation applies not only to the average church member, but also to its leadership. No priest in the royal priesthood of the church is prior to or above the church, whether that priest is a layman or a minister.

PRIESTLY ACTIONS

What are the functions of the royal priesthood of the congregation? What does Christ intend for his priests and kings to do? It seems clear that there is one primary function under which several activities may be classified. The royal priesthood offers spiritual sacrifices to God. As delineated above, the seven types of spiritual sacrifice include offering one's entire life, engaging in good deeds, shar-

---

61. Best, "I Peter II 4–10—A Reconsideration," 286–87.
62. Martin J. Selman, "Sacrifice for Christians Today," in *Sacrifice in the Bible*, ed. Roger T. Beckwith and Martin J. Selman (Grand Rapids: Baker, 1995), 166–67.

ing material wealth, worshipping, proclaiming God's Word, seeing people believe, and accepting martyrdom. Peter certainly elevated the proclamation of the gospel above every other spiritual sacrifice, perhaps even making proclamation a singular function of the royal priesthood. Paul, John, and the author of Hebrews also stress verbal proclamation above any other spiritual sacrifice (1 Peter 2:9; Rom. 15:16; 1 Cor. 16:15; Phil. 2:17; Col. 1:8; Heb. 13:15; Rev. 5:8; 8:3–4). By virtue of being a sacrifice, spiritual sacrifices must in some way point to God, for they are offerings made to God. Spiritual sacrifices must say something about God.

Every priesthood exists in a mediatorial framework. Although there is one mediator between God and humans, the man Jesus Christ (1 Tim. 2:5), the church also functions in a mediatorial manner in the proclamation of the gospel. Of course, the mediation of the church is entirely instrumental: the church is a tool in the hand of God and has no independent and no propitiatory role. Yet Paul sees the church's proclamation as absolutely necessary for lost humanity. The church mediates salvation by proclaiming the Word, yet the church is the mere instrument of the Spirit. The church is secondary but required by divine provision. Commenting on the call to proclaim Isaiah's vision,[63] wherein a prophet was needed for the people, Paul writes,

> For "whoever calls on the name of the Lord shall be saved." How then shall they call on Him in whom they have not believed? And how shall they believe in Him of whom they have not heard? And how shall they hear without a preacher? And how shall they preach unless they are sent? . . . So then faith comes by hearing, and hearing by the word of God. (Rom. 10:13–15, 17)

A LIMITED CONGREGATIONAL KINGSHIP AND A FULLER ESCHATOLOGICAL KINGSHIP

Perhaps the most neglected aspect of the royal priesthood is its kingship. This is a difficult issue to discuss for Baptists. On the one hand, Baptists who subscribe to Anabaptist origins for Baptists must deal with the specter of Münster in Anabaptist history, where the saints tried to bring in the kingdom of God by the sword.[64] On the other hand, Baptists who subscribe to English Separatist origins have the specter of the Fifth Monarchists, that generally neglected revolutionary group that included Baptists (who obviously had not learned that the separation of

63. On Paul's heavy dependence on Isaiah in Romans 9–11, see E. Earle Ellis, *Paul's Use of the Old Testament* (Grand Rapids: Baker, 1957), 160–70.

64. C. Arnold Snyder, *Anabaptist History and Theology: An Introduction* (Kitchener, Ontario: Pandora Press, 1995), 192–95, 201–7, 211–20.

church and state is a cardinal Baptist distinctive).[65] Leaving aside the problem of coercive apocalypticism, how does the congregation exercise its kingship?

First, it should be clear that the kingdom has not yet come in its fullness. The thrones of the saints will not be erected until the millennial reign of Jesus Christ, which follows his return (Rev. 19–20). Second, there is still some present earthly aspect to the kingdom of the saints, because they have already been made a kingdom by Christ (Rev. 1:6; 5:10). Paul indicated that the congregation should govern itself through discipline, as a precursor of their future exercise of judgment (1 Cor. 5–6). And Jesus declared that the church must exercise a form of discipline over its membership (Matt. 18:15–18). From these passages, we gain a view of Christian kingship as carefully exercised through church discipline now. The visible rule of the people of God over the world is reserved for the Millennium.

This is the biblical doctrine of the priesthood of believers. At the turn of the third millennium, Southern Baptists took a giant step toward rediscovering the biblical doctrine of royal priesthood by recognizing its communal dimension. One wonders if Baptists will embrace the doctrine in its entirety by maintaining the primacy and uniqueness of Jesus Christ as our Priest and King; by stressing the church and rejecting the modern libertine interpretation; by offering spiritual sacrifices to God, especially by proclaiming the Word in the power of his Spirit; and by restoring church discipline, which is reserved for the baptized and completed in the Lord's Supper. Only then may Baptists begin to claim the biblical doctrine of royal priesthood.

---

65. Mark R. Bell, *Apocalypse How? Baptist Movements During the English Reformation* (Macon, GA: Mercer University Press, 2000), 163–204.

CONCLUSION

Maintaining the Integrity of the Church for Future Churches

JASON G. DUESING

CONSERVATION AS A NATIONAL DUTY

Gathering together in May must have seemed a bit peculiar to America's nobility. Rarely before had the governors of each state convened at the White House at the request of the president of the United States. Never before had they met to discuss the topic at hand. The air in the East Room surely stirred when the president, full of energy and vision, stood and explained through his trademark clenched teeth:

> This Conference on the conservation of natural resources is in effect a meeting of the representatives of all the people of the United States called to consider the weightiest problem now before the Nation; and the occasion for the meeting lies in the fact that the natural resources of our country are in danger of exhaustion if we permit old wasteful methods of exploiting them longer to continue.

With these words, President Theodore Roosevelt not only began the address, "Conservation as a National Duty," but also brought national awareness to the fledgling conservation movement.[1]

It was the first time that the 132-year-old nation had to face the depletion of its natural resources. Land, forests, and fuels were seemingly in abundance, yet Roosevelt saw the expansion of industry and increasing population as very real threats

---

1. Theodore Roosevelt, "Conservation as a National Duty," in *Conference of Governors* (Washington: G.P.O., 1909), 3–13.

to a limited supply. Roosevelt was not concerned with any immediate threat to the existence of the growing nation, but rather with the present population's reckless indifference toward a vital problem that threatened its future existence.

This culprit called "indifference" lies at the root of many of the difficulties present throughout the Christian world today. Believers, acting under various constructs—from liberalism to ecumenism to even evangelicalism—also have engaged in "old wasteful methods" with regard to the "natural resources" of the doctrine of the church. What exists today within evangelicalism is largely a climate of ecclesiological relativism. Indifference abounds toward doctrines that many claim are biblically ambiguous.

It has been the purpose of this book to combat this indifference by seeking to revive an interest in theology of the local church. When a church preserves the "natural resources" of the local church found in the priesthood of the believers, the mode and subject of baptism, the participants in the Lord's Supper, and how all of this relates to church discipline, the church is practicing what is essential for maintaining its integrity in an ecclesiologically indifferent world. However, a final question needs to be asked: How do the churches of today that heed this call to church integrity ensure that these "natural resources" are preserved for the churches of tomorrow?

While there is room for debate in any discussion related to the doctrine of the church, the distinctive that is more often overlooked than deliberated is the doctrine of the believers' church. The believers' church is the resource the Bible gives for serving as a vehicle to protect and deliver the gospel to future generations. To follow Roosevelt's lead, this present situation of ecclesiological indifference, "calls for common effort, common action."[2] What is needed is a new movement of a different kind of conservationism. For the sake of future churches, the people of God need to take action to preserve the integrity of the church by maintaining the doctrine of the believers' church.

Is Ecclesiology a Nonessential?

The present evangelical environment rightfully regards the gospel as the culmination of biblical essentials, but it simultaneously disregards the biblically designed vehicle for protecting and carrying the gospel to the next generation— the believers' church. The result of this lack of emphasis on the local church has been impure churches that more often self-destruct from internal disputes and doctrinal deterioration than are compromised from an outside attack. As a result, the testimonies of these churches are lost in their communities, and the gospel is often carried by individuals independent of the local churches rather than by the

2. Ibid., 6.

churches themselves. Scores of believers today trusted Christ through an evangelistic rally or a college parachurch outreach event rather than through a local church within close proximity to their home. While one would be foolish to criticize the fruitfulness for the gospel of these other ministries, it appears their success is an exception to the New Testament pattern of a local church-based gospel witness.[3] While the gospel still thrives in this climate of ecclesiological relativism, an undefined doctrine of the church leaves no guarantee that the next generation will have the opportunity to say the same.

The current climate developed as the result of evangelicals embracing a modified ecumenism that relegates doctrines such as the believers' church to the realm of "nonessentials." Citing the popular seventeenth-century slogan, "In essentials, unity; in nonessentials, liberty; in all things, charity,"[4] many find broad agreement for exercising liberty with regard to "nonessential" doctrines such as ecclesiology and eschatology. Certainly, lockstep uniformity over the majority of doctrines traditionally classified under these headings is not essential for salvation, nor are they a necessary prerequisite for eternal life with Jesus Christ. However, it appears that this relegation of many ecclesiological distinctives to the realm of acceptable ambiguity is not consistent with the New Testament witness.[5] By recovering or conserving ecclesiology, and especially the believers' church, not as gospel essentials but rather as the vehicle to protect the gospel essentials, contemporary believers can have a sure foundation through their local church not only to proclaim their faith to their neighbors but also to deliver to their children's generation the faith they received—the faith that was initially delivered to the saints (Jude 3), protected (2 Tim. 1:14) and passed down through the churches (Eph. 3:10, 21).

THE ANABAPTISTS: THE FIRST ECCLESIOLOGICAL CONSERVATIONISTS

Perhaps the greatest champions of the believers' church since the days prior to the Constantinian synthesis were the Anabaptists of the sixteenth century.

---

3. For one example, see 1 Thessalonians 1:6–8.
4. Although often attributed to Augustine, Hans Rollmann rightly posits the genesis of this saying with Peter Meiderlin of Augsburg, followed by increased popularization by Richard Baxter. See Hans Rollmann, "In Essentials Unity: The Pre-history of a Restoration Movement Slogan," in *Restoration Quarterly* 39, no. 3 (1997): 129–39. Also available at http://www.restorationquarterly.org/Volume_039/rq03903rollmann.htm.
5. The commands of the Great Commission are intrinsically ecclesiological (Matt. 28:16–20). For instance, the book of Acts is centered around the establishment of local churches. Paul's foundation for and recipients of his theological commands are local churches (e.g., Rom. 16:4, 16; 1 Cor. 1:2; 2 Cor. 1:1; Gal. 1:2; Col. 4:15–16; 2 Thess. 1:1), as he provides clear instructions for the ordering, structuring, and practice of local church ordinances, leadership, and congregational life. And John sent the contents of his vision to the seven local churches in Revelation 1.

In Zurich on January 21, 1525, the first Anabaptists left the prevalent and state-mandated tradition of infant baptism and followed their biblical convictions that true baptism should be administered solely to believers,[6] and that such believer's baptism should function as the entrance into membership of the local church.[7] William R. Estep recounts the significance of this event:

> On this fateful night the concept of a Believers' Church based upon a voluntary confession of faith confirmed by the act of public baptism found concrete realization in history. Thus, from a handful of radicals in Switzerland and South Germany who preferred to call themselves Brethren in Christ, the Free Church movement sprang.[8]

But in Switzerland and South Germany in 1525 the distance between believer's baptism, the believers' church, the gospel, and death was short. The Anabaptists lived in a state-church environment that did not tolerate those who advocated and advanced biblically driven ecclesiological absolutes. The price to be paid for defending biblical church distinctives in this climate was more often than not the ultimate price. In the truest sense, the Anabaptists were the pioneers of ecclesiological conservatism in an age not of ecclesiological indifference but of ecclesiological intolerance.

Leonard Verduin describes the developments among the Anabaptists as the "second front" of concern for magisterial reformers such as Martin Luther and John Calvin. On the one hand, the magisterial Reformers' first front of concern was clearly the actions and reactions of the Roman Catholics to their call for church reformation. The magisterial Reformers desired to *reform* the Catholic Church in all areas of corruption by rightly establishing the gospel of salvation in Jesus Christ by faith alone as the center of faith and practice. On the other hand,

---

6. The early Anabaptists in Zurich were trained by Zwingli in the humanist tradition of returning to the original sources for doctrinal development. Thus, careful study of the Bible in its original languages led several of the Anabaptists to press Zwingli for New Testament fidelity when it came to ecclesiology.

7. In light of the order given in the Great Commission, the Anabaptist leader Pilgram Marpeck articulated that one was made a disciple (i.e., conversion as the result of the placing of one's faith in teaching received) before receiving baptism. Combined with the statement of Jesus inaugurating the church upon the confession of Peter in Matthew 16, believer's baptism served as the public confession of faith for the believer's entrance into the local church. See Pilgram Marpeck, "The Admonition of 1542," in *The Writings of Pilgram Marpeck*, ed. William Klassen and Walter Klaassen (Scottdale: Herald Press, 1978), 227. See also Jason G. Duesing, "Pilgram Marpeck's Christian Baptism," *Faith and Mission* 23, no. 3 (Summer 2006): 3–16.

8. William R. Estep, "A Believing People: Historical Background," in *The Concept of the Believers' Church: Addresses from the 1967 Louisville Conference*, ed. James Leo Garrett Jr. (Scottdale: Herald Press, 1969), 45.

the magisterial Reformers were concerned with the Anabaptists' desire to move beyond church reform to complete *restoration* of the church to its New Testament origins.[9]

By and large, the magisterial Reformers were not looking to make many ecclesiological changes. They saw the economic and political ramifications of separating the church from the state and looked at the melding of these two under Constantine as a fit exercise for Christian civil and religious expression. Therefore, they retained two things as a part of their ecclesiology. First, membership in the church (as well as recognition of citizenship with the state) was contingent upon one's baptism as an infant. Second, just as the state carried the sword for the purpose of maintaining and establishing justice, so too did the church support the sword for the purpose of maintaining and establishing truth. Capital punishment was the sentence for acts or beliefs that many evangelicals today freely endorse. The Anabaptists attempted to conserve the doctrine of the believers' church in a climate far more hostile, yet they did so, not because they saw it as a gospel essential, but because they realized that the believers' church functioned as the vehicle to protect gospel essentials.

THE BELIEVERS' CHURCH: THE VEHICLE FOR ESSENTIALS

While Western theologians today are quick to place doctrines such as ecclesiology, eschatology, and perhaps even variances of anthropology on the lowest rungs of what is essential for twenty-first-century New Testament Christianity, it is a mistake to view the cultural climates of past periods, such as the sixteenth century, as operating under the same doctrinal classifications. To be sure, in modern America, where differences over the doctrine of the church do not merit the sentence of capital punishment, such issues do not seem as essential as how one answers the contemporary evangelical question, If you died tonight, how certain are you that you would be in heaven? However, because the Anabaptists' cultural milieu was far more complex and costly, ecclesiological distinctives became the battleground for conserving the gospel essentials.

The Anabaptists saw the marriage of church and state under Constantine as both harmful and unbiblical. One can articulate a pure gospel, as the magisterial Reformers did, with great effect, but to do so within the confines of a corrupt and false church only convolutes the message one hopes to proclaim. In addition, by allowing unregenerate individuals into the membership of the church, and even mandating it, the magisterial Reformers left themselves open to further corruption.

---

9. Leonard Verduin, *The Reformers and Their Stepchildren* (reprint, Sarasota, FL: Christian Hymnary Publishers, 1997).

For the Anabaptists, the only way to accomplish biblical purity in the church was to separate completely from the existing institutions and establish a believers' church. These early baptized churches no longer supported the use of the sword in church matters and refused to call for the death penalty even for those with divergent doctrinal views. Entrance into these new churches was by profession of faith (something infants could not do) in the form of believer's baptism. Furthermore, the purity of these churches was protected by the regular practice of the ban, or church discipline, on those members who continued in unrepentant sin and thus showed themselves not to have believed what they had professed.

Therefore, one can see how the organization of a believers' church was not only a radical departure from the societal status quo but also the symbol of one's commitment to a greater ideal of church and gospel purity rooted not in the sacramental tradition but in the text of the Bible. The Anabaptists were not fanatics so preoccupied with their specific preferences that they no longer saw the forest for the tree in front of them. They did not represent the type of Christian who is so enamored with his peculiar theological eccentricities that he alienates himself and thereby ruins his gospel witness. Furthermore, Anabaptists were not experimenters in the avant-garde, simply going against the grain to stir up trouble or draw attention to themselves. Rather, these believers were standing under the conviction of what they perceived to be the biblical means for protecting gospel essentials: the preservation and right articulation of the gospel can be accomplished only through the preservation and right articulation of the church.

A church comprised of an unregenerate membership several generations removed will no longer care about proclaiming such essentials as the exclusivity of Jesus Christ as the way to salvation, much less the subjects discussed in this volume. One only has to look at the results of the Halfway Covenant among New England Puritans in the seventeenth and eighteenth centuries or mainline Protestantism's increasing indifference to the gospel in the twentieth century to see the effects of the failure to maintain a pure church. The gospel ministries of John Knox, Jonathan Edwards, John Wesley, and George Whitefield strengthened and established various denominations, but the churches within these groups failed to use the vehicle of the believers' church consistently to deliver a pure gospel message to future generations of saints.

ECCLESIOLOGICAL CONSERVATION AS A CHRISTIAN DUTY

At the 1909 governors' conference, President Roosevelt called the nation to awake from its reckless indifference toward the wasteful use of America's natural resources. The nation responded, and a system of National Parks, new legislation, and general awareness of the importance of conservation was born. Likewise, viewing the present climate of ambiguity toward the doctrine of the church through the spectacles of Anabaptist history, contemporary believers can see the importance of conserving the believers' church to aid in maintaining the integrity of the church. For preserving what is essential for salvation for the next generation, a new call is needed to awaken all evangelicals from a state of indifference toward ecclesiology and the believers' church. Just as Roosevelt's address called on the governors and the nation to see "Conservation as a National Duty" for the sake of future Americans, the purpose of this collection of essays has been to call on believers to see "Ecclesiological Conservation as a Christian Duty" for the sake of future churches. May the Lord continue this work of church preservation through such ecclesiological conservation.

Author Index

Scripture Index

Scripture Index